This book has been donated

in memory of:

Arnold Scacchitti

Celine

Center Point
Large Print

Also by Peter Heller and available from
Center Point Large Print:

The Painter

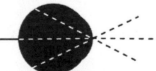

**This Large Print Book carries the
Seal of Approval of N.A.V.H.**

Celine

PETER HELLER

CENTER POINT LARGE PRINT
THORNDIKE, MAINE

This Center Point Large Print edition
is published in the year 2017 by arrangement with
Alfred A. Knopf, an imprint of
The Knopf Doubleday Publishing Group,
a division of Penguin Random House, LLC.

This is a work of fiction. Any resemblance to actual
people living or dead is coincidental, except for Celine
and Pete and Hank, who are based on real people.
There is a lot of Celine's family history in this novel.
Much of it is true, and some of it is imagined.

The text of this Large Print edition is unabridged.
In other aspects, this book may vary
from the original edition.
Printed in the United States of America
on permanent paper.
Set in 16-point Times New Roman type.

ISBN: 978-1-68324-364-9

Library of Congress Cataloging-in-Publication Data

Names: Heller, Peter, 1959– author.
Title: Celine / Peter Heller.
Description: Center Point Large Print edition. | Thorndike, Me. : Center
Point Large Print, 2017.
Identifiers: LCCN 2017003216 | ISBN 9781683243649
    (hardcover : alk. paper)
Subjects: LCSH: Women private investigators—Fiction. | Large type
books. | BISAC: FICTION / Literary. | FICTION / Thrillers. | FICTION
/ Family Life. | GSAFD: Suspense fiction. | Mystery fiction.
Classification: LCC PS3608.E454 C45 2017b | DDC 813/.6—dc23
LC record available at https://lccn.loc.gov/2017003216

With all Love

To my Mother, Caroline Watkins Heller—
Artist, Spiritual Warrior, Private Eye.

And to Lowell "Pete" Beveridge,
The Quiet American.

prologue

It was bright and windy, with the poppies flushing orange down the slopes of the bluffs, all mixed with swaths of blue lupine. The Pacific was almost black and it creamed against the base of the cliffs all along Big Sur. He loved this. He hitched the rucksack higher on his shoulder. Since Jence had died in the war it was the only thing he really loved. Good haul today, too, a solid handful of jade pebbles from the cove below. He stopped to catch his breath. The trail was steep here, the rocks like steps, his pant legs soaked to the thigh and heavy. Just a second here, he was in no hurry this afternoon.

He heard the click of rock and voices and looked up the trail and saw the family. The little girl was practically running down. She was wearing a yellow-and-blue summer dress a little like the flower-covered cliffs and she was yelling. Must be her mother right after, trying to catch up, trying to watch her step in her leather sandals, her arms held out for balance like wings. She was calling "Gabriela! Gabriela! *Cuidado*! *Querida*!" She was very pretty. She wore the same dress as her daughter and when the two got close he noticed they were like big and little twins: olive skin and green eyes, long black hair in ponytails. Well. It

7

was a day for beauty. The father came after. He took his time. He wasn't worried about a thing. He wore a black T-shirt and he was handsome like James Dean—older than Jence, maybe ten years, too old for the draft. The girl Gabriela yelled "Hi! Hi!" as she breezed past, and the mother brought herself erect when she saw him and flashed a shy smile. He held up his hand for the dad and spoke.

"Pretty good today. The rougher seas have brought down more stone. But be careful with the tide."

"Thanks. We will. Thanks." The father touched his arm and continued down, out of sight.

The man hooked his thumbs in the rucksack and climbed. He got to the top of the bluff and sat on the little bench that was just a slab of wood on two rocks. He closed his eyes against the sun and smelled the warming yarrow, the salt. Nice seeing the family. He and Jence also came here when Jence was a kid, and when they got home they covered the kitchen table with bits of jade. He still did that now. He came home and he didn't think about his son blown to shreds fifteen months ago in Vietnam, and he pieced the stones close together like a jigsaw, like a growing green island, so there was no room to eat anymore. He ate his meals on the porch.

He thought he heard shouts. Shouts and cries. Hard to hear over the wind and rush of surf. People got so excited about jade. Well.

• • •

Gabriela screamed. The foam rushed cold over her bare toes and as it slid back it vanished in a million tiny bubbles. What a glorious afternoon. White seagulls lifted off the boulders and terns dove. The waves broke and spumed over the outer boulders that were covered in shiny dark kelp. The waves rushed white through the rocks right up onto the gravel of the tiny cupped beach and turned the stones black and when they all glistened was when you could see the bits of green.

"Gabriela," Amana said to the girl. "*Querida.* This one—exactly the color of your eyes! See? But it's shaped like a bird! Here's a little fish, look. I am going to find one that looks like your eye."

"*Your* eye!" The girl shrieked with delight. "One that looks like your eye! I am going to find one for *you.*"

They kneeled, heads almost together, black hair flying in the wind, and sifted the stones. They raced. Paul helped Gabriela a little, but mostly he sat on a rock and closed his eyes. The wind was almost cold. He was thinking that he should have brought some sausage and cheese, that they could stay here maybe till sunset, when he heard the girls scream. He opened his eyes. A bigger wave had pushed whitewater right over the entire swath of gravel, right up to the wall of the sheltering cliff, and his wife and daughter were standing, soaked, and laughing.

"Hey! Hey!" he yelled. "Come higher!" He laughed too, but what he felt was alarm. He looked past Amana and Gabriela to the outer rocks and saw the dark swell. It was the next wave and it was the second in a set and he watched it as if in slow motion: the wall lightening to green as it rose, rising impossibly tall, the guarding boulders out in the cove dwarfed beneath it, the quivering top frayed by wind and then a piece of it curled and collapsed and the wall fell: a surge of whitewater chest-high roared in over the black slack water of the inner cove and he was slugged and knocked over, his shoulder and neck hit rock, he came up lunging out of ice foam to see the tumult sucking back.

Then he saw his daughter. Heard. Gabriela was screaming, the whitewater rushed back and she was in it, it was taking her, and the wall—a bigger wall was rising out there, steepening, green— *"Amana! Where—"* He took two steps and dove. His chest hit hard and he was flailing toward his daughter, her head, and then he saw his wife farther out and she was swimming. She was a strong swimmer and she was swimming! In the sliding rush beneath the next wave he saw the rhythmic beat of her arms—and the wave suspended and crashed and then he was tumbled. His back struck sharp rock and he cried, no breath, and she was somehow against him. Gabriela! His little girl was against him, the weight for a moment, and she was pulling away and with everything he could summon he flailed and reached and somehow grabbed her arm and held. And held. Grip like a claw. The charge of whitewater sucked back and he rolled, he rolled with her, and then somehow felt the bottom, loose gravel, and he scrabbled for a foothold and then the water was only knee-deep and he staggered and stood and she was in his arms. He was hugging her tight, she was bleeding from somewhere—was she breathing? She was blue—and he saw with a black terror the next wave and he could not see his wife. He scrambled back. Back against the cliff as the froth sucked on his knees and he ran. He half fell, half stumbled around a spur of rock holding his daughter, and he knocked shins and knees, elbows on the boulders and then he was at the foot of the trail and climbing and in the blank static of panic he turned once and saw something that might be the dark head of his wife, an arm—being tugged swiftly toward the point.

one

The call had come while she was at her workbench wiring the naked taxidermic form of an ermine onto a rock, beside the skull of a crow. The plan was to have the skinless ermine looking down at his own hide tacked to the rock. Her sculpture had a distinctive dark streak. When Celine wasn't solving cases, she made pieces from anything at hand, which often involved skulls. The year before, the window washer had been fascinated by her art, which was displayed throughout the open studio, and the next day he brought her a human skull in a bucket. "Don't ask," he said. She didn't. She covered it immediately in gold leaf and it stood now on a pedestal by the front door, looking elegant.

Now, she felt like this ermine. She felt skinned and lost, without protection.

Her own fur had been her family. She had Hank, of course, but a son, no matter how old, was someone to be protected, not the other way around. When the phone rang, she almost didn't answer it, but then she thought it might be Pete calling from up in the Heights, needing grocery-shopping help.

"Hi, Celine Watkins?"

"Yes?"

"This is Gabriela. Gabriela Ambrosio Lamont."

"Gabriela," she whispered, trying to place the name.

"You don't know me. I went to Sarah Lawrence. Class of '82. I saw the story about you in the alumni magazine: 'Prada PI.'" Gabriela laughed, clear, bell-like. Celine relaxed.

"That was silly," Celine said. "I mean the title. I've never worn Prada in my life."

"Chanel doesn't alliterate."

"Right." Celine closed her eyes. The name was distinctive and it sounded familiar. Hadn't the girl had her own small story in the magazine?— about a show of still-life photographs in a gallery in San Francisco. Celine seemed to remember a portrait of the woman and bits of biography—she was pretty, maybe partly Spanish. Her father had been a photographer, too, hadn't he? Famous and very charismatic. The story had interested Celine.

"I remember you from an article."

"Hah! The exclusive club of the alumni magazine profiles," Gabriela said.

"Yes."

Pause. "I hope it's okay that I called you. Out of the blue."

"Yes, of course." Celine had been in her business a long time; she knew that nobody ever just called out of the blue. They had been on a certain trajectory for a while, they deliberated, they picked up the phone. They were like the pilots of small

13

planes approaching an airport who call the tower, finally, for instructions to land.

What Celine didn't know was if she had the strength. It was one year and one day after the Twin Towers had fallen. She could still almost smell the char, still see the air gritty with ash, and remember how the wind blew bits of charred financial statements and Post-it notes across the river where they fluttered over the dock like lost confetti. She could not have imagined a sadder finale to a grim year.

Her younger sister had died that May. She remembered how bright, how tender seemed the cottonwoods along the Big Wood River in Ketchum, Idaho, the morning Mimi left. She had helped her go—the handful of pills, the long kiss on the cheek. How she had walked down the drive, how the leaves spun in the wind, and how when a gust came through it swept the old trees to a darker green like the hands of a harpist lifting a somber note off the strings. And then in July she got word that her older sister, Bobby, had a brain tumor. It was a flare-up of a cancer five years in remission. Celine went to Pennsylvania to visit, to help, and there was not much to do as Bobby died within three weeks. It was almost as if the youngest sister's death had given the eldest sister permission to take the deep rest she had longed for.

And then the first plane hit and Celine went to

her window and watched the plume of black smoke rise into a clear sky. She was riveted. She lived fifty feet from the pier in an old brick loft building kitty-corner to the River Café. It was almost under the Brooklyn Bridge, Brooklyn side, thirty yards from the East River, and with the windows open she could hear the current rip and burble against the pilings of the dock. She pursed her lips and tried to get enough air. She did not move. Pete left her alone. When the second plane tore through the sister tower to the south she shuddered as if it were she herself who had been slammed and ripped. Lying in bed that night while she cried silently beside him, Pete realized that Bobby was the North Tower and Mimi the South. And of course the collapsing buildings were much more than that, too. They were a burning message that a certain world had passed. Her sisters had been the last of the family she'd been born into. Celine's inner and outer world mirrored each other.

Celine was sixty-eight then. Her body was more frail than it should have been for an active strong-willed woman as a result of four packs a day for thirty years, and though she had quit ten years ago, the smoking had ravaged her lungs. She usually refused to wear oxygen, she was too elegant, or vain.

So she had stood in the window and struggled to breathe. She stared at the skyline where the two improbable towers had been and felt the constriction in her chest: the grief of this unreal, this towering loss that just then seemed the sum of all loss. She was aware of the half-full bottle of morphine pills she had in her gun safe upstairs, the pills in their labeled orange plastic bottle that bore Mimi's name: "Mary Watkins, *For pain, one pill every four hours, not to exceed six pills per day.*" But she would never go that way. Nor would she use one of the four handguns from the same safe, not on herself. She was too curious, for one. About how everything unfolds—and folds back up. But she didn't know if she had the will to do any longer the work she was born for. Which was saying, in a way, that she no longer had the will to live.

Celine Watkins was a private eye. It was an odd vocation for someone in the *Social Register* who had grown up partly in Paris, partly in New York. She may have been the only PI on earth whose father had been a partner at Morgan's in France during the war. The only working PI who had come to New York City when she was seven and attended the Brearley School for girls on the Upper East Side, and then Sarah Lawrence. Where she studied art, and at twenty-one spent a year back in Paris, where she apprenticed with an expressionist and was proposed to by a duke.

She also had what Mimi called the Underdog

Bone. Celine always rooted for the weak, the dispossessed, the children, for the ones who had no means or power: the strays and homeless, the hapless and addicted, the forlorn, the remorseful, the broken. One couldn't count the skinny trembling dogs her son ended up loving, nor the chaotic families that stayed with them for days. So she was not a PI like most PIs. Most people think of them as hired guns—jaded, mercenary, tough. She was tough. But she did not take jobs for the rich, she did not spy on wayward spouses or stake out anyone's pied-à-terre or recover the missing family jewels. She had literal family jewels of her own, which she hauled out and wore with a faint embarrassment to appropriate gatherings— Cartier diamonds and Breguet watches. She had engraved silver from the 1700s. She understood the shallow prestige of the aristocracy, as well as its responsibilities. Celine had inherited the mantle of a family who had come on the first boat and worked hard and made good, and often the mantle chafed, and she was happiest when she took it off and tossed it on a hook with her beret.

The cases she took were for the Lost Causes, the ones who could never afford a PI. They were never about leverage or retribution or even justice, and they were often performed pro bono. They were usually about reuniting birth families. So she found the missing, the ones who could not be found—she gave a mother her lost son, a daughter her lost father—and her success rate was a staggering 96 percent, much better than, say, the FBI. She had worked for them, too—once, and she would never do it again.

Gabriela said, "I'm staying with an old college friend up in the Heights. On Garden Place."

Celine was still holding a pair of small wire cutters in her right hand. She set them down. She closed her eyes. She hadn't been to Garden Place in years, but she had gone often when her son, Hank, had had playmates on the street. Those years. Of early marriage and motherhood. She could almost smell the streets on the south side of the neighborhood, eroding brownstones, maple leaves, and the brown crunchy seedpods of the locust trees. Wilson, her first husband, was living in Santa Fe now, with a woman thirty years younger.

"Right. I know the block well."

"Well. I . . . I called because I thought—I have a story to tell you. Is this a good time?"

"Please. I was just finishing something up."

A beat, she could hear Gabriela trying to decide the best way in.

"I was going to start by telling you about something that happened while I was at Sarah Lawrence. But let me back up. I should begin earlier so you understand. My mother's name was Amana Penteado Ambrosio . . ."

two

"Amana, in Tupi-Guarani, means rain. That is how I thought of her when I lay awake at night in my apartment—just a sec."

A rustling, the sliding of maybe a chair on a wood floor.

"Okay, I'm back. I want to—I don't want to intrude."

Celine shook her head. She felt fully awake for the first time in weeks. "Intrude? You've pretty much set the hook. I just had an idea. You said you were up in the Heights?"

"Yes."

"It's very close. Why don't you join us for dinner? My husband Pete just went up the hill for provisions."

"I—"

"I think he's going to make his famous Wicked Mac and Cheese."

"Hah!"

"He's from Maine," Celine added, as if that explained it.

"I just got back from a run. A two-second shower and—you live on the dock, don't you?" Gabriela had done her homework.

"At 8 Old Fulton. It's the red door, you can't miss it."

• • •

The young woman who showed up at the door must have run. It didn't seem that even fifteen minutes had passed. She was wearing a loose cotton mid-length summer dress with a batik pattern of tiny elephants, and running shoes. Her wet hair was tied back in a ponytail, her face was flushed, and she came bearing flowers that she must have gathered in passing from the gardens that overflowed the wrought-iron fences en route. Celine approved: Stealing roadside flowers was a family tradition; her own mother, Baboo, would gather up her work gloves and clippers on Fishers Island afternoons and tell her daughters it was time to go "highwaying and bywaying," which meant appropriating bouquets from the generous hedges and thickets that crowded the country lane. Celine noticed that Gabriela also carried a thick manila file tied with string.

Celine took the handful of wild roses and tall grasses and the girl leaned down and kissed her on both cheeks. She was much taller than Celine. She was not a girl, of course—if she'd graduated in '82 she'd be in her early forties, the same age as her son, Hank—but Celine could not help thinking of her as a youth. Her tan, oval face, her green eyes full of lights, her bowed mouth. On her left temple was a scar, a ragged arc like the edge of a leaf. Gabriela was one of those women whose beauty could not be parsed because it was mostly energetic—it hit one like the first scent of apple blossoms.

"Thank you." Celine took the flowers to the sink where she filled an empty olive oil bottle and snugged them in, hastily arranging them with her mother's swift eye. She turned. Gabriela was taking in the room with an expression Celine was not unused to seeing in her friends' first visits. The girl's eyes traveled to the gold-leafed skull, to another human skull emerging from a rock hollow with a barbed-wire crown of thorns, to a black altar cluttered with knives, bottles, dolls, crosses; the stuffed crow with a doll in his beak; the totem pole of human and animal bones.

"That altar," Gabriela murmured.

"That's to Baron Samedi, the Haitian voodoo god of the underworld. That's him in the corner in the top hat. Two visiting Haitian friends became possessed walking in here. I thought we might have to call a mambo."

"Gee."

"Gee is right. Come, come, sit. Here." Celine led Gabriela to a wrought-iron café table. "I heard you eating crackers on the phone and it seemed like a good idea." In truth, Celine never went too long without eating. HALT. It was her AA training. Hungry, Angry, Lonely, Tired—don't let yourself become any of those, if you can help it. Her favorite snack was a chunk of Lindt

21

chocolate bedded on a tablespoon of peanut butter. She could have lived on it.

They sat. Gabriela said, "I loved the article about you. I called an old friend, a retired dean who knew you, and he said that you were one of the best in the country at solving very cold cases, cases many years old."

"Renato? He's sweet. Searching for birth families is by definition a wading into cold cases."

"He also said you can go incognito anywhere, and that you once attended a diplomat's party dressed as a man. He said you were an amazing shot and owned an armory of handguns."

"Well. We shouldn't get carried away. You were telling me a story," Celine said.

Gabriela set the file on the table and drank a whole glass of sparkling water, refilled the glass. Her scar blazed. "You had cats," she said. "I count two, in framed pictures."

"Two loves of my life."

Gabriela hesitated. "In San Francisco, the year of Miss Brandt—so it was second grade, I was seven—we had a little cat named Jackson. He was spotted like a cow, all black and white, but fluffy. So small he fit in my mother's palm."

Celine nodded. Everybody can agree on a kitten.

"Amana called him Moto, which is short for motorcycle, because of the way he purred. I said that he didn't look anything like a motorcycle, and Mom said, 'You probably want to name him something all-American like Jackson,' so that's what we called him."

Celine smiled.

"He slept with me. I remember he would stick his wet nose in my ear as hard as he could like he wanted to crawl in and live in here. I wish he had." Gabriela rubbed the corner of her eye and Celine thought she was exceedingly lovely.

"Why did you wish that?"

"He got lost."

"Oh."

"We used to let him go out into the back garden, which I guess was dumb. One day he didn't come home. He was so small, he must've gotten over a fence and been nabbed by a neighbor's dog. I like to think that someone thought he was a stray and just adopted him. For years afterward I prayed for that. I also left my window open. When I had my own apartment, my bedroom faced the gardens and I left my window open winter and summer so that he could smell me and maybe jump up onto the sill and come home."

Celine could feel heat climb into her own face.

"And Mom, too. Rain. After she died I opened the window a little wider and when it rained I'd let the drops spatter on the brick sill and bounce onto my face and in the dark I'd imagine it was my mother coming to touch me. Maybe it was her in the rain. I used to think that maybe at night things could happen that aren't allowed in the daytime."

Gabriela reached for the water and refilled her glass, drank the whole thing again in one go. She looked out the windows to the bridge.

"Mom's paternal name was Ambrosio. Very Brazilian. I loved that, too. When I was finally out of school, out of college, and had a minute to take stock, I made it my middle name." She turned back to Celine. "I didn't cry every night as a kid, I wouldn't want you to think that I did. I was pretty tough."

"Wait," Celine said. "Wait. Your mother was Brazilian and she died when you were like—what?"

"The same year, second grade. In February."

"Right. So you were—"

"I was seven. Well, eight. She died on my birthday."

"How? I can't re—"

"She drowned. On Big Sur. We were in this cove called Jade Cove, hunting for bits of green stone that looked like our eyes."

Celine nodded.

"We all almost died. Pop tried to save her. A stranger drove me to the hospital. A cannery worker from Monterey. I still get letters from him. He lives in Santa Cruz with his niece."

Celine felt herself inclining forward. In her experience stories fell into two phyla: those that

24

followed predictable contours like the track of a game trail along a hillside, and those that were stranger from the start, more feral, and that struck out cross-country on the merest whim. The strange ones had a certain scent. She handed the girl a cracker with blue cheese.

"Thanks. We were living in the Haight, in San Francisco, and it was my eighth birthday. It fell on a Saturday in February when the poppies would be blooming, so we decided to make the drive down to Big Sur, which was our favorite place. I remember I rode on Mom's lap the whole way, just because I wanted to, and she squeezed me and was singing a Brazilian song in my ear. The song was about a rabbit who wanted the rice in the rice paddies but couldn't swim. They grow a lot of rice in Brazil." Her face blurred with whimsy. "Too much information, I guess."

"Not at all."

"Well." Gabriela twisted the strap of the athletic watch on her wrist. "We got to the cliffs and they were on fire with poppies. I remember we ran down the trail, we were so excited. It's a little pocket cove and it feels very wild but also sheltered, and I remember thinking this was our own private beach, just for us. The water rushed onto the pebbles and made the jade shine. Amana and I were racing each other to find a piece that looked like a green eye. She kept tickling me so I wouldn't beat her. And then a rogue wave hit and swept the beach and knocked us off our feet and we were pulled in. I remember the shock of the cold and screaming for Mom and I don't remember much after that. I guess we all got swept. We didn't know it but a storm was coming in."

"Whoa."

"I know. I guess Pop somehow grabbed me and hauled me out. I was covered in blood and unconscious. Apparently he saw my mother trying to swim in the cove and more waves were coming, and he saw me all bloody and barely breathing and he made a split-second decision he would have to live with for the rest of his life. He gathered me up and ran up the trail and there was this older man there, the stranger. Pop shoved me into his arms and yelled to take me to the hospital, and then he ran back down the trail and dove in and actually swam after Amana. It was crazy. He had seen she was being swept north and he swam that way. I guess he almost drowned himself. He washed up on another beach two miles away."

"Jesus."

The girl nodded, her eyes focused on a place beyond the room.

"I woke up at Community Hospital in Monterey. All the blood was just a head cut. I guess they can bleed a lot."

Celine nodded.

"The nice man waited by my bed. Pop didn't show up all night and then the man had to go. I found out later he was a supervisor at one of the last docks along Cannery Row, and he worked Sundays. He promised he'd be back after work."

Celine closed her eyes, conjured the hospital rooms.

"Pop didn't show up that morning. I remember that with more terror than the accident. Where's Daddy? I remember the confusion the way we remember some smells, the confusion and what must have been fear on the faces of the nurses. Where's Mommy, I want Mommy! I began to cry, to wail. They kept asking me my name, my full name, I kept saying AmanaAmanaAmana, maybe they thought I was saying Mama I don't know."

Celine opened her eyes. Gabriela was speaking now to the tall windows, the dusk over the dock, and the East River, the wider world. Her fingertips rested lightly on the edge of the wrought-iron table as if she were playing a piece on a piano, counting the beats of a caesura.

"He showed up sometime in the afternoon. I was hysterical when I saw him. They told him that I was basically fine and coming around, and that it was clear he needed stitches in his head right now, and probably other places. I think they tried to make him sign some papers, they were tugging on his sleeves and he pulled away from them and carried me out of that hospital. He

27

was never the same. I can't have realized that then, but I know it now. He had swum and swum in the rough water and twice he thought he saw her ahead of him and tried to sprint there and lost her. And I guess he lost his mind."

She turned to Celine, shook herself. "It's a lot, I know. I can finish another time."

They often said that. When they were getting to the part they least liked to tell, or had never told. Celine said, "I'm fine. Would you like some tea?"

Gabriela shook her head. The young woman looked around the big, airy studio as if seeing it for the first time. "Your art is kind of terrifying," she said. "Did I already tell you that?"

"I think you might have. Do you want to take a break?"

"I'm okay." She tucked a strand of black hair behind her ear, gave Celine an uncertain smile. "Well. Pop did the best he could. He was unhinged. We both were—"

The brass bell on the front door jingled and she saw Gabriela huff out a breath with what must have been relief. Round One, saved by the bell.

Pete carried in two cloth tote bags. Celine could see bunches of probably kale sticking out the top of one and rolled her eyes. For twenty years he had been trying to get her to eat a vegetable with little success. His tenacity was superhuman. Pete tipped his chin and gave his wife what no one else in the world would know was a smile, and he set the bags on the counter and took off his tweed newsboy cap. He cocked his head at the young woman and gave a friendly wave. He didn't say a word. Pete, who the rest of the family called Pa, had grown up on an island in Maine where Reticence was the state bird. The rest of the family also called him the Quiet American. Celine waved a cracker at him and said, "Whew. I'm starved. Pete, this is Gabriela Ambrosio Lamont. She went to my alma mater and she is just telling me the most remarkable story. She'll be joining us for dinner. Can you whip up one of your Blue Plate Specials?"

"We can probably do that."

Cooking was one of Pete's many skills. On North Haven, as a boy, he had learned to pitch hay, milk cows, and build small boats. Also, to feed a family of nine when his mother was busy doing something else. Now, in Brooklyn, he channeled his talents into making healthy dinners that his wife would half eat, and into carving unabashedly erotic sculptures that the cleaning lady refused to dust.

Pete had attended Harvard like his father and all his uncles. He was an athlete and played football for a year, and while in Cambridge he became a card-carrying Communist, when being a card-carrying Communist could seriously screw with one's prospects. After college he had enlisted in the army and promptly married a black civil rights activist named Tee, and when he got out of the service he moved with her to Brooklyn and edited the revolutionary civil rights magazine *Liberator.* Some of the most heartbreaking letters Celine had ever read were from Pete's parents, asking him not to come back to North Haven in the summers with his Negro wife, and trying so hard to explain that it wasn't because any of them were racist. The correspondence was eloquent and awkward by turns, and so hot with love and shame the stationery almost smoldered. This was all before Pete's career as a Wall Street architect, an amateur historian, a long-haul backpacker, and a legen-dary drinker. Which brought him into Alcoholics Anonymous where he met Celine. The man was definitely a strange cat.

Pete cooked up his Wicked Mac and Cheese, with a side of optimistic sautéed bok choy, and tiny side salads, and the three ate mostly in easy silence. Gabriela seemed happy for the respite. One of Pete's other talents was to allow long conversations to be nonverbal and to have his companions be comfortable with it. They finished, made a fresh pot of coffee, and put up the dishes. Celine and Gabriela walked slowly out onto the rough planks of the dock across the street and leaned against the railing. Night had settled. The incoming tide was tearing against the pilings, and the lights of Manhattan and of the great bridge were as grand and familiar to Celine as any constellation.

Gabriela said, "You can almost still smell it. Like embers."

Celine waited. The Towers, their absence, would have had an effect on the girl, too. On everyone . . . *she feels the dark / Encroachment of that old catastrophe, / As a calm darkens among water-lights.* Those gorgeous lines from Stevens kept surfacing, like the refrain of a pop song.

Gabriela said, "I'm torn. The time with you has just flown. I haven't felt so good in someone's company since I can remember."

Celine felt the same way. She also knew the grip of an irresistible story. "There's so much," Gabriela said and glanced at her watch. "I promised Callie we'd play Scrabble at eight." She turned to Celine. "It was our ritual at Sarah Lawrence, every night before finals." She smiled. "Other students would be cramming and we'd have these killer games, head-to-head. It was our way of staying calm, I guess."

"You want to keep the date?"

"I want to figure out how to tell the rest. Without—"

Without eviscerating the people in the world you love the most, Celine thought. She knew a little about that.

"Can you give me a day or two?"

"Of course." Nothing surprised her. So many

31

of her clients had come right to the brink. "I'm on the hook, you know."

Gabriela's smile brightened. Celine wondered if she had carried her own grief with as much grace as this young woman. Gabriela said, "I left my file on the counter. I'll just go pick it up and say thank you to Pete."

three

Hank lived on a lake in Denver, on the west side of town. He was a magazine journalist, a closet poet, and until recently he had shared his house with his wife, Kim. He was also an outdoorsman, something he attributed, oddly, to the influence of his cosmopolitan mother. Well, he was named after her father, Harry, who was a legendary sportsman. Over many summers it was she who had taught him to fish, and to swim, and to make the calls of a bobwhite, a whip-poor-will, a barn owl. Hank's father had taught him to throw a football and to write a sonnet, and had read Jack London and Faulkner aloud to him when Hank was a very young child, but it was Celine who taught him to love nature in all her moods. And so, though he lived in the city, it gave him great solace to sit on his front porch and see almost nothing but grass, trees, water, mountains. His favorite part of the day was to drink coffee out there as the day was breaking, and watch the first light flush the snows of the Continental Divide. He was doing that when he heard the phone ring inside.

"It's Mombo."

"It's early for you. Even for New York."

"I can't sleep."

33

Hank braced himself. That could be a prelude to many things, the best of which was the story of a stubborn case. Other possibilities included anxiety about his marriage or his next assignment. Or simply that she was too brokenhearted. She hadn't been herself for months. Hank was one of the rare young men who was fascinated by his mother. Her life often seemed much more interesting than his own, which he thought was an inversion of the natural order, and may have been part of the reason he got into writing adventure stories. Well, he had also inherited his mother's restlessness. He refilled his mug and took the phone back out to the Adirondack chair.

"And?" he prompted.

"I was wondering how you were doing," she said.

"You mean am I eating a vegetable?"

"That, too."

"You should try one, it's kind of fun. Full of vitamins."

"Hank—"

"Kim'll come back, Mombo. I think."

Silence. His mother cleared her throat. "Are you—"

"Drinking? Not yet."

"Please don't say that."

"Sorry."

"Well, I just had the most interesting talk with a young woman exactly your age. Very pretty."

"Whoa! Are you trying to set me up? Has it gotten to that?" He almost laughed.

"No, no. I just—"

Hank set his cup down on the arm of the chair. The mug said *Trouts Fly Fishing* and had a watercolor graphic of a speckled rainbow leaping for a mayfly. It was corny but he liked it. It gave him some comfort, especially on waking to a half-empty bed.

"This woman called you?"

"Yes."

"She wanted to tell you a story?"

"Yes."

"She wanted to hire you?"

"I'm not sure. Yes, probably. I haven't heard the full story, but there's something about it."

"If she does—want to hire you—will you take it?"

"That's what I'm not sure about. It's been an exhausting year. Are you eating regular meals?" she said.

"Mombo, I made green chili yesterday. And I got an assignment from Brad at *BusinessWeek*. About the surfing industry, go figure."

"Oh, *great*. How's the poetry?"

He deflected the question. "I caught a twelve-pound carp below the stadium yesterday."

"In the Platte? *Wow*. On what? Remember when you took me down there and we caught a body?" She had taught him to throw big streamers in the

Ausable when he could barely hold a rod, and a few years ago in Denver they *had* snagged the body of a young man one morning. She had. That was another story.

"How could I forget? I got the carp on a Clouser crayfish. Number eight. Mombo?"

"Yes?"

"Don't worry," he said.

"Why on earth would I ever worry about you?" She kissed the phone and hung up.

The second morning after Gabriela's visit, Celine woke to breakfast in bed. She had dreamed of a big hospital on an empty gray beach. The hospital didn't seem to have any doctors and there were hundreds of empty rooms. Musical scores were taped onto the green doors instead of charts.

She sat up and felt for her oversize tortoise-shell reading glasses.

"Oh, Pete." She reached up for a kiss. On the silver tray was a soft-boiled egg in its cup, the tiny spoon, toast, marmalade, coffee, and an envelope. On the envelope her name, in blue ink, in a free and flowing hand. She ate the egg, drank half a cup of coffee, and then opened the letter with the penknife she kept on the bedside table. Inside were five or six sheets of fine, pale blue stationery, handwritten, and she didn't have to flip to the end to know who it was from.

"It was under the door," Pete said. "She must

have come very early." Celine heard a trace of respect. For some reason Pete always admired people who got up even earlier than he did. She read:

"Dear Celine, Thank you. For the wonderful dinner and for your kind attention. Your willingness to listen. It means the world to me.

"I was telling you about the death of my mother. What happened next. Easier, I think, if I write it. After the accident, Pop tried. He did. The next two months after the funeral are a blur. I remember that we flew out east and spent a few weeks up in the Adirondacks at a cabin a friend had loaned us. Near Keene Valley. We spent a lot of time swimming in icy-cold water beneath a waterfall and we didn't say much. I remember the way these tiny bubbles came up through the black depths of a stone pothole." Celine let a warm memory overtake her: She might have swum in that very pool, it was probably on Johns Brook, beside the first lean-to shelter. She so loved that country. She had taught Hank to fish there, and to start a fire, before he entered first grade. She continued reading: "He took me canoeing on Saranac Lake and we caught fish. When school started, I know he must have been getting drunk at night because he forgot to wake me up.

"Sometimes I had to pull and drag him out of bed. He would resist and moan and then when he woke up and his bleary eyes focused I would see that he was awake and that he was seeing me and he would stare. Not like at me, Gabriela, his daughter, but like down a long street where he would find me and search my face, at first desperately, then with some kind of relief, then with growing anguish, and I knew he was not seeing me but the face of my mother.

"I cannot describe the effect this had on me. It made me feel both desperate to be consoled and also like a ghost. I would tell him that I was hungry, and often there was nothing in the fridge or pantry and he would take my hand and, still wearing the same clothes he had the night before, he would walk me down the hill on Clayton. He'd take me to the bakery on Haight and buy me a blueberry Danish and a carton of milk and then walk me to the French American School. That was the year of the Summer of Love, which of course I didn't know then, but I remember the colorful clothes, and all the smells of what must have been pot and patchouli and sweat, and people playing guitars and all kinds of drums, and handing out food. There was this one kid with beautiful blond hair to his waist who handed out apples. It was his thing. He gave me an apple almost every day. Sometimes we took the streetcar on Divisadero for a few blocks just for fun. I didn't care that Pop was unshaven and rumpled. I would cling to his hand. He was a very handsome man, even with a three-day beard, and I could see the way the young mothers looked at him and talked to him when he dropped me off, a mixture of maternal pity and lust. I could not name it then but I felt it—that he was desirable. I could see the way women, even my teachers, lit up, the way they changed when they talked to him.

"Well, he was a *National Geographic* photographer and an adventurer and just so handsome and he had just lost his beautiful wife."

Celine closed her eyes. Nineteen sixty-seven was the year Hank had started at Saint Ann's, which had recently opened. There was no Summer of Love in Brooklyn Heights, but it was a wonderful, exciting time. They were living on Grace Court and her own marriage was still strong—she would not have felt the pull of the dashing photojournalist. Everything with Wilson would not unravel until Hank was at boarding school. That's when the drinking started. A few years she would rather forget.

"In the afternoon it was the same," Gabriela wrote. "He often forgot to pick me up. There was often no dinner. When he came out of his reverie and realized that an eight-year-old girl can't live on vodka the way he did, he would rouse himself and off we would go to the Mediterranean restaurant on Haight, or the Japanese place on Cole that's gone now and I would eat nothing but tempura. God, I would have been roly-poly but for all the meals I missed."

Celine paused again. She could see it—there was something ascetic in the beauty of the young woman, and now she knew where it had come from: deprivation.

She continued reading: "Did I ask him about Mom? I don't remember ever asking. Is that crazy? Maybe not. There was a hole there, it spoke for itself. I didn't want any other explanation, I guess, anything at all that would get the Absence vibrating any more than it was, because the Absence was an utter ache, a black ball sitting very still in the middle of my chest. I knew that if it moved too much—that the vibrations of questions and half answers would tear me apart, cell from cell. I intuited this.

"That was third grade, with Miss Lough. I remember it was on the second floor of the new building on Grove." Celine had heard of the French American International School. It was a very progressive private school that started about the same time as Saint Ann's, and like Hank's school it began with just a few kids. "She was very tender with me. Sometimes when Pop forgot to pick me up she would wait with me outside, and then she would glance at her watch and try not to look too sad. She was very kind. Then she would whistle out a sigh and take my hand and say, 'What shall we sing while we walk?' It was lucky she had a boyfriend in the Haight. I took it all in stride. When you're that

40

little you don't know any better. I don't even think I was unhappy, I don't remember that as a particularly bad year. I missed Amana terribly. Jackson, too. As far as I was concerned this was the way life went when you were seven or eight. Sometimes your mother didn't come home for good, forever. Sometimes your father forgot stuff, sometimes you went hungry.

"And then one evening, at the end of our year with Miss Lough, Pop came home with a loud buxom cigarette-smoking nurse named Danette and they got married at city hall and she cleaned him up and put food in the cupboards. Not long after that she caught him looking at me across the dinner plates and she went and plucked up the picture of Amana on the hall table—she's on the deck of some ferry, smiling into the wind with the hair blowing across her face—I loved that picture so much—and Danette stomped back and held it up to my own face and practically spit at Pop, 'Every time you look at her you see her,' and jabbed her finger at Mom. I felt as if she were jabbing it into my own chest, I winced and started to cry.

" 'That's enough!' she said. 'I can't live like this. You'—she aimed her finger at Pop and her chest heaved, she was wearing a low-cut V-neck thing with no bra and there was a lot of chest to heave—'you figure out how this is going to work!' and she slammed out the front door.

"The next week they put me in my own apartment downstairs. With my own key and my own food. I was eight."

Celine set down the page. "You lived in your own apartment in third grade?" she murmured to no one. She drained her coffee cup and refilled it from the carafe Pete had brought with the tray. "You're kidding."

Why didn't her teachers know that? she thought. They should have. Well. Gabriela's words didn't feel like an indictment of her teachers or her family, but Celine might have taken them that way. Gabriela must have realized it, because the next line read: "Maybe I didn't know how screwed up that was. Pop told me the building was one big house and I was going to have a special treat usually reserved for older girls, I was going to have my own big room and even my own kitchen. You know, I could always tell when he was lying. Especially to himself. Sometimes I felt that way when he talked about his travels."

She thought about the young woman she had met the other night. Gabriela had a remoteness and a self-reliance that might make her unapproachable. And a sadness, she realized now. Very quiet, underneath it all.

Celine continued: "Pop was often in Ecuador shooting for the Smithsonian, or in Guatemala for *National Geographic*. He loved to ski in the Andes. The other parents had a heroic picture of him, I could tell. He spent a lot of time in South America and someone later told me that the rumor was that he worked for the CIA. Ha. What people always thought about someone who had a life that was just a little interesting or exotic. And when they saw him—this was later, after the first months of sodden grief—in his tight black T-shirts with his strong arms and clean jawline and his hair like James Dean's with the swept-up wave in front, his easy laugh, and especially with the air of having just been somewhere exotic and dangerous—it was like a breeze that came off him, you could smell it—everyone was charmed by Pop."

I bet, Celine thought. She always thought it was interesting that the most charming people—if you scratched the surface—were often the saddest. Celine topped her cup to warm it up and found her place at the bottom of the page.

"Well, that was the part I wasn't sure I could get through. Not so bad after all. I think I realized as I was writing it that every family is screwed up once you scratch the surface. After all, how many little girls before me had an evil stepmom? Ha!"

That was one way of looking at it.

"It never got easier with Danette. I kept trying to think of her as a mother, but it was too painful, and as young as I was, I think I understood that some relationships are as inevitable and unchangeable as the seasons. I gave up. I spent time with Pop whenever I could, I kept a protected space in my heart for him, for us, but I had to be almost surreptitious. I lived downstairs, I went to school, I grew up. And then something happened.

"Thank you for reading this. I'd like to tell you the rest in person—the reason why I looked you up. I'll be here until tomorrow afternoon. If you think you have the stamina—there's not much more—I'll run down to see you.

"With gratitude and affection, Gabriela."

And her cell number. Celine set down the letter and reached for the phone on her bedside table and called.

Gabriela literally ran. She met Celine on the dock at the same spot they'd been two nights ago, but now she was in pale green running shorts, training shoes, and a fitted T-shirt of an Alaskan salmon colored in blocks like a Rothko. Fine beads of sweat misted her cheeks.

A warm, mid-September late morning, the dock bustling with tourists. Celine said, "You didn't bring the file." She stretched up and kissed the girl on both cheeks.

"I'm sick of carrying it around. I thought that if you wanted to see anything I'd copy and send

44

it. I'd like to hold on to the originals anyway. Where were we?"

"You had your own apartment. You were all of eight."

"Okay. Whew." Gabriela blew a stray hair out of her face. She leaned on the railing and watched snowy gulls gyre out from under the bridge. "I missed Amana terribly. But I didn't feel—I don't know—like an outcast or anything. When you're little you accept things, as I said. I guess I thought that this was something that just happens to some little girls. They get their own apartment. They cook their own meals. Some days I even got myself to school. Thinking about it now, that was crazy—"

"Back up. You didn't join them for dinner? You didn't go up for breakfast?"

"I had a key. It was a big, pale blue Victorian with a few apartments, it wasn't like it was supermax or anything. And I did sometimes. Dinner, never breakfast, because in the morning they were usually hungover and a little mean. She was, and Pop in his morning-after fugue was helpless to protect me. So I ate cold cereal for breakfast, I mean I had a fridge and all, and Danette made sure I had generic cornflakes and ramen and cheap hamburger. She clearly didn't want me to show up at school looking starved and then have Social Services come in. Remember she was a registered nurse, she had a professional reputation, and I guess she had her pride. A monster never sees itself as a monster. Remember poor Grendel."

"Right. Poor Grendel."

"I had a step stool, the kind little kids use to brush their teeth, and I had it by the stove so I could stir the noodles and cans of soup. I learned to fry eggs. For my ninth birthday Danette got me an omelet pan."

"What did your father get you?"

"A trip to the Ice Capades."

"Did Danette come too?"

"Yes, of course. She would have never let us go off to something as celebratory as the Ice Capades alone. It would be like letting Pop have some kind of ghost date with Amana. I know, it's so fucked up. He couldn't get three seats together because of course he remembered and got the tickets at the very last minute, so I sat in front of them. Pop bought me like three cotton candies and a tub of popcorn because I guess he felt guilty and I got sick. I threw up on the sidewalk and Danette threw a fit."

"Wow."

"I know. But before I got sick, Pop used his press pass and we went backstage and I met the Hula-Hoop lady."

"Who was that?"

"She was a Romanian, tall and blond and sequined, terribly glamorous, perfectly in the

Olympic figure-skater vein, but she did her act with Hula-Hoops! She could twirl, like, a dozen, on her arms and everything, while she skated. I thought she was the most queenly thing I'd ever seen. I still have a picture Pop took of me in my pink princess dress with a plastic tiara on my head staring up in unadulterated awe at this six-foot ice queen."

"This all sounds like some strange nightmare. It almost makes me woozy."

"I know. Please don't hate my father. I'm coming to understand. That he did the best he could. I'm convinced that he loved my mother more than anything on earth. More, even. With more love than can exist in the universe. It was too much. To lose her. Which makes his running with me up the trail even more heroic." Her tone shifted. It deepened and saddened like rain when the wind stops and it falls straight down through trees. "I think he tried to live every day just so he wouldn't die."

I think he tried to live every day just so he wouldn't die.

The line would become a refrain Celine couldn't shake, like the chorus of a song. That was one way of putting it. Why some of us put one foot in front of the other. Celine had done enough of that in her own life. She wasn't much older than the little girl in this story when she lost, for all intents and purposes, her own father.

And just a few years later, something much more devastating.

Now, on the dock beneath the Brooklyn Bridge, warmed from a breakfast cooked by the man she loved most in the world, Celine listened to Gabriela and could not countenance the image of the child on a step stool at the stove, age eight, alone, stirring herself a pot full of ramen or minestrone. Taking it to the table, pouring it into a bowl, eating it, alone. Alone alone alone.

"Okay," Celine said finally. "Tell me the rest."

"There's not a lot more to tell. That's how it was. Danette tossed the photo of my mom on the ferry into a drawer where I retrieved it and hung it up over my bed. Right where some people hang a crucifix. Pop traveled a lot and the witch and I settled into a mistrustful détente. She kept me fed and clothed and walked me to school when Dad was home and too hungover. I think she was afraid that I would get bigger in some growth spurt and wreak unimaginable revenge. I don't know. She treated me like a dangerous reptile, with respect and wariness. She was all hip sway and boobs at the school and she flirted with the young dads outside, and I don't know for sure but I sensed that she had affairs with a few of them. Anyway, when I saw how they responded to her I wanted to kill her."

"Right."

"The years passed. Pop traveled and I heard

rumors that he did work for the government, clandestine work, but he always laughed it off. I'm still not sure, but there was one thing—" She stopped short, shook herself off.

Celine raised an eyebrow. "One thing?"

The girl shivered. "Nothing. Sometimes I think my imagination runs away with me."

Celine let it go. She knew when and when not to press.

Gabriela said, "He and I developed ways of communicating that circumvented her rage. Like when he gave me one of his favorite new photographs in a little frame—of a horse, a Chilean cowboy, a regatta—he always slipped another picture behind it. Hidden in the frame, behind the backing. Of Amana. Of the three of us camping or in a canoe. I don't know where he had these stashed, but it was his way of saying, 'We are still a family. Don't forget.'

"Or maybe he was trying to tell me that somewhere inside him was my old father and that one day he would be back. I don't know. Anyway, I hung them up in plain sight, knowing that Amana, that our real family, was behind them and they gave me strength.

"You know I went on to boarding school at St. George's. I got kicked out for doing acid, but they let me back in after I wrote a long letter of contrition and described my circumstances. Makes me shudder now, those lies. I was not contrite at all, but I could not go back to Danette. I did more drugs later, but was more careful about getting caught. Jesus. Got into Sarah Lawrence. Being away at school was like five-star, to me, after life at home. I already knew how to live on my own. The hard thing was that I was away from that open window, the one by my bed that opened onto the gardens. Because what if little Jackson decided to come home one night while I was gone? What if he jumped up onto the sill and the window was closed and I was nowhere near to hear his meows. I almost ran away several times in the first year and a half. Of course I realize now that missing Jackson was—that he was a surrogate for something else.

"One day at college I called home to tell Dad that I had gotten an honors in photography. Danette said that he'd taken an assignment to Yellowstone to document the grizzly bears and that no one was picking up at the motel or at the biologists' center in the Lamar Valley, she'd tried. And I tried and tried both numbers anyway. And he never came home from that trip."

"What?"

"He never came back."

Celine was standing at the rail looking across the East River to two tall ships, square-riggers, docked at the Seaport. The current seemed to be flowing faster now and kicking up waves under the bridge. At some point in Gabriela's story she

50

had closed her eyes for a moment and lifted her nose to the river and the harbor where she always went to get her bearings. The wind had picked up and it came from the open ocean and it smelled of salt.

"Where'd he go?" she said.

"I don't know."

"What do you mean, you don't know? Like, you never saw him again?"

"No. I never saw him again."

Just when she thought Gabriela's story couldn't get any stranger or more sad.

"Did he die?"

"I don't know."

"What do you mean, you don't know? Didn't you talk to the biologists or park rangers or whatever they were?"

"Of course."

"And?"

"He drove into Cooke City one night, just out of the northern boundary of the park. Said he was going for more batteries and bourbon—his words. It was a rainy early-October night, the rain turning to snow. They found his truck at the Soda Butte Creek bridge, just off the park boundary."

"You're not joking. Of course you aren't. I mean—"

"No."

"Give me a sec." Celine turned her back to the

railing and leaned against it. She labored for breath. It was like a hot flash. She broke into a sweat and her head throbbed. At the same time, the harbor breeze raised goose bumps along her arms. Better. What was it about the story? Had what happened to Lamont struck in Celine some deep primal fear? She didn't think so. It was that Gabriela had lost her mom, and her cat, and then her father. And in each loss was some further exile. Celine wondered just then what the word "home" must mean to her. Probably a space within the relative safety of her own skin.

"Is that a sec?" Gabriela said after what may have been several minutes.

"That was, like, twenty-odd years ago, right?"

"It's been a while."

"And nothing's surfaced? There was no investigation, no findings?"

"Of course there was an investigation. It made the news and everything. All the evidence pointed to a bear."

"A bear. A grizzly?"

"Yes. Pop had that Invincibility Gene. He took pictures of wildlife no one should ever take—with no zoom lens. He was crazy. Nobody should take a portrait of a wild hippo with a twenty-eight millimeter lens. He said he could sing to crocodiles. When I ask myself if he really loved me, those dangerous wildlife pictures go in the No column. He was that careless with his life."

"Huh."

"There had been a big boar grizzly marauding right in town, in Cooke City, that very week. Locals told tourists that if they went out on the town at night—ha! there's one main street—to go in pairs and bring defense. To a local that means at least a .44 Magnum, what they like to call the Bear Minimum. To a tourist it means pepper spray or more probably a cell phone and a scream."

"My son, Hank, had a .44 Magnum once. Told me the same thing about Bear Minimum. Sounds like you've been there."

"Three times. I didn't have a last name up there. It was Gabriela Whose Dad Disappeared That Time."

"That Time? Was there more than one?"

"Two or three people disappeared like that."

"Really?"

"Yep. Over, like, fifteen years. If it was a bear it was one ornery old SOB."

"Huh. Were there any signs, signs of—"

"A struggle? Robbery? A note? Suicide? Nothing. His keys were in the ignition. His wallet was in the glove box. Along with a handmade hunting knife he always carried. He took his down sweater and his Carhartt. He was an outdoorsman. If he'd been planning on being out in the woods any length of time in the snow he would have worn a Gore-Tex shell or some-

53

thing, not a canvas work coat. It's like he stopped to pee, or check out an animal."

"How about tracks? Up there they must have all sorts of Grizzly Adams tracker guys."

"His name is Elbie Chicksaw. He's like half Blackfoot, half mountain lion, half pine bark, half quartzite. He's like five two and his card says *Tracking, Hunting, Spirit-Travel.* Not joking. But he's pixilated. His spirit animal or totem or whatever is a guppy. He had one in an aquarium growing up in Teaneck."

"The tracker grew up in New Jersey?"

"Yep. His mother was Blackfoot, she was a traveling nurse. Like Danette, but I bet a lot nicer."

"So there must have been tracks."

Gabriela nodded. "So Pop was supposed to meet the bear biologists at daybreak on the road at a spot just below Druid Peak. When he didn't show up they figured he was hungover. He had a bit of a reputation. When he hadn't appeared by midday they got a little concerned. One, an Ed Pence, ran into Cooke City in the afternoon on a mail run and saw Pop's truck just off the road and radioed the cops. Cop. Who called the State Police. Who waited a day and initiated a search. The weather did not cooperate. It had been raining, and the night he went missing it got cold and snowed. By the time Chicksaw got there he was looking mostly for signs like scrapes and broken twigs. He did find grizzly tracks, drag marks, blood, but no Pop.

"It's a story, huh?" Gabriela said.

"I don't know. It seems stranger after all the rest of it."

"You mean the way I was brought up?"

"Yes."

"I know. It's not like life gets less strange." Gabriela reached back with both hands and pulled her ponytail free of the band. Her thick hair fell to her shoulders and she shook it loose. It reminded Celine of something but she couldn't say what. "It's why I called you."

"It is?"

"Nothing about Pop's disappearance has ever sat right with me. There was a sheriff up there, a man named Travers, who was very kind to me, and I'll never forget how he looked when he surveyed the scene. It didn't seem to sit right with him either. When I saw that story in the alumni magazine about the Prada PI, I thought about calling you. The story mentioned your friendship with Dean Renato, whom I knew, and I called him instead. When he said you were maybe the best anywhere at solving cold cases—I came to Brooklyn." Gabriela stopped. She was looking north, under the bridge, away. "I have a son," she said. "He's eight. I'd love for him to meet his grandpa." She didn't turn around and Celine thought that Time Does Not Heal All Wounds, not by a long shot.

four

It has almost never happened that a grizzly bear kills more than one man. Or woman. If they do, it's usually in the same incident, a mama bear's rampage protecting cubs or, as in the terribly sad incident featured in Herzog's movie *Grizzly Man*, a furious attack on a couple in their camp by what was probably a gaunt and desperate boar arriving at the end of the salmon run and wild with hunger. The history books are not replete with serial grizzly man-eaters. Pete checked it out after listening closely to Celine tell Gabriela's story. There was the famous vengeful Old Two Toes, who killed and partially ate at least three men in Montana, and was probably responsible for two more deaths, but that was in 1912. In Alaska, in 1995, a pissed-off boar grizzly attacked and killed one hiker, then his friend, but the incident was a response to being surprised on a moose carcass— a crime of passion so to speak. The incidents of premeditated, or habitual, serial assaults were very rare. No: Human beings, by orders of magnitude, remained the most vicious animal on the planet.

Once, in northwest Montana, up near Glacier National Park, Pete had flown into the Bob Marshall Wilderness for a three-week backpacking trip with a legendary backcountry pilot named

Dave Hoerner. Hoerner had told him how a very large boar griz had been disrupting camps on the Middle Fork of the Flathead, and had been shot with a tranquilizer gun and captured. It was Hoerner's job to move the bear from a mountain airstrip called Schafer Meadows. Hoerner flew a Cessna 185 single-engine workhorse, and the tranquilized bear was so big that when the Forest Service crew loaded it into the back of the plane it stretched through most of the airframe and the huge head lay against Dave's right hip where he sat in the pilot seat. In his lap was his .44 Magnum. Hoerner taxied back to the downwind end of the strip and was ticking off his run-up checklist when he looked down and saw the monster griz's mouth twitch. Holy crap. He pulled back to idle, set the brakes, ran around, threw up the cargo door, and hauled on the bear's legs and paws with all his might. The bear hit the grass with a thud and got to his feet and wobbled. By then Hoerner was back in his seat and throttling forward and the last he saw of the animal it was glaring back at him and striding toward the woods. Damn. Imagine if all that had happened five minutes later at two thousand feet above the ground. Mayhem.

Pete got a kick out of that story. But the fact remained that grizzly bears, like most predators, were smart enough to know that tangling with humans in any way was a bad idea. It was very hard to believe that one bear might have killed and vanished three people over a fifteen-year span. But not impossible. One thing Pete had learned over the years as a participant in so many disparate cultures, and as a family historian, is that almost nothing that can be imagined is impossible, and that, in fact, most of those things, in one form or another, have occurred. Scary, really.

He and Celine talked about Gabriela's case over several nights, and Celine wondered if she had the strength. The last year had taken its toll. Pete was more concerned than she was. When she was upset she struggled to breathe, and he watched her with concealed alarm. One night over Wicked-Good Green Chili—her name, not his—he reached across the café table and put his hand on her arm. "Maybe this is one to let lie," he said. "We'd have to travel, probably for more than a few days." Her lips compressed. She was annoyed. She picked a piece of broccoli out of her stew. What was broccoli doing in chili? He was always trying to sneak something in.

She narrowed her eyes at him. "The reasonable thing is not usually the right thing. Why is that?"

Pete had not fallen in love with Celine Watkins for her timidity. He dutifully picked up the discarded broccoli and ate it.

There was something in the case she could not relinquish, and the more she mulled it over, and the more she thought about Gabriela's shadowed life, the more energized she became.

On September 19th, Celine called Gabriela in San Francisco and told her that she would try to find her father. Or confirm that he had died. Gabriela would have to prepare herself. The young woman answered as Celine knew she would: with relief. She had money, she said, and insisted on paying expenses and the going rate of New York PIs. Celine could tell this was non-negotiable and she did not object.

Next Celine called Hank in Denver and asked if they could borrow his truck and camper for maybe three weeks; could they fly out to Denver in a few days to pick it up?

"And Hank," she said, "the little Glock 26 I gave you for your birthday that time? Can I borrow it, too? I'd rather not fly with mine. I have to declare it and everyone can see, and I'm always terrified it will get stolen by some baggage handler. Like that time Bruce Willis made such a fuss."

She made Hank laugh. *That time* was a family legend. She had been struggling with her bags through LaGuardia when a hand had joined hers on the handle of the carry-on and a voice had said, "Allow me, ma'am," and it was the movie star himself. He eased away the roller bag, too.

That was good enough for a good story. But then they had arrived at the check-in counter together and she had pulled the little lockbox out of her checked bag and declared the Glock, and Mr. Willis had cracked his signature smile—the warm one, not the one before he blows you away—and he'd become enamored with Hank's mom. It was a few weeks before the New York City Police Department was to switch over from revolvers to the Glock, and so several curious airport cops came over, too, and autographs were signed, and when Willis heard Mom was a PI he gave her his personal card with an assistant's phone number. He said, "I wish you were *my* mom," which always made Hank a little jealous. Willis said that if she and her husband were ever in L.A. to please look him up. Maybe he thought her story would make a good movie.

Anyway, when she arrived in Maine to solve the case of Penobscot Paul, which became another favorite story, her treasured Glock was missing from her luggage. She always attributed it to the fuss and bother famous people leave in their wake. She considered fame to be a terrible and irresistible trap. Once she told Hank, "Hank, if you are going to do something—say, writing—do your very best, and if it happens that you also become the best in the world, that's wonderful, but try not to let too many people know about it."

But what made Hank happier when she called him was to hear the new tone in her voice. There was vigor there, a contained excitement he hadn't heard in a while. And he knew that it was because she had committed again to do the work she was born for. He told her she could borrow both the truck and the gun.

Celine hadn't ever really needed to carry a gun. The type of investigative work she did rarely involved dangerous perps. She had tried that and didn't like it. After working for a detective agency that mostly handled domestic matters—yuck—and learning her trade and getting her PI license, she was almost immediately contacted by the FBI. The bureau, it seemed, did not have many agents who were comfortable moving in the milieu of the investment banker–Fishers Island crowd. Well, Celine had spent every summer there for most of her life. The bureau needed an associate who could call someone in the Connecticut Blue Book and ask delicate questions, and who would be trusted—the two families might even know each other, perhaps they were even second or third cousins. They were going after a man who had perpetrated a very large fraud on the Bank of New York, and they thought he might be in the environs of his family in Old Greenwich or Darien.

No one realizes the power or extent of the aristocracy in America; it exists and holds enormous sway despite the inroads of all the techy, sneaker-wearing New Money. Celine was born into it. Fourteen of the governors of the Plymouth Colony were her ancestors, and their families had continued to consolidate and expand their power for more than three centuries. They summered on Nantucket and Fishers and Islesboro, Maine; their sons and daughters attended Ivy League colleges and had careers with Big Banks and Big Oil and the International Monetary Fund and the Federal Reserve; and the most daring and radical of their children became artists and filmmakers or worked for the Nature Conservancy, and these were everyone's favorite cousins and nieces and were endowed with a certain mystical reverence—they were not so much the black sheep of the family as special children who were indulged like the shamans of other cultures who only walk backward. Celine was one of these. Perhaps even farther afield than most. She was not exactly an outcast, but she had deliberately stepped out of the fold, and so she could see it with an outsider's perspicuity.

It had begun with her mother, Barbara. She had done something unheard of in her society during the war: Soon after returning to New York from Paris just before its occupation, she had set in motion the divorce from her husband, Harry, who was the father of her three daughters. And then almost as soon as the Japanese surrendered, she had taken up with Fleet Admiral William F. "Bull" Halsey Jr., the five-star admiral who had commanded the Pacific's Third Fleet and is considered by some to be the greatest fighting admiral America has ever had. They became lovers while he was still married—horrors!—and though Halsey's wife was committed for life into what was then called an insane asylum, he would never divorce her. He visited her once a month until his death.

Complicated. Her children called Barbara "Mummy," but Hank and everyone else called her Baboo. WASPs have these names. Every year Baboo brought her three daughters to Fishers Island for a long summer season. Admiral Bill joined them. He was there, ostensibly, to visit his daughter who also had a house on the island, and he always kept a room at the club to keep up appearances, but everyone knew. Three and a half months, early June through the middle of September, and they repeated this sojourn for the next fourteen years, until his death. It was a longer stretch of summer than almost anyone else ever took, and it was because the island was a partial sanctuary, away from the more codified strictures of New York. On the island, in the summer, with the sound of waves heard through the screens of almost any house, and the weather sweeping in from the Atlantic with winds that flattened the dune grass and dusty miller, and thrashed the bayberry and squalled rain against the cedar shingles of the roofs, well. Certain allowances were made for the unpredictability of nature, both human and maritime, and people were generally more forgiving and relaxed. It didn't hurt, either, that Baboo was almost universally adored. She had been the wild sister, the heavenly dancer, the legendary waltzer, the mischievous joker, the girl who had swum from Simmons Point to Ty Whitney's dock, around the Race. Her father, Charles Cheney, had founded the Fishers Island Country Club for God's sake. But. Well. Baboo's domestic realignments were more than the idiosyncratic decisions of a well-bred young woman who had always been seen as warm-blooded. (Her mother, Mary Bell, was from *California,* after all, Santa Barbara, and had Spanish ancestry mixed with those flinty Scots.) Baboo's decisions were more than peccadilloes; they were tectonic transgressions: She had initiated a divorce while her husband was still in Paris trying to safeguard Morgan Bank's assets from the advancing Nazis. And then only five years later she took up with a professional *soldier.* Well, he was a five-star admiral, one of the towering commanders of the Pacific fleet, who stood beside General MacArthur on the USS *Missouri* at the Japanese surrender. Celine had the famous photo signed by Admiral Nimitz and the others. But Halsey was a bit rough-hewn and Not Our Class, Dear. NOCD, the mildly uttered and searing brand, always casually tossed off, one of the most vicious and eviscerating curses most people have never heard of. A final judgment of relative inferiority that no store of accomplishments or merit or even wealth can ever wipe away. Ludicrous. Halsey had the inborn class and dignity one would expect of a great commander, and he had more courage and native intelligence than almost any man alive.

Baboo was still invited to the parties and the clam bakes, still brought her famous fried chicken and deviled eggs to the beach picnics, was still held in certain awe: She was the scion of the family that had founded the club and had lived a life abroad that was so dazzling and glamorous not even Hollywood could have done it justice. She was still adored, but from a certain distance now, as one would a colorful fish behind glass. She continued to command the devotion of friends who would never forsake her—Ginnie Ackerman, Ty Whitney, Penny Williams. But a subtle coolness overtook her, an almost imperceptible shouldering to the colder outer edges of the inner circle in which she had grown up. No one on earth is better at death by a thousand slights than the WASP aristocracy of the East Coast. Or death by very gradual hypothermia. It can be delivered in the most nuanced tone of voice: the barest lift into the next octave when speaking of personal matters, of, say, the troubles of someone else's family—most listeners wouldn't notice it. But it means the loss of the most natural and intimate *lower* register, the one reserved for only the most trusted cohort. The omission—Oh dear, *how* could I have forgotten?—of an invitation to a daughter's wedding in Delaware. It was, it could feel like, the most devastating fall from grace. A woman of lesser character might have quietly killed herself, or worse, become bitter and vengeful. Baboo carried her changing status with a dignity and grace that made her more regal in the eyes of her children and, later, her grandchildren. *She* was the great love of our greatest admiral; *she* had skied the Streif at Hahnenkamm in one fell swoop; *she* spoke beautiful French and could compose an occasional poem of great wit and bawdy humor; *her* ancestors had founded this country. But she had the mildest sadness, like the faint scent of honeysuckle or the fluttering shadow of a bird at dusk, and it felt to Hank, as a child, noble and trustworthy, like the sadness of an exiled queen. Of course as a child he had no idea where it came from, but somehow it made her laughter more rich, her delight in him more poignant. And to her three true friends, it gave them access to a friendship and a loyalty that was more real than anything they might have found in their unfor-giving society.

The costs to Celine and her two sisters are hard to assess. They all attended Brearley, that very fancy private girls' school on the Upper East

Side, and they had no dearth of friends. It was as if the children of Barbara Cheney and Harry Watkins were offered conditional reprieve—after all, *he* had done nothing but be the youngest partner in the history of Morgan's and escape Paris at the last possible second, on a bicycle he traded for his gorgeous Hispano Suiza when he realized the roads were too clogged with cars to get out in time—and he was too handsome for words, and a spectacular natural athlete—no, the children should be put on an indeterminate probation, the unspoken terms of which would be lifted when . . . well . . . when they were lifted. Probably when they married some up-and-coming banker from Williams.

Celine did not get the memo.

She begged to be sent away to a boarding school in Vermont where her beloved first cousin Rodney was a sophomore, and so Baboo relented and sent a scrawny fourteen-year-old girl off to Putney. The school had been started by an avowed sympathizer of the China experiment and was one of the first New England boarding schools to admit boys and girls in equal numbers. Not many: two hundred students on a dairy farm, on top of the most picturesque southern Vermont hill, with a view to folded ridges quilted with orchards, fields, sugar bush. The students, mostly from the New York and Boston elite, were required to do barn chores and cut firewood, which was a novelty they learned to relish.

Celine rose at five a.m. in the winter dark with the ice chips of stars deeply set in the patterns of constellations for which she did not know the names but that were starting to seem like friends—the billion stars that breathed a faint luminosity onto the snowy hill, the snow so cold it squeaked underfoot as she walked to the big barn whose lights already burned. The clank of stanchions and scrape of shovels and shouts already drifted across the field; she entered the barn and was hit, then enveloped in the warm heavy scents of cows and manure and lime, rotting sweet silage and dusty hay and sawdust. Celine was converted. The Putney School did not have to emulate the precepts of the new Chinese collectives—of Communism—to be subversive: It was enough to take a girl from the Upper East Side and give her a silage fork and a wheelbarrow and ask her to sweat in a crowded barn with her friends as steam came off the cows and a below-zero North Country dawn doused the stars and washed the wooded hills in a tide of blue-gray and burning rose. That was enough.

And then at ten a.m., after the first two classes, they put her on a wood bench in a creaky oak and pinewood hall and had her sing: Bach and Handel, hymns and four-part rounds. Not just for the glory of God but for life. For the joy of it. For being all together and creating music.

It was more powerful than any church. And better than any pamphlet or soap box at throwing an unflinching light on the values of patrician society. Poor Celine. Whatever wariness she aroused by simply being the offspring of Barbara Cheney Watkins, she compounded by returning to Manhattan for Thanksgiving break with an ax sticking out of her rucksack.

And then she did the unthinkable. She missed her period.

Then a second.

She had just turned fifteen. And she was pregnant.

Hank picked Pete and his mother up at Denver International Airport on the morning of September 22nd. On the way into town Celine asked Hank about his marriage, his poetry, his diet, all of which she thought would eventually come around. Pete sat in back, reassuring everyone with his dependable reserve. Hank had huge affection for his cryptic second dad. His first, who left for New Mexico when Hank was about to enter college, was the antithesis to Pete in almost every respect: Hank's father was a gregarious storyteller, a great wit, he could do accents. He adored Edith Wharton and a good old-fashioned, and he didn't know the first thing about building a boat. Hank loved him fiercely. It was almost like having two fathers from two different species. Hank appreciated the diversity.

He turned off the highway and drove up into his neighborhood on the edge of the lake. Celine said, "The young woman, Gabriela, whose case we're taking—her stepmother put her in her own apartment when she was eight. And then when she was in college her father went missing in Yellowstone. Presumed dead."

Hank passed a truck loaded with crates of live chickens. "And?" he said. He was interested.

"She grew up and raised a son mostly on her own and became quite a good fine-arts photographer. A single mom."

Hank laughed, he couldn't help it. His mother was a truly wily investigator, but when it came to trying to disguise a message to her own son she was hopeless. He knew that she wanted to be a grandmother more than anything on earth.

"Wow," he said simply. "She devoted her life to her art and decided to go ahead and have a kid."

"I know," Celine said. She patted his knee.

The tour of the camper was perfunctory. Hank pulled the Tacoma long-bed pickup around to the front of the house. Celine always thought it was a wonderful spot, with a big view to the west of water and mountains, and it was five minutes from downtown's Union Station and the Tattered Cover Book Store. Until the spring he had lived in the house with his wife, Kim, but she was gone now in a trial separation—partly, she said, because she was sick of trying to be married to someone who was away half the time on assignment. Well.

The camper was one of those that fitted in the bed of the truck and extended over the cab. Hank unlocked the little back door and invited his mother and Pa in at a crouch and showed them how to unlock the latches and pop the top. He'd installed pressurized struts so it didn't take much more than a gentle push to lift the roof about three feet. Now they could all stand and light poured in through the lemon canvas. Celine uttered a happy cry. "Oh, look," she said. "I thought we'd have to crouch like when we lived in a shoe."

"When did we live in a shoe?" Pete said. Hank stared at him in wonder: He speaks!

"That time we slept in the back of the hearse. When we found Jerry, the Elvis impersonator."

"Ahh," said Pete.

Pete wore a tweed newsboy cap, the kind worn by Welsh Mountaineers and the guys driving the butcher trucks in movies about 1940s New York. His bushy gray hair stuck out around it so that it looked a little like a life raft riding a choppy sea of furry whitecaps. He also wore a corded charcoal wool vest, the kind loggers and trappers used to wear. Hank never stopped being intrigued by the man he could never get used to calling his stepfather. He thought Pete wore the cap in solidarity with the proletariat who no longer seemed to exist. Or maybe it was simply water resistant and warm and kept the sun out of his eyes. Pete stood back holding a steno pad and took notes on the operations of the camper. He was a very fine woodworker, and he had been a small-boat builder growing up on North Haven; Hank could see his appreciation of how all the storage and utility compartments in the camper fit together—the cabin was like a small yacht.

Celine politely listened as Hank explained the propane shutoff for the two-burner stove and little furnace and fridge, the operation of the hot water heater and outdoor shower—"It's already getting chilly up there," Hank said, "I doubt you'll use the shower. But anyhow, here." Celine glanced at Pete, and Hank saw the slightest smile pass between them. *What does he know? We come from northern people,* they seemed to say. They were still in love, that was always so clear. With a pang, he thought of his own wife. He quickly banished her image, along with the image of his mother and Pete prancing around the Montana woods naked.

"Hank, what season is it up there?" Celine said, running a hand over the quilt on the cab-over bunk above her. Hank had given them his moose and bear quilt, to get them in the mood.

He looked at her, puzzled. "It's—it's early fall, Mom, same as here."

"No, I mean is it deer and elk season yet? Or what?"

"Ah, that wouldn't be for, like, another month. Probably archery now, and upland game birds— grouse, turkey, partridge."

She bit her lower lip. "A bow is so cumbersome. Okay, can I borrow your twelve-gauge?"

Hank stared at her.

"And an orange hunting vest. And a hat, too. Do you have one of those funny neon-orange ones with flaps?"

He stared at her.

"Second thought," she said, "we may still be up there in a month. I better take your .308, too. I always felt more comfortable with high-powered rifles."

He stared at her. Celine ruffled his hair.

"Hunters go everywhere. They get lost. They tromp across anyone's land, traipse right past anyone's front windows, apologize later. It's also a very good reason to be in a place. Perfect guise." Her eyes crinkled. "Furthermore, hunters are well armed. Always a plus, I've found."

When they drove away that afternoon Hank was minus a duffel full of hunting clothes, two turkey calls, and more than half his armory.

five

When Celine found out at fifteen that she was pregnant she saw only darkness ahead and she prayed. When Celine prayed, she reverted to her beloved French. Her first language and her secret dialect with her two sisters and apparently with God. She and Bobby and Mimi spoke rapidly, in the colloquial French taught to them by their nannies, and they could conduct a running commentary on the people around them in the middle of a party, standing so close to their subjects that they might be touching, and do so in such a way—with small smiles covering laughter, with subtle eye rolls, with pursings of lips and biting of tongues—that their targets never knew. Of course most of the children in their circle studied French, and most of the parents had, too, but the rapidity and cadence and peculiar turns of phrase left no hope of decoding. Now she knelt by her bunk in her dorm at the Putney School, an old clapboard cottage with a little bell tower, and she prayed for her future child.

Mon Dieu, le Roi du ciel, appuyé sur ta puissance infinie et sur tes promesses . . .

She prayed fast and she prayed hard, and the sobs that racked her frame as she knelt did not slow her down, but she did not pray for guidance. For she had made her decision.

That morning she had seen the school doctor on the pretext of having a splitting headache. He was a kind elderly country GP of the old school, a man who had retired but had taken the sinecure as school physician because he could not imagine not helping people in need of care. Celine breezed in and sat on the edge of the examination table and tilted her chin up with pride and looked straight at the old man with steady gray eyes and said, "I think I am pregnant"—in this case he was the perfect shepherd.

He was not a fundamentalist in any way except in the interpretation of his oath, and he generally took the Long View. He had seen pretty much everything one human being might do to another. Dr. Watt examined Celine in the two-bed infirmary above the assembly hall and told her he had little doubt that she was halfway through her first trimester. At fifteen, Celine seemed too skinny to carry her own frame, much less another life. She had the gangly coltish gait, the high cheeks, prominent nose, and large eyes of a girl who was not beautiful, nor perhaps even pretty, but who discerning adults could tell would grow up to one day be gorgeous, even startling. But now she was only a waif who kept a plush mouse named Myriam in a tiny basket under her bed and who spent half her time at the swimming hole below the barn rescuing moths trapped on the surface of the black water. And she was a long way from home, and she was watching the life she had planned as a secret agent and resistance fighter flicker and sputter and go blank like the broken ribbons of film in the school's Friday-night projector.

Under the nonjudgmental ministrations of the old doctor her guard finally cracked. Her lips trembled as she buttoned the waist of her loose wool pants and slipped on her leather lace-up boots, and she hung her head and her hair covered her face, but the kindly Dr. Watt saw a tear hit the linoleum. He tossed the towel he'd just used to dry his hands into a wicker basket and put a hand—a hand that was arthritic from building woodsheds and auguring sugar taps—on her thin quaking shoulder and said, "You will have choices to make. You will want to talk with your parents today."

"My mother." Her voice, faint out from under her hair.

"Your mother, I see. I will let you talk to whomever you decide. I will not inform Mrs. Hinton." He was talking about the headmistress. "I'll leave that up to you," he said, "in your own time. I suggest that you do it soon, though, as your, ah, symptoms, will become more apparent, and arrangements will have to be made. It depends—I mean—"

"I know what you mean."

God only knew how she knew what he meant. She lifted her head and straightened her back and brought the fingers of both hands to her cheeks and gave one swipe outward, as if wiping away all further weakness, and blew a long sigh out of pursed lips and said, "Thank you, Doctor. I will never forget your kindness."

He smiled sadly and told her that he would help her with whatever decisions she made, and she put on her short wool jacket and walked straight to the library building and straight into the office of the headmistress and school founder, Carmelita Hinton.

Mrs. Hinton liked the scrawny, shy girl who spoke perfect French when pressed and who drew and painted with a sensitivity that was truly rare. At an exhibition in the student gallery at the end of the fall term, Mrs. Hinton was struck by Celine's compositions; she had an eye for the odd angle, the whimsical moment, and some pieces had the rare beauty that cannot be unwoven from a very subtle wit. It was as if Celine were trying her hardest to hide her true talent and failing, and Mrs. Hinton appreciated the instinctive modesty. But the headmistress also understood that the health and vigor of the community always came before the enabling of an individual and that sometimes terrible sacrifices had to be made. As soon as the child came through the door, she knew that life as this girl had come to understand it was about to be shattered. "Please," she motioned to a heavy wood chair and stood and came around her desk and took the other flanking chair. She turned to face the girl.

"Something has happened."

Celine had steeled herself and vowed not to asseverate or bargain. She admired the head-mistress and would not disrespect her. She studied for a moment the general area where her womb would be, trying to locate the mystery of the life inside her and to draw from it some sense of proportion in the face of the judgments that were sure to be laid. She nodded to herself, took a deep breath for both of them, and met Mrs. Hinton's eyes.

"I will have to leave school, I'm sorry."

The headmistress raised an eyebrow. That may have been a first: stoically taking on the punishment before arraignment or trial. Mrs. Hinton realized with a certain sorrow that she now liked and admired this girl even more. She knew that Celine was happy at the school: not at first, but more and more so with every passing month. She could see the girl finding her place and flowering in her work and enjoying the society of two or three classmates, also artists and sensitive; one was a dancer, another an accomplished violinist. She had not noticed her suffering the attentions of any particular boy. Sexual intercourse between students was strictly forbidden and the punishment was immediate expulsion. It must be remembered that a coeducational boarding secondary school, where students of both sexes shared not only classes but also work and sports and camping trips, was at the time a novel and brave undertaking that required the clearest rules. Carmelita Hinton was a rare commanding officer: She was a humanitarian with a kind and generous heart as well as a fair and unwavering disciplinarian.

"I see," she said. "Can you tell me why?"

"I'm sorry."

Mrs. Hinton picked a pencil off the blotter and shaved the lead with a thumbnail.

"You're pregnant," she said finally. The girl's eyes widened with surprise, then instant fury.

"Dr. Watt called you."

Mrs. Hinton shook her head. "No, he did not. Though he is required to do so. I have been doing this a long time. I knew the moment you walked through the door." She reached a hand out to Celine who hesitated and took it. Mercifully, Mrs. Hinton gave it one reassuring squeeze and let it go. Celine thought it was like the handshake the captains of opposing sports teams give each other before a match, to show that it was nothing personal.

"I will be very, very sorry to lose you. Do you wish to call your mother? I'll ask Loreen to go out and fetch the mail and you can use the phone in her office. When you're done you can tell your mother that I'll be calling her this afternoon."

Celine did not quiver or cry once during the entire visit. She called Baboo who took the news with surprisingly brisk pragmatism, the kind you'd expect from a mother who had once run a household with seven servants and raised three daughters in the shadow of a Nazi invasion, and who was the lover of a married fleet admiral. Celine took great strength from her mother's response and was immensely relieved. She understood for the first time in her young life what mothers were really made for. When Celine told her that Mrs. Hinton had expressed real disappointment in having to expel her, Baboo snapped.

"You are not going anywhere young lady. She threw all of you boys and girls together and assured us that it was *tout à fait bien*. This mess is her responsibility more than yours and she will clean it up. Now please tell her to come to the phone. I will not be available later, I plan to be busy this afternoon." Celine wanted to cry and laugh at the same time. With wonder at her mother's moral authority. Well, she would certainly not shed tears in the presence of the headmistress, not after her mother's display of regal sangfroid. She handed the phone to the one other truly strong woman she had ever known and waited for the fireworks.

There weren't any. Celine heard Mrs. Hinton say, "I see. I understand that you feel that way and I am sympathetic, I truly am, but that is our policy . . . Yes, yes, I understand . . . No. No, well . . . I would be happy to talk . . . No. Tomorrow afternoon? Well . . . I . . . Well. I see. Mrs. Watkins? . . . Yes . . . Okay, I look forward to it."

Did the ruddy-cheeked Carmelita Hinton look slightly pale when she hung up? Celine thought so. The headmistress rested the phone on the cradle and said, "Your mother is driving up to see us tomorrow."

On April 19, 1948, Barbara Cheney Watkins was driven from East Sixty-Eighth Street to Putney, Vermont, by William F. Halsey's driver, and she was accompanied by the admiral. Admiral Bill may have thought that he was about to witness one last epic engagement. The man told Baboo more than once that his life's greatest sorrow was having to sail away from sinking ships and leave his men drowning in the burning slicks and drifting in their Mae West lifejackets, terrified and abandoned while sharks circled. A horror that never ceased to haunt his dreams. And so he can be excused if he took Celine's hand while her mother met with Mrs. Hinton, and walked with her slowly, in his suit, up a dirt road muddy with snowmelt and seemed to be thinking of distant things.

Celine would never know what was said in Mrs. Hinton's office, but Baboo emerged in her long sable coat that gleamed and ruffled in the cold April wind, and Celine could tell by her bearing that if she chose, she could return one day to the Putney School.

Aside from Celine, the only one alive who knew this story was Hank, and it came to him in pieces. Celine told him some: how she had been expelled for one single day from the Putney School for fraternizing with a boy. The image he always had—and it may have been, of course, because he was her son, and the imagination of a son will only go so far when it comes to a mother—of "fraternizing" was her climbing trees with a fellow student. Birch trees, probably. He saw the two of them perched in a leafy canopy sharing a cigarette and a kiss. Certainly grounds for expulsion in the old days.

Celine told him how the sentence had lasted only as long as it took for Baboo to drive up to the school and give Mrs. Hinton an earful. Hank loved that. To him, Baboo had always seemed august and he loved to imagine her words in that office: "My dear Headmistress Hinton, what did you *think* was going to happen when you threw a hundred hormone-addled adolescent boys together with a hundred *unchaperoned* young girls? On a *farm?* I've never heard of such a thing . . ." Baboo had the authority of someone with immense personal discipline who adhered rigorously, unwaveringly, to how things *ought* to be done. She was also adored by her many grandchildren because it was clear to even the youngest that she had seen almost everything in her long life and understood how complicated and many layered people were, and it was obvious, above all, how much she loved them, an adoration beyond reckoning, and sometimes she could give the wink and tolerate a bit of foolishness because, Lord knows, she had been foolish enough at times.

Baboo told Hank some of Celine's story, inadvertently. She said something once after they both had had several cocktails and were sitting on her porch that overlooked the little marsh above her beach. It was right after he graduated from high school. Moths batted at the porch light and herons croaked from the cattails, and frogs boomed, and the tiny intermittent lanterns of the fireflies blinked. She said that she was glad he had had such a fun and easy time at Putney, because she had been terribly afraid after Celine took most of her sophomore year off that she would never graduate.

Hank said, "She took most of the year off? She never told me that. Why?"

Baboo rattled the ice in her vodka tonic. She glanced over quickly and pursed her lips. "Well, they tried to expel her."

"I know. And you stormed up there in a sable coat like Anna Karenina. Mom told me."

Baboo laughed. "I'm not sure Anna Karenina had a sable coat. It seems to me that that awful anemic husband of hers was very cheap, wasn't he? Karenin? I will never forget the description of the blue veins in his pale hands." She shuddered dramatically. Baboo always amazed him. She was Catholic in temperament and seemed to have read everything. He knew that she had attended Vassar for a year over the objections of her father, Charles Cheney, who felt that girls from good families should not attend college, and he knew that she left halfway through when she married Harry Watkins. She sipped her drink. "No, your mother had decisions to make and she was as obstinate as a camel."

That expression. Had she said "mule" it would have glided by unremarked like any hackneyed turn of phrase, but leading in a camel with his hump had the effect of inviting a certain association and he may have nearly jumped out of his seat. Somehow he saw the camel with its oddly swelling back and he saw young Celine standing beside it with her swelling belly and decisions to make. It was the first time he was certain that his mother had gotten pregnant, and

84

this revelation was followed immediately by the certainty that she had taken time away from school because she had stubbornly decided to take her baby to term.

Which meant that somewhere Hank had an older sibling.

Baboo must have noticed his shock. She said, "Well, it must be time for dinner. I'm famished, aren't you? Joan is probably baking the lamb chops to death again, I can smell sulfur." She pushed back her wicker chair.

"Baboo?"

"Dear one?"

"Were you just trying not to tell me that Mom was *pregnant?* Is that what 'fraternizing' means?"

"Fraternizing means fraternizing. Now, would you take your drink to the table and try not to upset an old woman?" Discussion ended, case closed.

The next spring, Celine drove up to visit him at Dartmouth. She drove the red VW bus. He loved her in the Beast, the elegant private eye in the hippie bus. She pulled up in front of his dorm, the engine roaring happily away with the signature bravado that was 80 percent bark, and she stepped down in a khaki jacket and jeans and he thought she looked like a movie star relaxing off-set. That first afternoon they drove across the river and up into the hills above Norwich, Vermont, and set up cans on a log against an embankment so they could shoot the .44 Magnum he had bought with money from his summer job at the cannery. He had bought it for bear protection. She popped in a stick of Juicy Fruit, which always helped her concentrate, and shot first and didn't miss. She neatly flipped open the cylinder and ejected the brass onto the mat of old leaves. "We'll pick it all up later. It's nicely balanced. You should really get some ear protectors."

Now or never: "Mom, why do you reunite birth families? You're an incredible investigator. Why not go after perps?"

She jerked her hand over and flipped the cylinder home and handed him the gun, barrel away. "They may call this the Bear Minimum, but if it's a grizzly I think you'd better hit him in the head." She walked across the turnaround and set up the line of cans.

"Why not perps?" Hank said. "I should think it'd be more of a rush."

"It's not. I tried it once, and I thought it was sad."

"Sad?"

"You don't remember the case? It was the one I did for the FBI when I was just starting out."

"Vaguely. Do you want to shoot again?"

"You go, I'll coach you. Just a sec." She went to the bus and came back with two packets of Mack's foam earplugs. "Here. You might want to hear your child's first utterance." She screwed one into her right ear. "Like this, good"—raising her voice—"now take them out! I want to tell you a story."

He took the earplugs out and they sat on a moss-covered boulder. She took out her gum and stuck it behind her ear for later. It was a fifties bebop gesture Hank thought he had seen in a Gidget movie.

"It was bank fraud," she said. "A lot of money, really a lot. The man was from a good Hartford family—you remember the Brainards—and the bureau needed someone who could blend in and make some calls. Well, it took about twenty minutes. His aunt had a house next to Tauntie's at Woodstock and they all played tennis together. She was so glad to hear from me. 'Why on *earth* do you want to get in touch with Franklin after so long?' the aunt said, a bit suspicious. I told her that I was embarrassed to ask, but that he was an old beau, one of those a girl never forgets—she twittered and said something like, 'I have one or two of those, dear,' and I said that I had been packing up my desk for a move to Newport and found his old dog tags from the Tenth and I thought I better return them, and did she have an address. I'd done my research. He'd been in the Tenth Mountain Division with your uncle George. 'Oh, he'll be *thrilled,*' she said. 'Best years of his life, I'm sure of it. To tell you the truth, he's in a bit of a funk, a rough patch, I'm sure it'll lift his spirits,' and she gave me an address in Old Greenwich. So I felt like a shit to begin with."

His mother told him how she had not gotten her kit together yet for stakeouts and had to use a pair of opera glasses. Celine got in her old Volvo wagon and drove up to Connecticut and spied on the place from a hill—it was a fancy horse property with barns and white rail fencing—and she said she was proud of herself when a warbler landed on her shoulder. Finally Franklin emerged from the house. It was him all right, the felon and fugitive. Matched the photo in her dossier. He didn't look like a hardened criminal, he looked like a rather sad man in early middle age wearing a light cotton Lacoste sweater, navy blue. He got into a Mercedes and she followed him through the genteel back roads of Greenwich. At some point he must have realized he was being followed because he goosed it and they had a "high-speed" chase through the well-kept countryside, Celine clinging to his taillights for all she was worth—"I must've nearly rolled that clunker three or four times"—until the man was just overcome with curiosity: Who the hell *was* that well-coiffed lady in the Volvo who could barely see over the steering wheel?

"He pulled over and got out looking confused

and perplexed and a little scared. I walked up to him and I said I was Marybell Hampson's niece and I had been engaged by the FBI to bring him in and that what he was doing was simply wrong. 'What you are doing is just wrong, Franklin. You need to make this right. It will be best for everyone. You're a decent man and you need to behave with decency.'" Hank could just see petite Celine. The moral certainty she had inherited from her mother. The poor man didn't stand a chance. She brought him in. She said, "Let's take your car back to the house and you come with me to the City. We'll have a good talk on the way."

He followed her like a puppy and she drove him to the bank where they met the branch manager and several agents. "The way he looked at me when they put the cuffs on him. Like a beaten dog, Hank. I never want to see that expression again." She breathed out a long sigh. "On second thought, let me have that gun." She took it from him along with the six bullets he had in his hand and she thumbed them in swiftly without thought, her mind on something else, and she blew the six cans away in six of the fastest shots he had ever seen.

It's a wonderful thing to be in awe of one's mother, but she had not put him off the scent. She seemed distracted by memory, maybe vulnerable, so he said, "Whoa. Nice. So no perps any more, but why birth families? I was thinking maybe once you had a baby—"

She whirled around. Her breathing was labored, maybe from her incipient emphysema, maybe from emotion.

"I'd like you to never mention that again. Okay?"

"But if I had an older brother or a sister—"

She compressed her lips and her breathing quickened. Her eyes were big and bright and they were wet and he shrunk from her pain. He nodded. "Okay, sure."

But it wasn't really okay. For days, weeks, years he couldn't put out of his mind the certainty that he had an older sibling. He got more of it later from his aunt Bobby right before she died, but that would not be for twenty-two more years.

SIX

A road trip frees the mind, revitalizes the spirit, and infuses the body with Dr Pepper and teriyaki jerky. That's what Celine had always found, and what could be better? She and Pete drove around the hulk of Denver's football stadium and pulled onto Interstate 25 and headed north. Celine drove. She was a very good driver. Pete had given up cars when he moved to New York City as a young man. His license had expired and he'd never renewed it. Pete liked to imagine his mind as the interior of a great house, one in a constant renewal of design, and he found that not driving somehow freed up a lot of mental square footage. They had a road atlas and gazetteers with detailed topographic maps for both Wyoming and Montana. These blood-red atlases were wonderful and indispensable as they showed every ridge and creek and old logging road. As they passed the Downtown Aquarium, Celine motioned to the sign and said, "Did you know that the aquarium was bought by a seafood restaurant chain?"

"Why am I not surprised," Pete said.

"It's true," she said. "Imagine! You can view all those fish while you eat their cousins. Seems to me it would be nerve-racking for the permanent residents, don't you think? Here." She wormed a hand into the bag between them on the front seat and pulled out a plastic cylinder filled with strips of beef jerky. "Could you hand me one, please? Pete?"

Jerky was her favorite road-trip food. Maybe her favorite staple, period. If she had to live on jerky and marzipan she'd be totally happy.

Pete asked her if she'd like him to figure out the navigation screen on the dash of the truck and Celine waved her hand no. "They make me nervous," she said.

"Really?"

She bit off a hunk of dried beef. "I think it's a terrible invention. Nobody knows how to read a map anymore. You chase down a blue line but you have no idea where you are in the world. Like a rat in a maze. How do I ever know where I am in relation to Pikes Peak, or the South Platte? Or God?"

Pa had grown up on an island in Penobscot Bay, Maine, where everyone knew where they were in relation to God pretty much all the time; he saw her point.

"With regards to the wider context," Pa said, "do you think we should talk about what we're doing?"

Celine allowed her eyes to leave the road and to appraise her husband for a full beat. To continue the conceit: For twenty years now he had been spreading these maps on her table, always reminding her of the wider territory. When she lost her bearings he helped her find them, and gently suggested that there were probably many ways to move forward. Pete was a very rare bird.

"Okay," Celine said. She loved this part. Pete would lay out the facts of the case. His mind was particularly well disciplined and she loved how he chose to organize everything, whether they be the chisels and hand planers he used in the shop in the basement at home, or the threads and stray leads of a case.

Pete took out his reporter's notebook and hooked his grandpa half-glasses over his ears. "Well, we don't have much. But then . . ." He frowned.

But then they never did. Have much. Celine was most happy when they had close to nothing. They had solved dozens of cases when a young adult came to them seeking a birth parent and had nothing but the name of an adoption agency, a town where the handoff had occurred, and perhaps one shred of maybe false information—the rumor, say, that the mother had been a lounge singer. Nothing but sealed records and a young life clouded by questions.

Pete cleared his throat. "Gabriela's father was Paul Jean-Claude Lamont, born 1931 Sausalito—" Pete rarely editorialized during these recitations but now he did: "That might explain some things."

"What do you mean?"

He took off his glasses and wiped them on the white handkerchief he always kept in one pocket of his vest. "It's just a hunch. At the time, Sausalito was a hotbed of smugglers and rumrunners. It faced San Francisco across the bay, but it was isolated. The Golden Gate Bridge wasn't com-pleted until 1937. Trawlers loaded with liquor would come in through the Gate at night and unload their 'catch' and fast boats would cross early the same night or the next. It was dangerous work in the dark, in the fog. The crossing could be very rough and the currents are wicked. A lot of men died. Other things came in that way, too. Guns, opium, even fast women."

"You mean sad, desperate, exploited prostitutes."

"What I meant to say."

"And so?"

"I'm not sure. It was a town full of adventurers and adrenaline. Pretty tough. A lot of traffic moving through, too. There was a big ferry that brought cars across to continue north and south on old 101. We'll have to ask Gabriela if she knows anything about her paternal grandparents. They might have been schoolteachers for all we know."

"How does it bear, though? On the case?"

"Well, I just think if there was any town in the country that was truly Out of the Box, it was here. Constant movement, danger. A place perched between the wild sea and the civilized world, a portal. Some people lived on houseboats as early as the twenties. Nobody really did anything the way they were supposed to do it. That's the feeling I get. They had one of the world's great cities facing them across the bay, with all its riches and allure, a usually easy boat ride, and yet, here, there was this sense that nothing could touch them, they could play by their own rules. If an impressionable kid grew up there, he probably wouldn't do anything the way anyone else did either. He might march to his own drum. Have you seen Lamont's photographs?"

"Have *you?*"

"Well." Pete kept farmer's if not fisherman's hours. He usually woke in the dark a little before five. At home in Maine he might have milked the family cow or tossed chunks of firewood from the woodshed to a pile outside the kitchen door. Now in Brooklyn, in their high-ceilinged quiet studio with the bellied cable lights of the Brooklyn Bridge stringing their windows and a tugboat with barge gliding silently beneath it— maybe a foghorn blowing from over near the Battery—then, while Celine slept up in the aerie of their loft, in what he considered the very beating heart of the day he would sit at his computer beneath the big window and lit only by the blue screen of the laptop he'd pull up a current case and follow leads through one improbable leap to another, browsing the Web the whole time. He would let his imagination soar. Sometimes, on these flights of speculation, he would come upon something that would crack a case. The other night he had been perusing Paul Lamont's impressive catalogue—photographs of wild nature, animals unaware that they were subjects, expeditioners under extreme pressure, earthquake survivors, even war pictures. In the photographs, there was a sensitivity and a rare tenderness, a hewing to beauty that was remarkable.

Celine reached out and put a hand on Pete's leg. His private world—the one before daybreak that she would never witness—was one of the things she loved and treasured about the man. For Celine, love, the love of a partner, was impossible without mystery. "It's okay," she said. "I know you cheat on me early in the morning."

"Think about it," Pete said. "Lamont is scarily smart. We know because he came out of public high school and attended my alma mater in Cambridge for a year and a half before dropping out. I called your cousin at the Peabody Museum—"

Celine lifted her hand and waved with excitement. "Rodney!" He was her favorite first cousin. Another Out of the Boxer: the curator of manuscripts at Harvard's Houghton Library and a consultant at the Peabody—one of the great curating jobs in the world—who received his bachelor's degree from the Manhattan School of Music and never earned a graduate degree.

Unheard of in his position. A passionate viola player and amateur composer. And wonderful wit. Celine adored him. He came to Fishers Island for a few weeks every summer when she was growing up, and he acted very well as a surrogate older brother. He was one of those people who just seemed to make magical things happen. Once, just after Celine graduated from Putney, and during her particularly painful summer romance with a known cad, Rodney drove up island on an August night and convinced the miscreant to give Celine a station wagon. Signed title and all. She cried with delight and threw herself on her cousin's neck and declared the car much much better than the man. Of course Rodney would do anything for her, and to have a leading research librarian at her pleasure proved at times invaluable in her work.

"Rodney," Pete repeated, with no outward signs of jealousy. "And he got ahold of young Mr. Lamont's Harvard transcript."

"And?"

"He received straight As, three with honors."

"What were they?"

"Eastern Religions, Introduction to Ancient Chinese Literature with your old friend Lattimore, and Art History. He wrote an honors paper on Hiroshige."

"How does it bear?" On the case, she meant. Celine was tenacious.

"Well, think about the mind-set of the man. Not just mind-set but M.O., even spiritual orientation. He comes from a rowdy defiantly counterculture town, a place a little like a Dr. Seuss village where everyone lives in a crazy sand castle. On the edge of the sea, where everything feels possible. He goes to Harvard, probably the first from his school, and he doesn't concentrate on anything practical like premed or engineering or even political science, he studies a range of humanities with a bent toward the Eastern and the exotic. But even that is too staid. He drops out. Three years later he marries a Brazilian woman. She is from an aristocratic family, the daughter of a respected landowner in Mato Grosso, a father with a serious ancestry stretching back to the Reconquista. A self-styled anthropologist and thus the poetic Guarani name Amana. But still—Creole and Asian had mixed in over the centuries. She was a great beauty, very quiet and reserved, and an olive shade of brown. Imagine the stigma. Or, at the very least, the unwanted curiosity and attention. His marriage seems to express more of the Fuck-Off attitude, he was going to do things his way." Pete hummed a short bar. It was one of his ticks, something just shy of a laugh. He said, "He was in love, no doubt about it, this wasn't simply a political statement. The portraits are, again, extraordinary."

"Portraits?" Celine passed a VW Vanagon with

Minnesota plates and mountain bikes and the young couple smiled and waved—camper to camper. Celine waved back. Midwesterners were so friendly.

"There is an archive of some two hundred nudes he took of Amana. And dozens of portraits—just a face, hands, ears, the back of her head. As I said, she was very beautiful. Dozens more shots of her arranging flowers. She was a master at flower arrangement, an art she learned from friends of Japanese ancestry when she was studying in São Paulo."

"Hmm." Celine was traveling now, he could see it. When she got caught up in a story she let her imagination range in much the way Pete did early in the morning. Their minds were quite different—very—in how they approached a problem: He was analytical. She could be, too, but she trusted most her intuition, her sense of smell, which were almost infallible. She saw the peculiar, the motive no one else could see, the odd touch of grace; he followed the trend lines of certain behaviors, the probabilities of effects leading to further causes. But they both thought creatively and let their imaginations roam.

"I know a little about her, too, you know," Celine said.

Pete raised one bushy eyebrow.

"While you were cheating on me with your sources, I called Cece. Remember, she lived in the

Richmond District and sent her son to the French American School? We often talked in those early days, because Saint Ann's was just starting, too. She said Amana came to a parents' meeting. It had to be her—a stunning Brazilian with green eyes, very reserved, with a daughter in second grade. Everyone was excited about this experiment in education. The feeling was that they were giving the benefit of the doubt to their children, to an extent that perhaps had not been tried before, while also giving them a fully cross-cultural education. They would all share in the excitement of them revealing themselves, while at the same time immersing them in French language and culture and being careful to train them in the expected disciplines—math, science, history, English."

"And she remembered her?" Pete leaned forward. His interest, too, was piqued.

"She remembers that she sat very straight."

"And?"

"She had a vivid picture of the sweep of her dark hair. It was all of a piece, like a curve of the richest wood. She seemed like that—almost sculptural. Very refined. And Cece thought she detected a nearly concealed skepticism. Her education, of course, would have been the polar opposite of what was then being celebrated."

"Anything else?"

Celine shook her head. "Not really. She had green eyes, as I said, and she was very quiet. She doesn't remember her saying more than two words. She remembers a smile. Shy but sincere. Some kind of purity there. It struck Cece that she was one of the most beautiful women she'd ever seen. Not just her looks but her bearing, the hint of what one saw inside when she smiled. She must have died a few months after that meeting."

They drove in silence for a minute or two, ruminating probably on the resounding properties of fate. They were in the open-range country north of Denver, running parallel to the mountains off to their left, the piled ranges of Rocky Mountain National Park dusted with new September snow. The hayfields were brown and stubbled after the last cutting, the ranch ponds a dark, cold blue. The hedgerows and windbreaks of the old cotton-woods were just starting to turn the tenderest of greens. In another month they would be the color of flames. Celine pushed the truck past the seventy-five-mile-an-hour speed limit. Traffic was now sparse.

"And so what were you thinking, Pete?" Celine said finally.

"Well, imagine it. This man who refuses to do anything conventional. He marries a refined and shy South American beauty who excites attention and speaks English more properly than any of his friends. He worships her as only an artist can, as only a lover with a fierce eye for beauty. He earns a living as a freelance photographer—no surprise there—and travels to the most exotic distant places and puts himself in extremely dangerous situations—again no surprise—in order to bring back award-winning photographs. They have a child. Whom he esteems just as beautiful. There are almost as many pictures of Amana with Gabriela and Gabriela alone as of his stunning wife. When the child is old enough they enroll her in a brand-new experimental school—knowing what we know of the man, how could he resist it? And then Amana dies. Sudden and unexpected. The one thing aside from his young daughter that he has loved unequivocally, without reserve."

Pete paused. The import of what he had just told seemed to stop him in his tracks. He took a second to clear his throat, regain his composure. Celine glanced over. Beneath Pa's Old Mainer reserve was an impressionable soul.

"So." Pete cleared his throat. "What does he do? He is, literally, at a loss. He can't do anything but drink, which, by the way, he is especially good at. He is so overwhelmed with loss and grief he can no longer keep track of the one other thing he loves. Imagine the terror of that. He loves Gabriela, he loves her. But his faculties—the ones we use for day-to-day survival—are broken. I tracked down Miss Lough, the third-grade teacher—" Now Celine turned her head in surprise. Her lips tightened.

"I was going to tell you, but you were in one of

102

your states getting ready for this trip. I thought I'd better wait until you could really hear it."

Celine's face relaxed. She forgave him. Phew.

"The former teacher told me that he often forgot to pick Gabriela up at school, that she would call him at home and if she reached him he was often slurred with drink and that when he did show up to get her he hugged and gripped Gabriela like a life ring. Her words: 'He held her like one of those life rings you throw to a drowning man. And sometimes I could see he was crying, though he tried to hide it.' Think of the nightmare, the loss he could not abide and the confusion and self-hatred caused by his own incapacity as a father. Miss Lough, now Mrs. Khidriskaya, said that she kept food in the classroom because Gabriela often showed up hungry. He must have seen in flashes of clarity the harm he was doing to the only other thing he cherished. It may have only been Gabriela that kept him from suicide. So what else does he do, a man desperately clutching a life ring? He scrambles into the first lifeboat that comes along. Danette Rogers. ICU nurse. Specializing in bringing patients back from the precipice of death. Certified sexpot. I also talked to her supervisor at San Francisco General"—Pete held up a hand (peace!) and chuckled—"just day before yesterday. Marie St. Juste told me that Nurse Rogers had a reputation for putting powerful doctors into situations they could not easily wriggle out of. 'She was a man-eater!' Marie said in a baffled Haitian accent. 'I can't count the doctors, good Lord!' I recorded the conversation, it was wonderful, you can listen to it later."

Celine could only forage in her bag for another piece of jerky. This was too good.

"Danette bragged one afternoon that she had met a *National Geographic* photographer at a bar on Haight Street. She lived in the Mission but came into the Haight to hunt, I guess. When she was tired of doctors and wanted a big strong free-loving hippie." Pete managed to look bemused. "She said Lamont was the most charismatic man she had ever met, one of the most handsome, too, and the saddest. And drunk. She bragged that she screwed him in the telephone booth in back of the bar. But she couldn't stop thinking about him. Marie St. Juste said that she was really bothered about this man. 'She could forget anyone!' Marie declared. 'Drop him like a Kleenex, you know? But this man, he really bothered her. Every day she went on about this photographer. One day she told us she was going to have to marry him! Ayee, imagine! Well, you should have seen our faces!'" Pa smiled an inward smile. He always took delight in the pure souls of the earth, wherever they shone.

"They married at city hall—"

"You found the marriage certificate," Celine said tartly.

"Well." Pa cleared his throat. His investigation partner really had been in a state the last few days. She always was before a trip.

"Continue, please."

"Well, Gabriela told you about living in her own apartment when she talked to you. How Danette couldn't stand the sight of her almost from the beginning and banished her and the photographs."

"You talked to Gabriela!"

"I was going to tell you last night but you kept asking me where the recording wire was and dropping shoes off the loft railing."

"Ha, wow. I guess I did. She told me about one photograph of her mother on a ferry."

"Danette sent Gabriela off with a whole box. Almost like having her mother in an urn. The nudes, everything. These were the ones the adult Gabriela so carefully catalogued online. Many had been in shows in San Francisco and New York, but many hadn't."

"Okay, so how does it bear? On his disappearance."

"I'm not sure."

"But you have an idea. Don't clam up on me now."

"Hmm," Pete said. "Give me a minute. I'm still arranging it."

Arranging it in his mind like one of the office interiors he used to design. Celine bit off a shred of jerky and decided to give her husband a break.

seven

The basin and range country of southern Wyoming is an acquired taste. Celine had not acquired it. She wrote to Hank in a letter a few days later, "The miles of rolling sage and rabbit brush, the surprising flecks of antelope like splashes of paint, red and white, the distant dry mountains and the incessant wind, they feel remote, untouchable somehow. They make *me* feel remote. They are like true mountains that have been drained of moisture and color, though I know people that go on and on about the subtle shades of that country. Almost like a compensation, an apology. Well. They make me tired. I never wanted to meet a landscape, or a person, more than halfway. If one is to dance one needs a dancing partner, don't you think? Which made me think of Gabriela. I was getting the sense that, like these parched and far-off hills, she was withholding something.

"That's what I puzzled about as we drove through gritty, windbeaten Rawlins and stopped on the old main street at a Chinese restaurant across from a building painted entirely in jungle camo. Not kidding, can you believe it? The whole building. Welcome to the West. What I thought about as we folded our pancakes around the moo shu pork and sipped the scalding jasmine tea . . ."

Celine often said it was the one drawback of working pro bono: When people put up good money for an investigation they had usually committed to their decision and rarely got cold feet. But if all they had invested was a phone call and a story, sometimes it was too easy to back out. It was true, though—money or no money, many of those who enlisted a PI weren't fully prepared for what they would find. But Gabriela had insisted on paying and Celine never got the impression that she was in this search with anything but both feet.

When Hank had found his mother's letter in his mailbox he had put on a windbreaker and taken it with him for a walk around the lake. It was a cool fall evening, the clouds over the mountains burning with russets and purple shadows, and there were still a couple of snowy pelicans drifting slowly on the dark water like fat schooners. Hank loved how the huge white birds took on the hues of the sunset. They came every year to breed, and happily fished for crawdads and carp, and helped the lake's visitors pretend they were on the coast.

He carried the envelope to his favorite bench across from the little sanctuary island and opened it there. He and Celine still traded handwritten letters, a habit they began when he went away to Putney for high school. They had a bond, going to the same school, and more than once she wrote to him of secret spots none of his peers had known about, like the flat diving rock in Sawyer Brook. He remembered his joy when he went to his mailbox in the lobby of the dining-hall building and found one of her square envelopes. She did not write to him the way other parents wrote to their children—of commonplaces, weather, pets—she wrote of the problems confronting her in her current case, and he read the letters with the avidity some read detective novels. She often asked for his thoughts, and more than once his insights had led to a breakthrough. His roommate, Derek, insisted that he read those parts aloud so that they could ponder the puzzle, like young Watsons, while they lay in their bunks before sleep and a winter wind howled in the eaves of their cabin.

He was not surprised that the sere landscape of eastern Wyoming was not to his mother's taste. She'd be happier as they moved north and west into the mountains. She was a New Englander at heart, a shaded-brook and hardwoods gal. He remembered the almost vertiginous sense of exposure he had experienced when he first encountered the vast sky of Colorado. Whenever he came to a grove of big cottonwoods that reminded him a little of the broadleaf forest of Vermont he had felt relief. The Putney hills were in their blood.

The summer after he graduated from high school, and was shocked by Baboo's partial revelation, he returned to Putney almost every day in his mind. He closed his eyes and put himself back on the campus, back on the country lanes and paths he knew so well; back into the classrooms and barns, into the routines of chores and classes and sports, of meals and evening activities. He traveled in his imagination to the fields and art studios, the sugar house and blacksmith shop, and tried to fathom who the father of his brother or sister might have been. Might be. Two years later, while at college in New Hampshire, he drove the hour down to the school and took a tape recorder.

He interviewed two teachers who had taught both him and his mother, and the retired farmer, now an old man, who lived over in Dummerston. He had a journalist's instincts even then, and he conducted the interviews in a way that did not arouse suspicions of the real story. He told them he was working on a family memoir about Putney for a college writing project. And he did not tell his mother.

Celine didn't really relax until they turned up into the Sweetwater valley and the ranges on either side got close, and their flanks were dark with timber and the meadows were green. So were the irrigated fields of the ranches lying along the river, the neat white ranch houses peaking out from groves of boisterous cottonwoods. She opened her window and let the late-afternoon wind pour in and it smelled of alfalfa and wet fields and the river. They drove into Lander just as the sun was settling into the long escarpment of the Wind Rivers.

Just three more latitudes north made a difference, here, at the end of September. The air pouring through the window was chilly with fall, and she could smell woodsmoke. The aspen were already turning on the higher ridges, slashing the shoulders of the mountains with ocher and gold. Glorious. This time of year. It was good to be out of the city now, good to be rolling, traveling, letting her losses toss in her wake. The cold currents would bring them around again, surely; probably tonight as she slept. And if she woke up to the strange silences of a new town and lay in the dark listening, she would welcome them home, and taste without bitterness the oddly sweet grief of missing those one loves. But now it was wonderful to forget for a few hours, to be traveling, to hear tires hum and thwop on cracks in the pavement, to come to a T in the road above a creek whose meadow was dotted with horses, roans and appaloosas, and smell smoke from the wood of trees that didn't even grow in the East.

Celine didn't feel like cooking. Pa offered but she waved him off.

"Let's have ribs," she said. "Isn't that what they eat in Wyoming? And then let's go find a pullout somewhere to make our new home. I feel a little like a hermit crab."

"Carrying his house on his back?"

"We had one as a pet, you know. Mimi brought it home from Simmons Point one day in her glasses case. Mummy had a fit."

"You were all suckers for a stray."

"He was not at all a stray. I'm sure she plucked him from a very fine family where he'd been quite happy. It made me mad. Kind of a lesson for me in not offering help where it isn't needed."

"Did you make her put him back?"

"No. She was irrationally attached. At the end of the summer I abducted him and put him right back in the little tidal pool where she'd found him. I'd been with her that day. Anyway, over the summer he'd been quite spoiled. She dropped all manner of food into the pickle jar. One Friday night she brought him to the movies. She swore to me that he crawled to the edge of the jar and came half out of his shell and watched. Ginger Rogers. She swore on the Bible that he moved all his little legs like he wanted to dance. She said he was an Almond and wasn't allowed to dance. I finally figured out that she meant Amish. I had learned about them from our nanny and I'd been telling her about how they don't have zippers, which she thought was hysterical. She changed Bennie's saltwater twice a day. When it was clear that he was actually growing she found several empty snail shells and dropped them in. He inspected them and found them lacking. I told her that probably they couldn't have holes. She thought he'd like to have windows in his new house. Finally she found a beautiful glossy symmetrical shell all covered in irregular black spots like a paint pony and with no pinholes. Bennie took one look and moved right in. Years and years later, as an adult, she told me she thought of that as one of her proudest moments. Isn't that odd?"

Pete half smiled. It was his way of giving vigorous applause. Finally he said, "I always thought of ribs as a Texas specialty. Or Louisiana. Though, come to think of it, Uncle Norwood could barbecue a wicked batch."

"Were you even listening? Of course you were."

"His son, Norwood Jr., kept a pet lobster one summer. That one didn't end so well."

"Ha!" How could she have doubted him? Of all the things Pete Beveridge was very good at, listening was perhaps the best. "Maine ribs?" she said. "You know, Pete, I've been cutting you slack all afternoon."

"I'm supremely aware."

This was how they sparred. It was a call and response, a little like the cries red-tailed hawks screed across a valley to their mates: *Are you there? Yes, I am here.*

They passed the Pronghorn Lodge and came down the hill onto Main Street, a straight mile-long prospect of mostly late nineteenth-century brick buildings with tall front windows and ornate front doors. They passed the Lander Grill and the Noble Hotel and two outdoor sport shops with tents and fleeced-up mannequins in the windows. They passed a Loaf 'N Jug and the Safeway and a gas station turned burger joint and two stores featuring Native American crafts. It was that time of day, or night, that happens only a few weeks a year at a certain hour in certain parts of the American West. The sun sets behind mountains but the cloudless sky that is more than cloudless, it is lens clear—clear as the clearest water—holds the light entirely, holds it in a bowl of pale blue as if reluctant to let it go. The light refines the edges of the ridges to something honed, and the muted colors of the pines on the slopes, the sage-roughened fields, the houses in the valley—the colors pulse with the pleasure of release, as if they know that within the hour they too will rest.

Maybe Celine thought this way because she was exhausted. She was. It had been a long time since she had driven that far in a day. Main Street curved to the right and they passed the Double Ought Motel—which made them laugh as there were probably patrons doing things there they doubly ought not to do—and Celine abruptly threw the wheel over and executed a U-turn that startled Pa and squealed the tires.

"Practice," she smiled. "Twenty-seven miles

per hour. Pretty good. Didn't even think about rolling." She grinned. "Never know when we might need one of those. I was thinking we ought to head back to the Lander Grill. They might not have ribs but I bet they serve a mean steak."

The summer of Bennie the hermit crab was their first full summer at Fishers Island. It was also the summer Celine discovered that fathers don't always behave like fathers—that they might actually choose to be far away from their daughters.

When she first came to this country she was seven. It was mid-May 1940. The Nazis were steadily marching toward Paris, and the season at Fishers Island would begin in a few weeks, and Baboo's mother, Gaga, said yes, of course they could come early. Baboo and the girls' father, Harry, were still very much together, and the plan was that he would hold down the bank's office in Paris until things got very bad, and then he would come over and join them. If Baboo were to have planned their middle-of-the-night flight from Marseilles she could not have picked a better time. Over the course of their seven-year sojourn in France, they had been back to Baboo's parents' villa on Fishers Island twice, both times when Celine was too young to remember. Maybe she did remember. She had been four the last time, and she could, when she closed her eyes, recollect the sounds of seagulls, the rising laughter. She thought she could remember a smell of drying seaweed and ocean and the cold onslaught of waves. A wood balcony with a view of treetops and blue water. Her grandmother Gaga speaking to her in an accent she would later find out was touched with Spanish. That was all. The memories were somehow delicious. Somewhere in the background of all of it was her mother's laughter, her grandmother's delight chiming in just after, the two overlapping like waves. Now they were refugees, sort of, and they were returning home for good.

What was perfect about the timing was that the three sisters spoke only French. Mimi was five and precocious, rattling away in a constant soft-spoken soliloquy on the world around her, Bobby was eleven and already willowy and tall for her age and terribly practical—and perhaps a better judge of adult character than even Celine would be—and Celine was Celine; at seven she was quiet and shy and kept her many impressions mostly to herself, humming as she drew figures of birds and horses, and usually only voluble when it came to the subject of animals. Silent Celine would turn into a nonstop, exuberant commentator, for instance, at the Paris Zoo. But. They only spoke French. And so having a summer with Gaga and Grandfather at Fishers would be the perfect acclimatization.

Baboo hoped that by the time they hit their various grades at Brearley they would be fluent in English. They weren't. Probably because all that summer they stuck mostly to one another. They had their own small beach below the house, and their grandparents and their mother often invited other families over to swim and picnic and so the girls got away with learning a few necessary phrases and yammering among themselves. When they all drove over to the club beach in the Packard and trekked across the sand with their baskets and towels—"like Lawrence in Arabia," according to Baboo—the girls hung together. Bobby and Celine did, and Mimi ran after and lagged behind and rarely cried, and was so often covered head to toe in fine white sand she looked like a powdered doughnut. Not to say that they did not understand English, they did. They just refused, or did not know how, to speak it.

During that summer Celine remembered that Baboo communicated with their father by regular mail, by telegram, and by the rare phone call, which he made, because of the disruptions caused by the war, from the American embassy in Paris. Harry had stayed behind. He was safeguarding Morgan's interests in what was left of Europe and making preparations for his eventual flight. Celine remembered her mother bent over the rolltop desk in her room carefully writing letters to her husband. The room had a little balcony just big enough for two people to stand on, and it faced north toward the sound and the Connecticut shore, which could be seen over the trees if someone hoisted Celine. Through its screen door came the perpetual angelus of the bell buoy in the channel.

Celine has an image of Baboo bent over the small desk composing her letter—her handwriting was perfect, Victorian: It unfurled itself across the pages in ruled lines of slants and loops where there had never been a ruler. The oversize capitals at the beginnings of paragraphs had the formality of chess pieces. The signature below "Your Ever Loving Wife," *Barbara,* spun crisply through the *B*s and twirled away through the last *a* with the self-discipline of a great waltzer—which she was—and the flourish beneath it had the surprising dash and speed of passion.

Celine thought later that all love letters should look like that: that the recipient need not read the content but only glance at the hand to feel its impact. And then, in the middle of writing, her mother would stand and stretch, open and close her cramping fingers, and go out to the balcony for some air. Sometimes she seemed wrapped in fog, hazy, distant. Sometimes she pulsed like a firefly. Celine remembered.

And then one afternoon while Celine was drawing egrets and crabs on her big artist's pad on Baboo's floor, her mother came briskly to the desk with a letter from Harry—Celine recognized the blue airmail envelope, heard the tinkle of her mother's bracelets—and Baboo took up a silver letter opener and sliced the top and drew out the single translucent sheet and began to read.

She was bent over the rolltop and Celine saw her shoulders begin to quiver. A movement that spread down her arms and back the way a sudden strong wind moves through trees. And then her mother stood abruptly, keeping her back to her daughter, and made her way to the little balcony, weaving almost like a passenger moving on a deck in a rough sea, and stood under the sky, her hands gripping the wooden railing, as if she were holding on for dear life.

Only for a minute. Celine saw her mother's back stiffen. Expand with a great indrawn breath, saw her mother stand erect and breathe. Saw her hands come to her face, which was by then lifted to the blue waters of the sound, and wipe her cheeks with a gesture Celine would never forget and only saw from behind: Unhurried, decisive, Baboo moved both hands in sync from what must have been the corners of her eyes, or the bridge of her nose—moved them over her cheeks outward to her temples and then lifted them away and held them up palms outward toward the sea and spread her fingers. Held them there for a moment as if to dry. Like the wings of a seabird. And then she turned to her daughter and in a voice that was pitched a little higher than normal, said, "What are you drawing, Ciel? Birds again? How beautiful."

The contents of the letter were never discussed, but the ramifications became apparent over the next months. Baboo, if anything, became more attentive to the girls. She took them more often to the island's beaches. They branched out from Gaga's little strand and the familiar white sand of the club beach. They drove a few miles up island just past the big painted footprint in the road to the long stony stretch of Chocomount, which always had rougher waves and felt wilder, and had the most gorgeous thicket of thorny wild rose. They had to walk through it on the narrow path and Celine always lingered, inhaling the fragrance of the delicate flowers whose petals folded back in the sea wind. She picked the berrylike rose hips that she chewed and spat out. She liked to pretend it was betel nut and that she was an Indian woman on the way to the shore to gather snails. For Celine, the sight of the pale pink flowers and their sweet scent would for the rest of her life remind her of this time.

If Baboo was sometimes distracted and seemed to move in a mist of sadness, she was also more tender with her daughters than she had ever been. She read to them from books more often when she put them to bed (one of the latest had been *Kim* from which Celine got the betel-nut thing); she often eschewed the formal dining room, with apologies to Gaga, and ate with the girls at the long table beneath the windows in the kitchen. She took them on walks to look for bird nests, and they all practiced together how to whistle like a bobwhite and a whip-poor-will, and hoot like a barn owl. Bobby could make the ugly alarmed croak of a heron, which got the biggest laughs.

Of course the girls could feel their mother's grief but they had nothing to attach it to and so responded with a tenderness of their own. They reached for her hand when they were walking over the uneven stones at Chocomount, and they curled up in her lap to shelter from the wind and sun in the fragrant shade that smelled of coconut Coppertone and the particular salty sweetness of their mother's freckled skin, and they breathed in her sadness with her love.

In mid-June Harry Watkins also fled Paris. Baboo knew how the girls pined for their father, and she loved them too much to ever let her own troubles get between him and his daughters; she told them that their father had left the house on rue de Lille and was coming across on a grand boat and was bringing their cat, Chat. They would see him in New York at the end of the summer. The girls were beside themselves. It would have been hard to say what caused more delight—the prospect of seeing Harry again or of squeezing Chat, who, remarkably, loved to be squeezed and seemed even to enjoy being picked up unskillfully by Mimi, under the forelegs, and run around the house, eyes huge and striped gray body dangling.

Bobby, who was hard to excite, and who had not been listening closely, asked excitedly, *"Et quand va-t-il arriver ici*? He promised he would jump with me off Grayson's dock!"

And Baboo stiffened and said that Papa had urgent business in New York and would not be coming to the island but would wait for them there.

The three girls looked at one another. In many ways, despite the span of their ages, they were as close as triplets. They had sensitive social barometers—even Mimi at five—and they were sensing the import of this statement without having a clue as to its meaning, and the pressure in the room dropped as before a nor'easter.

Celine, who was even more attached to Harry than the others, said, *"C'est entendu. Il peut venir pour le weekend! Il nous emmenera pêcher!"*

Baboo squeezed her hand and said that they would see him in just two months in the city.

And that marked the end of the Period of Tenderness and the Weeks of Wild Roses.

Not from Baboo's standpoint. She recognized the beginning of a transition that would be very painful for the girls and she was determined not to scar them, or, at the least, to minimize the damage. She was as attentive as ever. She insisted on forays up island to the village for ice-cream cones at Diana's and comic books at the drugstore; she organized picnics with just the four of them to Simmons Point and to her friend Ty Whitney's where there was a swimming pool with a diving board and slide, which were objects of endless fascination for the girls. But the sisters were keenly aware of a dark cloud of catastrophe hanging over their displaced family, and they had nothing tangible on which to pin their dread, and they began to act out.

The Lander Grill did serve ribs. So there. Celine was starving. She had a full rack and Pa had a chopped salad that, curiously, was blanketed in well-done burger. The only flora on Celine's enamel plate was coleslaw out of a can, which is the way she preferred it, but Pete dutifully picked a leaf of iceberg lettuce out of his bowl and garnished her pork, laying it down delicately like a proffered rose. "Geen," he said.

"I don't like geen."

"Well I know." It was their ritual. She would eat the single leaf last because she loved him.

It was a Sunday night and the grill was hopping. Most of the tables were full, and the mounted speakers played a mix of Mavis Staples and the Dixie Chicks, which was lively if not a little disconcerting. The crowd was burly oil-and-gas men—she could tell because their caps said stuff like *McIntyre Drilling* or *Hansen Well Services*—

a few young cowboys, anachronistic in their Wranglers and hats; a large contingent of very athletic and outdoorsy-looking young people, men and women; two Native American couples in Goth black; and a single pleasant-looking young man in the far corner, head down, concentrating hard on his double cheeseburger. Celine noticed that his Black Watch flannel shirt was very green in the greens and black in the blacks and creased down the breast—brand new. And that he sported a week's worth of whiskers but was otherwise clean-cut. She noticed these sorts of things.

She also noticed that the folks laughing the hardest and seeming to have the best time were the drillers. Maybe because they were drinking at twice the rate of anyone else. She noticed, too, that the sporty outdoorsy folks in their very expensive and colorful soft shells and fleece mostly ordered pitchers of beer—the cheapest option—and drank them at a judicious pace. Revealing perhaps a subconscious tallying of ounces-slash-dollars per minute per level of intoxication divided by the steadily decreasing time left in the evening. A couple of the kids were clearly wild and showed some promise, but mostly these young people were very smart and very controlled. There was one woman who was older than the rest, and more beautiful, very lean, her hands dark and weathered, and Celine studied her, the facial structure, the movements. Early fifties would be the age, just right. She felt the old swelling in her heart, but she shook herself— not a chance; just a habit, an old habit, that's all—and continued scanning the room.

The oil-and-gas men drank longnecks, some accompanied by amber shots—that would be Jack Daniel's, wouldn't it?—and they were supremely comfortable in their own skins. They drank what they wanted and didn't care what it cost. The Native Americans were in one of the far corners, at the dimmest table, and seemed insular and wary. They leaned toward each other when they laughed, as if trying to cover their humor. The single man in the new shirt in the other far corner was hard to read. He was eating with a purpose but not quite relish, and he seemed at the same time to be listening, the way a hunter would listen in a windy forest.

All of this was good information, probably. For context in a new territory if nothing else. One never knew. When Celine was on a case she observed many things closely, it was reflex— gathering everything up in the baleen of her intelligence. It both kept her in practice and sometimes gleaned useful and even crucial information. As for her and Pete, nobody seemed to notice them much, though they were clearly "from away" as Pete would say, and this was also good. One of the things that happens to people as they get older, and especially to women on the other side of middle age, is that people forget to notice. If Celine wanted to be virtually invisible she could be. She was also gorgeous and striking and if she wanted to make an impression she could do that, too. Also useful.

They finished their meals and Celine ordered a scoop of ice cream smothered in chocolate sauce for a nightcap. The warmth of the pub, the rich meal, the hiatus from the long day on the road—they suffused Celine with what these days was a rare fatigue that felt a little like contentment. She came around the table and slid a chair next to her husband. She'd been very patient with him all day.

"Okay, Pete," she said. "You've been 'arranging' all day, I can tell. Now tell me the rest."

Pete let his brown eyes fall gently on his wife. The wonderful thing about having a close and long marriage is that certain responses are as dependable as sunrise. He pursed his lips, which only meant he was covering another inscrutable expression, like maybe the beginnings of a laugh. He'd known this reckoning was coming.

"Well," he said.

"You need coffee."

Pete nodded. She managed to grab a waiter who brought two cups, one black, one with milk.

Celine nodded. "I can hear you, Pete. Even in the din. Any time."

Pete sipped and set the mug on the scarred wood table. "Gabriela's exile." He huffed out a breath.

"Paul Lamont let his new wife banish his daughter. Just downstairs, but still."

Pete glanced at her. She tipped her head forward: Go on. Sometimes Pete was a bit slow to rev up.

"The calculus may have been something like this: I need this woman. Without this woman I will drown. She is keeping food in the cupboard, in Gabriela's kitchen, she makes sure she gets off to school and back, she knows that is the bottom line, the bare minimum. That is the bargain. Without her my daughter may not eat and I may succumb. To oblivion. It was oblivion he was battling. A mortal battle. For him and his beloved daughter. Beloved, yes. May not seem like it at first glance, but if you look closely. Gabriela was his cherished daughter and also the living repository of his wife's heart. And her doppelgänger in some sense. She looked just like her, you should see the photographs."

"Well, I would have, if—"

"I know, I know. I'm catching you up now. There's nothing else."

"Yes, but—"

"I'm getting to that. He must have known right from the beginning that his bargain with the devil was a mistake. But he had no Plan B. Whenever he could—when Danette was working an afternoon or night shift—he would go downstairs and try to help Gabriela with her homework. He tried.

But he was often too drunk. And it wasn't often enough. When I called her the other day—you were having a fit trying to compress two suitcases into one—she told me that when he came to visit she pushed aside her homework and tried to engage him in a game of canasta. A fairly advanced game for an eight-year-old, my cousins and I played it for hours on rainy summer nights, on Aunt Debbie's porch on North Haven—"

"Why *rainy* nights?"

"Because on clear summer nights we were out frogging, or fishing with lights, or playing these big games of kick the can in the Beveridge cemetery."

"Was Norman Rockwell on-site? Or were those reenactments?"

"You're making me lose my train of thought."

Celine considered her husband's upbringing and felt again the pang that those with imperfect childhoods feel when confronted with one that seems idyllic. Or even normal. She marveled once more that his youth seemed to her so exotic, when *she* was the one raised in Paris who fled the Nazis on an ocean liner. Salvador Dalí was on her passage. She remembered him, he had a pair of ocelots on jewel-studded leashes, imagine.

"I'm sorry. You were talking about card games."

"Gabriela ignored the homework and tried to get her father to play canasta because even three sheets to the wind he was a competitive

127

sonofabitch and canasta can be a very long game. She wanted him to stay with her as long as possible."

Celine lit up. "We used to play it on Fishers! Same strategy: The longer the game, the more time Mummy would spend with us, and the later we could stay up."

Pete nodded. "She told me that she also visited her father upstairs. She would listen for the heavy clomp of Danette's clogs on the steps going down—Gabriela said she was sexy but not at all graceful—and she'd go up. She said she took little Jackson with her once, but only once because Danette came home and found cat hairs on the couch and freaked out. Gabriela said she was afraid her stepmother would get rid of the cat while she was at school. Ended up that Jackson took care of that all by himself."

"Whew." Celine could hardly bear it, the story. The predicament. Her finely tuned sense of empathy vibrated and hummed. It was the harmonic that ruled her life. The small child was visited by her father like someone in a prison, or a hospital. Or worse, a mental ward. *What is wrong with me?* Gabriela must have asked herself again and again. She knew that Danette was jealous of her, her and her dead mother, Amana, but the kind of isolation she experienced gets internalized. Especially by children.

"Another thing," Pete said. "When they visited

and he was warmed up, which was pretty much all the time, he would tell her this fairy tale that he'd made up: He said that way far north, up on the Canadian border, there was an Ice Mountain, and a lake the color of his true love's eyes, and there was a castle there for princesses and their families and he would take her there. He said the lake sounded like birds and the mountain was the king of mountains."

"I want to hate him," she said, "but somehow I can't."

"That's just it. And what I'm getting to. He must have known right away. He was not insensible, as I said. He was *too* sensitive. What I'm learning about the man. He was *too* heartbroken. He could not face life on life's terms after his wife's death. He tried every way: alcohol, immersion in work, travel, a plunge into an obsessive sexual affair that he allowed, unfortunately, to become a marriage. I imagine that Danette got him warmed up one afternoon and screwed his lights out and dragged him down to city hall. So there he was. Trapped first by overwhelming grief and then by marriage. And he was—really trapped."

"How do you mean? Was there a prenup?"

Pa let out one of his soft hums, part amusement, part pathos. He loved that his wife could often be a step ahead of even him.

"Yes there was. *She* wrote it, not him. Gabriela sued to see it after he disappeared. Lamont had not inconsiderable income from the royalties of a handful of his iconic pictures, which are everywhere. But, as you seem to anticipate, the prenup undid and reversed the usual protections. I mean that we think of a prenup as usually entered into in order to protect the rights of the party with a disproportionate share of assets. Well. It also protects the other, the one who has much less, in that it often stipulates a schedule of payments in the case of a divorce—so much after so many years of marriage, so much more after more time. But get this. This prenup said . . . let me see if I can remember the wording . . . 'In light of the fact that the grantee'—that's Danette—'has eschewed numerous lucrative marital options in favor of marriage to the grantor'—that's Paul Lamont— 'this agreement, legally binding under the laws and statues of the State of California, lays out the following terms . . .' "

Celine was wide awake. Unconsciously she was stirring her coffee, which didn't need stirring.

"You've got to be kidding!" she cried.

"No. Not kidding."

"In plain English," Celine averred, "it was saying that because she screwed so many surgeons in the broom closet and had them dead to rights in one way or another, and could have had her choice of a gaggle of rich doctor husbands—if Lamont ever divorced her she would pick his bones. Clean him out! Unbelievable."

"Yep."

"That's *legal?* I mean some lawyer actually typed out those words. My God."

Sometimes in the middle of the night when Pa couldn't sleep, which wasn't often, he liked to think about all the jobs there were in the world. He liked to take a tour of the workbenches in China or India where nimble-fingered women who would never see a free-running brook, much less a trout stream, tied fishing flies. He imagined someone cementing the gargoyles to the ledges of reconstructed churches. Someone adjusting the compasses that now come with cars. He could imagine many both wonderful and cruel jobs but he could barely imagine the conversation in some cluttered legal office— probably just like those in the warrens of the hack lawyers up on Court Street—that led to the crafting of those lines. Man.

"The terms set forth, needless to say, were draconian. Gabriela said she probably got him drunk and worked him up right to the threshold, so to speak, of sex, and then made him sign it. Most of his net worth was tied up in the upstairs apartment, the one the two lived in. If he were ever to initiate divorce she would get the place, plus half the value of the cash and stocks he had on the date of union. Lamont had bought the apartment outright after selling a coffee-table book on the wild horses of Monument Valley.

You've seen the pictures, some of the most iconic wildlife pictures ever taken. And there is the famous one you see everywhere of the fishing boat cresting the giant wave. Gabriela is still partly living on the royalties and subsidiary rights. As I said, they are not inconsiderable."

"Danette would have gotten those, too."

"That's right. But not if he died."

They sat in silence. The Dixie Chicks were wailing out "Travelin' Soldier." "I need fresh air, Pete," Celine said. "There was a bench by the door. It's not so cold."

They paid the check and buttoned up their coats. It was cold. They shoved open the heavy door and went back out into the chill night. Because it was night now and moonless and ranks of heavy clouds had marched over the country in just the last hour, and the stillness smelled heavy with rain. Not a single star. Still, the fresh air was clean and good.

Pete held her hand and they sat. "You were saying about what happened if Lamont died," she said.

Pa nodded. "Danette thought she had that covered too. Gabriela said she was practically licking her lips at the unsealing of the will in the lawyer's office on Howard Street."

"Ha."

"Yep. She gave Gabriela a look like, 'You poor thing. I've seen the will. You've always lost out in the battle for his affections, and you are going to lose out now big-time.' Gabriela told me she would not have been surprised if Danette had whispered, 'Don't worry, I'll send you a card from Acapulco, sucker.'"

"And?"

"And her expression changed gradually as the lawyer unsealed and read the document and she digested the words *sole heir* and then *Gabriela Ashton Lamont.* Danette stormed out. Later she locked herself in the apartment and Gabriela heard dishes breaking. It took about a month for the co-op board to transfer ownership to Gabriela, at which point Gabriela evicted her on the spot. She was only twenty, but she knew what needed to be done. The co-op board, none of whom had much stomach for Danette Lamont, had to call in the city marshal to drag her out." Pete lifted up his tweed cap and rubbed his forehead. The image was sad and amusing at once. It always amazed him that greedy people could throw themselves so headlong into acting against their own long-term self-interest.

"There was an insurance policy, too. That drove her wild. Wilder. One million. All to Gabriela. It seems trite, doesn't it? Like Dr. Evil putting his pinkie in the corner of his mouth and asking for a million dollars to ransom the world."

"Trite or not," Celine said, "it's a pile of cash for a college student on scholarship. But wait, how

133

long before Lamont was declared dead? It was pretty fast, wasn't it? I think she told me it was something like two months after his disappearance. That doesn't seem right. Without a body."

"Yes." She'd done it again. Worked out in a flash what had taken him not inconsiderable pondering. "A federal agent in Yellowstone National Park, and then a county judge, signed off. A smear of Lamont's blood was found on the bark of a nearby fir tree. The prevailing theory was killer bear. And there was this otherwise destitute young woman who stood to inherit. The intensive search lasted about ten days. It probably would never have lasted that long except that it was fueled by media coverage. The story was sexy. Lamont was a handsome and well-known *National Geographic* photographer who took the photo of the wild horses clashing beneath the towers in Monument Valley. An unexpected long shot from above, the two stallions rearing up and dwarfed by the rock. You've seen it."

Celine nodded.

"Gabriela said there were television vans all over Cooke City. The place only has one paved street and two motels. She said loggers and bearded recluses were renting out rooms to coiffed broadcast reporters in panty hose." Pa chummed—his trademark utterance, between a chuckle and a hum. "There's another detail."

Celine studied her husband, one eyebrow barely

deigning to rise. He had done a lot of groundwork on his own in just a couple of days. While she was, admittedly, on her own frightful tear to get ready and out the door. This was not their usual way of doing things, however, and she felt a mixture of hurt, if not betrayal, as well as admiration for his thoroughness. "Yes? Another detail?"

"An insight is perhaps better. Lamont disappeared just outside the boundaries of Yellowstone National Park. Half a mile outside. Had his car been found just south, within the park's borders, the case, and the search, would have automatically been federal."

"Ahh."

"You see? He avoids both the FBI and the prodigious search-and-rescue apparatus of the national park and the federal government."

"He does?"

"Yes. I mean if this was premeditated, if this wasn't actually a killer bear attack. Except."

"What?"

"Gabriela flew out from Sarah Lawrence as soon as she heard from Danette that her father had disappeared. She spoke to her professors and got deferments on the first papers and work groups. It was lucky that she had no labs. She landed in Bozeman, rented a Jeep, and drove down. She said she interviewed everybody, the biologists, the tracker, the cops and the searchers, park officials, even the people who ran the bar that Lamont frequented in Cooke City. She kept meticulous notes and a journal. And she kept running into a pair of officials she knew in her gut were feds and who would not talk to her. She said they avoided her."

"She brought the notes with her when she came to dinner," Celine said. "But not the second time she came over. Can you please hand me my phone?"

Pa's telltale eyebrow lifted and fell, a bit like a Maine coast groundswell. He knew that his wife was constitutionally incapable of staying out of the fray and that she would not be side-lined for another minute.

Gabriela answered on the first ring. "Hello, it's Celine. I hope I haven't caught you in the middle of dinner."

"No, no, we've eaten." That clear voice, like mountain water, Celine thought. A voice to love.

"Can you please FedEx a copy of your file of notes? The one I saw you with the other night?"

"I can't find it. I . . . I misplaced it."

"How? Do you remember? Can you tell me any more about that?"

"No." Neither woman was in the mood to beat around the bush. Celine knew there was more, but she also sensed that now was not the time.

"I see. Well tell me: You spoke of certain rumors

about your father. About his . . . his, ah, travel. All those places he went back to—Argentina, Peru, Chile. Do you think the rumors had merit?"

"I'm not sure, but—"

"But what?"

Gabriela hesitated. The girl was clearly conflicted. "I mentioned on the dock that there was one thing—"

"Yes, I remember."

"I told you that after . . . that I moved back into the larger apartment upstairs."

"Right."

"I did it on my Christmas break from school. My junior year at Sarah Lawrence. Not the funnest Christmas—"

"Of course. Very bleak. I can imagine."

"Well, I was cleaning out the upstairs apartment, trying to purge the residue of Danette before I moved in, and . . ."

"And?"

"And I lifted out the silverware tray, the one with all the compartments for knives, forks—"

Celine nodded impatiently into her phone. She knew what a silverware tray was.

"I lifted it up and underneath was a stained sheet of thin oilcloth. It was sort of etched with the outline of a rectangle. I peeled up the sheet and underneath was a current U.S. passport. It bore Pop's picture. But the name was Paul Lemonde Bozuwa."

• • •

Celine felt a rush, almost like the hit from a double espresso. Gabriela said she had put the passport back where she'd found it, she wasn't sure why.

They drove west up Main Street and halfway through town they saw a sign on the left that said SINKS CANYON—US FOREST SERVICE ACCESS. They turned. Bounced up the washboards for ten minutes and pulled off at a small meadow. When she opened her door the sound of a creek in a rock bed filled the night, and the smell of cold stones and water and sage, and she felt strangely elated.

eight

They woke to rain. It drummed on the camper's aluminum roof and pattered against the canvas walls of their upstairs bunk. She loved this as much as the presence of the stream. How long had it been? Rain on a tin roof? Except for the small incident in the night, she felt blessedly . . . something. Happiness was not a word that seemed to apply anymore, when she had lost so many close to her. There was a contentment that felt deeper, that acknowledged and accepted the quieter offerings of small joys—of love and occasional peace in a life that was full of pain.

The summer before last, between two sisters' funerals, they had gone back to Pete's family compound on North Haven and stayed in the Doll's House hard against the little inlet—just a clapboard cabin with odd-size salvaged windows, candles, a lantern, a woodstove—and she had loved it without knowing how much because the whole sojourn was heavy and darkened by grief. She must have loved it. It had rained there, hard, two nights running, and if she could love anything then she loved the feel of Pete warm beside her in the tiny bed, snoring with the peace of an elder who has come home after a long time away, and the sound of the rain sweeping against the mossy shingles. And walking slowly up the grassy track through spruce woods, holding Pete's hand, walking slowly and stopping to catch her breath— the trail was steep, her emphysema a nuisance— up to the Big House, which was just a clapboard saltbox fitted out with small rooms and book- shelves stuffed with musty first editions. And a view down the clearing to the slate blue bay and an archipelago of little islands.

There might not be a measure of happiness left in a life, but there could be beauty and grace and endless love.

A few miles above Lander, the whole making- camp part of the night had been surprisingly easy. They undid the six outside latches, and Pete crouched inside and pushed up on the roof expecting a hard lift and the thing swished upward on its shocks at the first touch. He locked the struts with two small levers and the canvas walls stood taut. The bed was already made thanks to Hank, with the moose quilt and a light duvet. All they had to do was toss up a couple of pillows. One step on top of a storage cabinet and they were up, and snug.

Celine slept well, better than she had maybe since those nights in Maine. She woke once needing to pee, and as she was lying there in the warm quilts summoning her will to take up the little head- lamp and make the climb down, she was startled by a sweep of headlights against the canvas.

Her first thought was lightning, but then she heard the soft crunch of tires on the dirt road maybe thirty yards away. Was that what had woken her? And not her bladder, which was admittedly tiny? Well, it was now grouse or archery season or whatever in all of these states, isn't that what Hank had told her? Some hunter was coming home late from the mountains up higher, or going out early.

She was the one with the keen nose, and none of this smelled right. She felt for the Glock in its paddle holster that she'd dutifully clipped to the edge of the bed platform, and she climbed down without the light, feeling the cabinet and then the floor with her bare feet, finding her sheepskin slippers by touch. She shrugged on a fleece jacket that she'd hung off a high cabinet handle, also at the ready. She found the latch and door handle without trouble and eased herself out into the cold damp night. The smells of sage and water and fog were even stronger now. As if the darkness had allowed them to breathe. No rain yet, but the little clearing was now in the clouds that had pushed down into the valley, she could feel their wet touch. And then she saw the blurred red glow of taillights descending out of sight through mist. Hunh. Whoever was passing was not simply traveling—the time between the first flash of headlights and the now disappearing taillights was too long. Someone was curious, or doing recon.

She peed, just squatted in the beaten grass and

listened to the creek rush in the dark. Amazing how many sounds when you parsed it: gurgles and spills, a rill like a flute, gulps and drums, even deep gongs.

Amazing, she thought: the layers of anything. The constituents that reveal themselves when you stop and pay attention.

She did not mention anything to Pete until they were both fully awake. They made coffee with the door of the camper open and the smell of the French roast filling their little house. A scrim of rain outside the door. The steady hush. Celine marveled. Is that all it takes? To rearrange the world? To sense again that everything is working as it should? They sat at what Hank had called the side dinette. He couldn't help but see Celine's flash of skepticism when he said it.

"I never in my life thought I would entertain myself at a *side dinette,*" she had murmured. "Sounds like Danette." Hank saw the slightest shudder.

But there they sat, drinking coffee at the vinyl table, and as at home in the swells of the hills as sailors on a little boat. She told Pete about the truck, she was sure it was a truck, and she said, "You know, you can tell a lot from the sound of tires on a road. Are they in a hurry or dawdling? Heedless of their surroundings or paying very close attention? You can even tell if the driver is mad. This driver was definitely not mad. Very cool. There was a distinctly surreptitious sound to the crunching of those tires."

Pete had long ago dismissed the notion he'd had in early days that he was indulging the active imagination of his wife. He sipped his coffee. "Mmm," he said.

"I feel something," Celine said. "Something is off. This thing about Gabriela losing her thick file of notes."

"She didn't say she lost it, she said, 'I misplaced it. I can't find it.' Her exact words. Seems to me there's a difference."

Celine chewed on the earpiece of her large tortoiseshell reading glasses. "There *can* be a big difference, can't there?"

"She sounded very upset," Pete said. "But as if she were trying to cover."

"That's just it. This feeling of cover. A cover-up." Celine sipped. Delicious. Why should coffee with cream and honey be better out here? "I'm not sure of anything," she said. "Which is almost wonderful."

They drank their coffee slowly and Celine wrote her letter to Hank. Then they buttoned up the truck and Celine picked up an animal bone that looked like a little mask—probably a pelvis, she'd use it for something—and they drove northwest toward Jackson Hole. The rain lightened then cleared and the groves of aspen running up through the slopes of black timber seemed to be a deeper yellow and the fields of wheatgrass tinged with faint green. Fall rain. They stopped for breakfast at the Fort Washakie Diner, which was crowded with mostly Native Americans eating breakfast after what looked like maybe night shifts working at the casino. A brown spotted pit bull snoozed contentedly in a corner and a round-faced Native girl served them with four curt syllables: "Can I getchyou?" She was almost as laconic as Pete.

She took their order without a hint of smile, but when she brought coffee refills she couldn't help herself. "You from L.A.?" she said. "He don't look like it, but you do." She pointed not quite accusingly with the pot.

That set them to laughing and the girl finally cracked a smile that brightened the whole room.

"New York," they said.

"Figured," she said.

"What's the dog's name?" asked Celine.

"Orchard."

"Orchard? Why on earth do you call him Orchard?"

The girl twisted her lips, " 'Cuz he looks like a apple." Her eyes sparkled.

Celine looked at the muscly, lumpy, snoring dog. "Hunh. He's about the furthest thing from an apple I think I've ever seen in my life."

"I said, *Richard,*" the girl chided.

As they got up to pay at the counter Celine noticed a youngish trim-bearded white man at a booth in the corner, wearing a creased and unfaded plaid shirt, this one red. She couldn't see his face because he was wearing a baseball cap and he was concentrating hard on a ketchup-covered omelet, head down.

nine

We have all seen the posters and prints of the bends of the Snake River curling beneath the sharp granite towers of the Grand Tetons. The water is black and the peaks are dusted with new snow and the cottonwoods along the banks are yellow, their smoldering ranks throwing the scale of the mountains into perspective. Because the tall trees look tiny running along the bottom of the picture. It may be morning and the river is covered in mist that moves over the water like smoke, and there may be one man fishing, his fly rod bent back mid-cast. If he is there, it is only to remind us that the grandeur and shocking beauty are not of human scale. That the most indisputable beauty may be the one that people cannot ever touch. That God exists up there somehow, in the peaks and remote lakes and the sharp wind.

Who knows why that picture stirs joy. It speaks directly to our impermanence and our smallness.

Those were Celine's thoughts as she drove along the river on just such a morning. The mist smoked and rose, the peaks towered, the cottonwoods caught the sun from the south and blazed and flamed. It was almost too grand. It could not be real.

"Look, Pete," she said. "There's a man fishing

down there in the fog. It looks just like that poster of Hank's."

"Aye-yup." Pa was speaking Maine this morning. Clearly the Washakie waitress in her reticence had reminded him of his first language.

They drove out into the open grass valley where a herd of elk in their hundreds grazed head down unafraid of bow hunters. "That's the National Elk Refuge," said Celine, pointing. "I remember all this. I took Mimi skiing here for her thirtieth birthday. I remember we rode a big cable car to the top—that mountain there, can you see it?—and once we got above the fog it was bright sun and blue blue sky, and as we neared the summit an announcement in the gondola said something about 'If you are not an expert ride back down.' It was glorious skiing up there, all those steep chutes. And down below the whole valley obscured by a layer of clouds. When we took our long run all the way to the bottom for lunch we skied right through that floor of clouds, right into mist and snow! We were like two little airplanes!"

"Mmm," Pete hummed.

"You're not listening to a thing I say this morning!" Celine cried, though she knew, of course, that this was not true.

"Hmph."

"Hmph is right. We have good cell reception. When we get to town, I'm going to call Gabriela again."

"Good idea."

Suddenly they were at the edge of it, the bustling town. They wound past the rec center, the first ski shops and cafés, and entered the flow of traffic around the central square. The town was packed. Trucks loaded with kayaks and bikes, campers with fly-rod vaults on the roof. Everybody seemed to be on the way to Fun. A sunny cool September morning, bracing for real fall but unwilling to let go of summer, the kind of autumn day that can only occur a couple of weeks a year. Tourists posed for pictures at the corners of the square, beneath tall arches made of elk antlers, their big smiles not at all fake.

"You'd think it was Fourth of July," Celine exclaimed. "Gracious! Don't any of these people have jobs?"

"Hard to say."

"Let's pull over." As soon as she said it, an SUV carrying a canoe began backing out of one of the prized parking spots. Right in front of them. Pete did not comment. This was another of his wife's talents: She had Parking Angels.

They got out, stretched, walked slowly on stiff knees across the street to one of the antlered arches.

"Pete, wait a sec. Let me catch my breath here. It's all the sitting. Can you please post this letter for me. It's to Hank. There's a box there." What a nuisance, emphysema. She thought she was a long way from having to carry oxygen, but higher altitudes could make things difficult, especially when she was tired, which she was. Her sleep had been troubled after seeing that truck vanish into the mist. She hadn't imagined it, and she was sure that whoever was driving the vehicle had been scouting them. God knows why.

Pete rejoined her and she glanced over her head at the gate of antlers. *"Come the True Dreams through Gates of Horn,"* she said.

Pete held her hand, barely. Moral support. *"And False through the Gates of Ivory."* He looked up. "Definitely qualify as horn," he said.

"Hmm. We'll take it as a sign. Old Penelope was even wiser than her husband, don't you think? Women usually are." She gave Pete's hand a squeeze, a sign that he could release her. "Let's sit on that bench in the shade." They did. Celine wore a small leather belt pack at her waist and she pried from it her flip phone. She called Gabriela, let it ring. Just before she thought it would go to voice mail the young woman picked up. Celine thought she had deliberated—*Pick up or not pick up?*—she could hear it in the sound of her "Hello?"

"Gabriela, hi, this is Celine. We are in Jackson on the way to Yellowstone. Are you well?"

"Fairly well. Yes."

"And your son?"

"He's—he's at school. Yes." She sounded nervous.

"Good. Before we get to Cooke City I'd like to know if you can locate your research file now. You know, it will be tremendously helpful."

The conversation began in fits and starts, which was another clue. Celine pressed about the file. How on earth could she misplace it? What did that mean, anyway? Gabriela at first was evasive. She tried to sound upbeat and clueless—"God, I have no idea. I wonder if I left it in the coffee shop at the corner, I was going over it, trying to organize it before I copied it to send to you, I just don't know. I've been by the place half a dozen times!"—and the more hapless she acted, the more seriously distraught she sounded.

"Just a sec," Celine said. She stopped the girl in her tracks. She had no patience for a bad liar. A good liar, on the other hand, was someone to learn from. She dug back into her belt pack, pulled out a red plastic inhaler, and sprayed herself one, then two full doses and held them in her lungs. *Pheeeeew* she let them out through pursed lips. "There. Better." She breathed two lungfuls of mountain air. "Now. I am an old woman, who knows how much time I have left. I certainly don't have enough of the stuff to tolerate deceit from the ones who should be telling me the truth. Gabriela, can you tell me what in God's name is really going on?"

Gabriela said she honestly didn't know. That rang true.

"Okay, tell me," Celine said.

"I—I don't know if I can. Or should."

"You are scared."

"A little, yes."

It was hard for Celine to imagine the intrepid bundle of energy she had met on the dock, the one with the clear laugh and the scent of blossoms, as frightened. Even the sadness that softened her seemed devoid of fear. "Well." Celine waited. One beat, then two. "Is it that we are on the phone?"

"Yes. Maybe."

Celine thought for a second. "You know," she said finally, "there is probably nothing you can tell me now, about the file, that Whom It May Concern doesn't already know."

Gabriela laughed, nervously, but it relieved the tension. "Yes, I guess that's true. Well, I put it on the coffee table in my apartment a week ago. To review, as I said. I went down to the athletic club on Mission for a yoga class and when I came back I couldn't find it anywhere. I went out of my mind. I was sure I'd left it there. And—"

"Yes?"

"My picture of Amana was knocked over. The one on the ferry. It is never knocked over. It sits on its own shelf. Nick can't even reach it. And in the kitchen, the silverware tray was over on the right side of the big drawer. I keep it on the left. And—"

"Go on."

"That passport was gone."

151

• • •

The phone was on speaker so that Pete could listen in. He had taken off his tweed cap and leaned his head in close, the side with the hearing aid. At twenty-two he had enlisted before he could be drafted for Korea, and though the war ended before he was ever shipped out, he went almost deaf on his right side from firing an M1C sniper rifle. He had been trained as a sniper, which was an odd specialty for a man with Pete's gentle nature, but maybe not so odd when one takes into account his boyhood growing up on a Maine island and plinking groundhogs from impressive distances with a .22. Pete's range instructors would have noticed it right away. His brother told Celine once that Pete could hit a flying chunk of two-by-four with a .22 just as if he were using a shotgun. A talent he never mentioned, which was not surprising as he never mentioned much.

Celine considered. If the file had been stolen, which sounded like the case, then this investigation had just become much more interesting. And they had barely started. A frisson of excitement went through her.

Celine's close friends had long ago determined that she was not constructed like other people. Where others might shrink or panic she seemed to get larger, to become more focused. Perhaps it was her years with Admiral Halsey, Baboo's longtime companion, who was known and feared for going straight into the teeth of battle. It was a trait his critics dissected with relish. But what they often missed in their analyses of battles and tactics was a streak of imagination and creativity that came straight out of a zest for boyhood mischief. Celine must have told Hank the story half a dozen times: When Halsey was an upperclassman at Annapolis he was given command of a patrol frigate during a live-ammo battle exercise on the Chesapeake. There were two teams. There was also heavy fog. The live ammo were rubber torpedoes. Halsey used his enemy's convoy as radar cover—they just assumed the blip was theirs as no enemy in his right mind would fall into the fleet like a duckling—and he maneuvered undetected so close to a Farragut-class destroyer—feet not yards—that when he loosed his rubber torpedo he put a hole in the hull of the brand-new ship. He was reprimanded and commended by the same commander—who had a distinct twinkle in his eye as he gave the cadet his dressing-down.

Hank, who loved to think about character, sometimes wondered if that spirit in the face of long odds, and the unorthodox approach, may have rubbed off on Celine when she was a child. He thought of the two of them walking up that dirt road together in mud season in Vermont, the distraught girl holding the old admiral's hand, the cold wind through the bare woods blowing her hair so that it covered her tear-stained face, the aged sailor barely noticing, his wandering mind maybe coming at last to focus on his young charge, this current mission: To console and protect. To educate. To love. Which he did. He adored Celine—Baboo had said so. He may have seen in the skinny girl—in her courage and mettle and imagination—a little of himself. What he might have said to her that afternoon: something about when we are most scared is the time to summon our clearest concentration and move forward, not back.

One of Hank's favorite stories of Celine was years after Admiral Bill died. She was in her forties. One of her cousins, the curator Rodney's younger brother Billy, was dying of pancreatic cancer at St. Luke's up in Harlem. She went to say goodbye. They had grown up together and shared many summers on Fishers Island and he was enduring probably his last day on earth and she stayed late and did not let herself fall apart in his room. And she lost track of time. It was two a.m. when she finally kissed his cheek and said, "I'll be seeing you, Billy," and went out into the November night. It was windy and cold, much like that day with Admiral Bill years ago. She was lost to memories of childhood as she made her way down a deserted Amsterdam Avenue. This was back when that part of the city was much more dangerous than it is today. She had a vague thought that she might catch a cab at 110th Street. Litter blew across the street. The heels of her pumps clicked on the pavement and her bracelets jingled. Suddenly two large men leapt out from a doorway and loomed in front of her. They were very rough. Without thought Celine said, "Oh! You must be freezing!" Addressing the larger of the two, she said, "You'll catch your death of cold. Your shirt is all ripped. Let me see if I have a safety pin." With that, she opened up her *purse* and began rifling through it.

The men stared. They were dumbfounded. "Here, found one!" she said and pulled it out and reached up and deftly folded back the edge of the rip, smoothing it carefully so that it made a neat edge the pin could catch, and she did the same on the other side of the tear, and with wonderful concentration pushed the pin through both sides and secured it. She patted it neatly down. "There," she said. "You'll be much warmer." The men stared. When they could speak they told her that this, ah, neighborhood was really really dangerous and what was she doing out here all alone?

"Saying goodbye to someone at the hospital who has been very special to me."

They insisted on walking her to the corner and waiting with her for a cab. Hank could see the two towering men in tatters, and little Celine in her long wool coat and beret and gold earrings. Of course no cab would stop, the men were too formidable. So she finally turned to them and said, "You two were on your way to doing something, why don't you go do it. I'll be fine. I can't tell you how much I appreciate your help." And as soon as they left she hailed a taxi.

She had not been in command of a frigate that night, and her motive was not a vanquishing of any kind, but the instinct to go straight ahead where others wouldn't dream to go seems in sympathy with her surrogate father.

Now she covered the phone in her lap for a second and was on the verge of speaking to Pete when she picked it up again and said, "I'll call you back in just a minute. I promise. Pete is right here and we need to talk it over," and she hung up.

ten

The chat may have lasted five minutes.

The deductions were obvious. If someone had stolen Gabriela's twenty-three-year-old research file on her missing father then 1) the timing suggested that they didn't want Celine and Pete to have it, and 2) they couldn't know that the two were just now launching an investigation unless Gabriela had told someone, or her phone was tapped. They'd clear that up in just a minute.

On the next bench, in full sun, was a family of four tourists feeding popcorn to Canada geese. The little boy was hurling the kernels overhead like he was trying to hit the birds with shot, and in his other hand he held a chocolate ice-cream cone that was melting all over his wrist.

"It's very hard to be a boy," Celine commented dryly. "You're never sure whether to love something or kill it." Pete followed her gaze. "This is a very self-respecting town, Pete. The pigeons here are wild geese."

"Hmm."

"Remind me to tell you a story later about peppering birds with shot."

"Hmm."

"Which, if you will stop interrupting me, brings us to further ideas on the matter. It's very hard to concentrate when you are so effusive."

He held her hand and rubbed the back of it with his thumb.

"Let's assume that the file didn't get up and walk of its own accord out of Gabriela's apartment. And that she didn't just leave it at the coffee shop. I'd be very surprised if she took it there in the first place. She would handle something like that with extreme care."

"It was stolen," Pete said flatly. "And I don't believe she told anyone about enlisting us. I didn't get the sense that she has a wide circle of confidants."

"Right. And we'll just ask her in a minute."

"Which means her phone was tapped—"

Pete was interrupted by an alarmed blatting and honking. The little boy, unable to arouse love or inflict death on the geese by hurling popcorn—they just happily ate the stuff—had dropped his cone and charged headlong at the little flock. He'd stubbed his toe on a root and hurtled like a surface-to-surface child at the birds who were at least as big as he. That was the first commotion. The alpha goose, if there is such a thing, was on top of the prone boy in a flash, beating his great wings and hissing and pecking at his neck. You could see that the goose had snapped. Psychologically. He'd had enough of obnoxious little boys and junk food, this goose was going postal. Enough was enough.

That was the second commotion. The mom screamed, the dad leapt up and rushed; the goose, to his credit, gave no quarter and flew into the man's face. The dad looked like he was beating himself about the head and shoulders. The goose landed on the grass, stumbled sideways, recovered, stretched his tremendous neck, took two strides, and in sync with his tribe, flapped his great wings, this time for flight, and with dignity and improbable slowness took wing. He and his flock rose over the trees muttering and circled north, out of sight.

In the shocked silence that often follows mortal combat, Celine and Pete looked at each other.

"Goose two, Smiths zero," Pete said quietly.

"I had no idea their wings creak like rusty hinges. Didn't it sound just like that, Pete? The boys look all right," she added, very dry, meaning the kid and his father who were taking their humiliation out on each other.

"A valuable lesson in Don't Feed the Animals. Could prove a lifesaver in bear country."

"We're going to bear country, aren't we, Pete?"

"Yes we are. I'm looking forward to it. I'm a little tired of being at the top of the food chain."

"You sound like that Neruda poem I love so: *It so happens I am tired of being a man* . . . Somewhere in there he knocks out a nun with a lily. Sorry, you were saying?"

Pete squeezed her hand. "Her phone is tapped."

"Mmm. Probably for a while, God knows why. And nothing happens, no trigger, until she hires us to find her father."

"Right. He disappeared twenty-three years ago. I think there's a good possibility that someone has been eavesdropping ever since."

"Wow."

"Wow," Pete repeated dramatically.

"Waiting for him to call. Because they don't believe he's dead either."

"Right. And there are scores to settle."

"Accounts to balance at the least."

"Hmm."

They listened to the vanquished little boy's older sister scold him for getting whipped by a bird and dropping a perfectly good chocolate cone on the grass, and they watched the Family Smith tromp off to their car and new adventures in engaging the world.

Celine said, "Instead *we* triggered the action. So then why . . ." Celine wore large glasses in dark tortoiseshell. They were a bit like Jackie O's sunglasses but bigger, even more of a statement. She didn't mean them to be, she shied from anything show-offy, but she had an innate and inarguable sense of style. She took off the glasses, eyed them critically as if they were smudged, which they weren't, and put them back on, settling them on her not at all diminutive, aquiline nose. "Why wouldn't they want us to have the file?"

"You mean if they wanted to find Paul Lamont?" The two were beginning to pronounce the "they" with vague distaste.

"Yes," she said. "They could simply follow us to him. After all, we have a better find rate than the FBI." Which was true.

"But do we have a better success rate than the CIA?"

They looked at each other. "Probably," Celine said. "That's just it. They can't find him. Whoever they are. And they've seen the file. You can bet they've broken in before and copied it. She didn't know but she does now because they *wanted* her to know. They wanted *us* to know. The fallen picture, etc.—that was a warning." Celine took a pocket mirror from her purse and checked her lipstick. "No, they've wrung the leads dry. The file is no more to them than an artifact. And we come along with our impeccable track record. They don't want us to find him or they'd let us have the file. The risk, whatever the risk is, is just too great."

"What's the risk?" Pete said.

"I'm not sure." She snapped the mirror closed and smiled at her husband. "I thought the silverware tray being moved was an interesting detail, didn't you? Spy craft is spy craft I suppose."

They had worked together for so long, had conducted so many of these inquiring conversations, that they knew the pacing down to the

161

last long notes. Like musicians who nod at each other before the final measures, they shared a long look that meant: *That's all for now. This too shall be revealed.* And then Celine raised the cell phone and called Gabriela back.

eleven

Jackson Hole was pleasant. Nothing more. Celine pointed out that an entire town bent on leisure and fun was very tiring.

"I take that back," she said as they strolled across to the Cowboy Bar for lunch. "*Pursuing* fun is exhausting. Having fun is just fun. Much more relaxing just to do your work, don't you think? I mean if you enjoy it."

"Well," Pete said. He held her hand and guided her across the street. He looked a little out of place in town, but only because he always dressed as if he were going to build a boat. In Maine. The attire did not change for formal affairs except that he might, just might, throw on an old tweed jacket. What he wore summer and winter, for woodwork in his shop, for dinner with one of Celine's fancy childhood friends, was loose khakis, often stained with a little varnish or a spatter of paint; worn leather deck shoes, often without socks; a canvas shirt, blue or green or cranberry, from L.L.Bean. That's it. A little like Fidel Castro always wearing army fatigues. Pete refrained from quoting Thoreau, but he told Hank once that his sartorial habits saved a lot of time and energy and expense.

Now he said, "It's why I always felt coming back

to the States after traveling was a bit stressful. I mean our job as citizens, apparently, is the pursuit of happiness. Something I always have to gird myself for. I'd much rather just *be* happy, or not."

To prove her point about the pursuit of fun, they had to wait for a table behind a group of road bikers who wore bike shoes that clumped and tight bike shorts that didn't clump nearly enough. According to Celine. "You will never ever be truly happy if you wear those shorts," she said. "You are telling your manhood that you wish he were an internal organ." One of the men overheard her and began to laugh, and insisted that the two of them slide in front of the group in line.

At the scarred wood booth where they ordered burgers, the young waiter told them that Celine looked like an old-time movie star. *Was she?* No, she was not.

"Dude, you could be," he said. "And I mean that as a compliment. We have a bunch in town."

"So I hear."

"Harrison Ford was in the other day."

"You don't say."

"He's a regular guy. He was even on the ski patrol."

Celine really could have used an ice tea. But the kid was warming to his subject. He told them that a skier from Texas or somewhere ran into a tree and was knocked out pretty bad, and when he woke up he saw Harrison Ford leaning over him, strapping him into a sled. The man began to cry because he knew he was dead. The kid thought it was so funny.

The burgers were excellent. The bar in the center of the restaurant was packed with locals drinking beer like it was a job, and Randy Travis sang about how his love was deeper than the holler. The din was so loud that Pete might as well have been legally deaf. Perfect.

Celine leaned forward and nearly shouted in his amplified ear: "Pete, we're being followed. I'm sure of it. FYI." She tipped her head toward a young man in a baseball cap and week-old dark beard at the bar. Pete nodded. Only she would have known that the bare twitch of his lip was a smile: He had come to the same conclusion.

Celine wanted to see Lamont's portraits. Pete had brought in his laptop, and after he'd eaten half his burger he scooted around to her side of the booth and opened it up, and using just the bar's open Wi-Fi network he found the first archive of Lamont's photos of Amana.

The first black-and-white portrait filled the screen. What struck Celine right away was the calm. A distilled calm radiated from the woman and formed a pool of quiet in the boisterous clamor all around them. It was a profile shot, slender neck and naked shoulders, head inclined, black hair tied back.

Where was the beauty, where did it begin? Celine, who understood the necessity and power of mystery, wouldn't know where to start.

It could have begun in the tilt of her head, the angle, the light tension it put on the neck so that she seemed at once poised and relaxed, the way a violin can look—or a bird. Celine thought of the great blue heron in Baboo's cattails, just below the porch. How the bird would stand, it seemed, for hours, neck stretched over the shallows in effortless balance between stillness and strike. Because the strike would inevitably come. Celine used to think that if eternity was anywhere it was somehow contained in the attitude of this bird. Everything the heron had done, and would do, and was now so perfectly not doing, was contained in her bearing. And so Amana. As she tipped her head she was both bowing to time—there is no mercy there, that is clear—but she was also gathering herself, her focus, for something that went beyond acceptance: She had acted and she would act, and there would be love in the action, and imagination. In whatever she did. That was also clear.

So that in a world whose onslaught was barely bearable there would be something new and lovely. The angle of her head suggested a promise.

Then there was the plane of her cheek and

where it softened and yielded to meet her eye, her temple. Her cheek was high but not severe. Pronounced but not insensitive to the soft skin below it. It suggested self-discipline and submission to duty—if she were asked to be a warrior, she would be a warrior—but also compassion and tolerance. Am I reading too much? Celine thought. No. This is what I do. I am not always right but usually I am.

Her mouth, the half that Celine could see, was relaxed, closed. Celine might have stayed right there. Made camp, so to speak, and dwelled on this aspect of the woman's glory. From the slightest downturn at the corner, her upper lip rose through a long double bow and into a fullness at the crest that was sensuous but held the faintest humor, too. There were many serious pleasures the mouth had tasted, but its favorite may have been laughter. The lower lip seemed like the serious younger sister—she was resolved to follow along and join the fun but was willing to stay back a little, and to be bitten. One wanted to kiss that mouth. To reach down and kiss even the edge. But it was Amana's eye that kept drawing the viewer: The intelligence there and the stillness. The relaxed concentration. The sense that whatever was seen and decided would be acted on swiftly. The photos were black-and-white, but Celine imagined that her eyes were a smoky green.

Celine had not even considered the fine nose, the smooth shoulders, or ever realized that a jawline could evoke such purity. Amana's temple slayed her. The vulnerability there, the stray hairs just before the perfect and odd nautilus of the ear. Remember that Celine had been a painter. She had been drawing and painting figures since soon after she could walk. When had she ever felt that a face could so effortlessly hold all her attention?

She was reluctant to leave the image but she nodded to Pete and the next came up, and the next. Portraits of Amana looking straight into the camera—the same distilled serenity but full face, the beauty now full bore, both barrels, the wide-set eyes looking straight at the viewer, who catches her breath—or Amana contemplating something humorous or faintly sad, or something inward and distant, the pictures almost hard to look at, not because they demanded some recalibration by the viewer, or obeisance, or envy, or anything at all, but just because simple beauty can be hard to bear. There were nudes, Amana stretched on her back and shot from behind her head, seeing almost what she might have seen. Or on her side, one knee almost to her chest, or the woman bending to test the water in a tub like a Degas. But these were not by Degas, the framing was not meant to flatter. These were transparent statements of awe. A few times Celine had to remember to breathe.

She found herself forgiving Paul Lamont a little. Good God. Whatever the man had done after the death of his wife, she could more than understand. A weaker man would have simply offed himself. And these were moments with Amana captured in relative stillness. What would it have been like to make love to such a woman? To receive her kisses? To taste her skin? To make her laugh? To listen to her tell stories to the child you had given her? To take the child from her arms? To share a meal? To hold hands and walk the neighborhood late on an August night, the light clapping of your sandals the closest sound? To watch her shed her clothes and dive into a lake and swim, steadily outward— she was a trained and strong swimmer, that was evident from many shots of her at a pool, a pond—leaving behind a spreading wake and tiny wavelets that touched the pilings and the shore long after? Celine could not conceive it. For Lamont, who clearly was so sensitive to beauty, it may have been like experiencing some kind of afterlife while he was still alive. Certainly it would not have been easy.

He would have wondered often if he were dreaming. And if the dream would one day vanish.

She closed the laptop herself. It was enough.

• • •

In the World According to Celine and Pete the very best part of every town was the library. And then the historical society, if there was one. Unless, of course, there was a discount gun shop (Celine), or a woodworking store (Pete) that sold fine hand planes and chisels. Jackson's library was just a mile down the road. They'd passed it on the way in and Celine had remarked the hand-drawn sandwich board that said BOOK SALE TODAY! MAGAZINES!

Now, as they walked to the truck, Celine popped in a stick of Juicy Fruit and said, "Pete, I'd like to see more of young Paul Lamont's photographs. I had an idea—just a sec." On a bench outside an art gallery crouched an athletic girl in running tights and training top. Celine had a hunch she was pretty but couldn't be sure because her face was in her hands and her very red shoulders were shaking. Celine stood over her and touched her heaving back. The girl's head jerked up. Her eyes were swimming in tears and they were confused and angry now and they tried to focus.

"Breakup?" Celine said. She had lived long enough to know that the tenor of the girl's sobs could only be one thing.

The girl wavered. The more she registered the handsome older woman, the less angry she became. She nodded.

"May I?" Celine said.

The girl hesitated, nodded, and Celine sat.

"You have the kind of loveliness that comes from inside," Celine said. The girl almost smiled. "Which means he is a complete fool, don't you think?"

The smile broke through, quivering. What the hell, was she dreaming?

Celine reached for the girl's wet hand, held it. "You know, I have lost three great loves. Loves that could knock the earth off its axis. Truly. Each time I thought my life was over." The girl was very still, she was listening. "I have finally found the one I am meant to die with. It's a love so deep I cannot attempt to fathom it, and I don't want to. I wish I could have told that to my younger heartbroken self. That everything would work out, more than work out, it would be glorious. So I am telling it to you. One day you will be grateful for this new chapter."

The girl was listening. Her hand rested in Celine's now like a bird that had nowhere else it would rather be. "Here," Celine said. She rummaged in her purse with her free hand and found a small tube of SPF 50. "Will you please wear some of this so you make it to a ripe old age. You look like a very lovely lobster." She gave the hand a squeeze and returned to Pete. She did not see, but Pete did, that the girl looked like she'd been hit on the head by a lily—or struck by an angel. A Day in the Life, Pete thought. He had

171

long ago admitted that when one moved through the world with Celine, well—it was simply more fun. A giddy concept for a seventh-generation Mainer.

"Where were we?" Celine said. "Oh, I had an idea. We passed the library just a mile back. Looks like they're having a cleanout. They would have old copies of *National Geographic*, don't you think? Maybe we can even buy some."

The Teton County Library was a long low building with log walls that looked a little like a ranch house. Don't let that fool you, thought Celine. This was one of the richest counties in the country and the inside did not disappoint: the computer area, the children's room, the Calder mobile hanging in the lobby would have been the envy of any city. It reminded them of the very fancy high schools on Fishers and North Haven: Where there are many rich folks "from away," their property taxes have to go somewhere. In the courtyard in back, in the dappled shade of an aspen grove, were tables and tables of old books and taped paper signs that said $2 EACH. They passed them with barely a glance. The farthest folding tables, beside a venerable old blue spruce and not far from the chortle of a small creek, held stacks of donated magazines.

Many were so old the covers were marbled by wear. There were the expected *Popular Mechanics* and *Better Homes and Gardens.* The *Modern Architectures* and *Flyfish Journals.* Celine glided by them without a twinge of remorse, but had to make herself ignore the surprising edifice of *Soldier of Fortunes.* Well, actually she couldn't. She stopped and pondered the issue on top with a picture of a commando in a floppy jungle hat and face paint emerging from a twilit river holding a camoed rifle with a double scope and the headline: NIGHT VISION LIKE NEVER BEFORE. Pete nudged her. "It's a very small camper." "But, Pete, just one?" His eyebrow did something minute, which was Pete's version of a shrug, and she picked up the magazine. What they were looking for was in boxes on the grass. Boxes and boxes. Clearly, the local Brahmins were drowning in *National Geographics.*

It took them all of ten minutes to locate the dozen years Paul Lamont was active, and to skim the tables of contents and pull out the issues in which he had stories. Celine decided it would be a good idea to jot down the dates of the ones in this period that they left behind. They grabbed a few more from later years for good measure and came away with an armful of thirty-one magazines, fifty cents apiece. The docent with the cash box by the glass doors wore almost as many gold bracelets as Celine. She looked up over her half-rim glasses and, recognizing one of her own, visibly relaxed, smiled, said, "Oh, don't you just love these? We wallpapered the ski room with old covers. Five dollars will do, take as many as you like." Absently she flipped through the old magazines and stopped cold at *Soldier of Fortune*. "Oh!" she peeped. "How did that get in here? I'm so sorry, I can put that one back if you'd like—"

"We'll take it," Celine said, smiling brightly. "You never know when you might need a night-scope." She gathered up the magazines and they left.

They drove north along Jackson Lake, through the National Park. Blowdown wracked the banks, piles of tangled driftwood logs silvered in the sun. Pink fireweed flushed the meadows and the mountains stood above their own reflections in the dark water. Celine wondered again what it was about beauty, and what it had to do with love. She thought that she was probably as sensible to its intoxications as Lamont. Artists, as a tribe, tend to share this dangerous suscep-tibility. She could sympathize. She would have gone crazy, too. The man had roamed the earth bearing witness to beauty through the lens of his camera, and Amana was maybe the most exquisite thing he had ever beheld. More even than those two horses pawing the sky at sunrise. She was more glorious than his famous ship cresting what looked to be a tsunami. Easy to love someone that beautiful. Easy to be obsessed.

And when Amana was being pulled by the current out to sea, he turned his back on her and swept up his daughter and ran with her up the trail.

To Celine, that was the bravest act of true love. It might seem contrary, mightn't it? She might have asked that of someone listening to her story. *No, not to me,* she would answer. Because he made himself an extension of his wife's will. Counter to his every screaming instinct, he did what she would have wanted, insisted, he do. And he did it in a selfless instant, without hesitation. Celine could not think of an act more truly heroic.

What he did after: disappearing into drink, exiling his little daughter to her own planet, maybe abandoning her completely twelve years later. She almost forgave it. After seeing the photographs of his first wife and the quality of the attention he had given her, she understood.

Did he finally abandon Gabriela for good, on the border of Wyoming and Montana? Or was he hauled away by a bear? That's what they had come to find out. Which was the worst outcome? Which would hurt the girl more? The revelations about the missing file pointed to a picture a bit more complicated than a bear attack. And she knew that simple death is sometimes the least painful form of absence.

twelve

That first summer, when the sisters were finally certain that their father really would not take the three-hour train ride from New York and the forty-five-minute New London ferry to visit them on the island, they began, in adult parlance, to act out. Bobby was the first to go to the hospital. Las Armas, Gaga's house, was a Spanish villa brought over from the old country brick by brick by Grandfather Charles. It had a courtyard that opened to the sound and an upper gallery that ran around the entire second story and looked down on the central fountain and flower beds. The upper rooms were serviced by two inner staircases—one from the kitchen and service quarters, and one from the main entrance—and two outer sets of steps with heavy, varnished banisters.

Las Armas ran with a spare summer staff. It was more a matter of aesthetics than economy. Gaga brought with her to Fishers a butler, who functioned also as secretary and valet; a cook; a serving maid, who did housekeeping; and a laundress, a chauffeur, and a gardener. The heavy landscaping and gardening that took place before and after the family left for Manchester were contracted out to an island crew who took care of a number of houses. At home in Connecticut this skeleton staff would be beefed up considerably to a full complement that included two grooms; though they drove everywhere in their Rolls, no one could imagine a house without horses.

Bobby, being the eldest granddaughter, had her own bedroom on the upper floor, which overlooked the lawns that ran down to the beach. Celine and Mimi shared a bedroom down the hall that looked out on the crushed-seashell driveway and the front gardens.

The two younger sisters were, as a rule, the first up in the morning. They were two years apart, but like twins, they tended to wake at the same minute, their bare feet hit the maple floor in a four-beat tattoo, nighties were shed and shorts and shirts thrown on in a blur, the water tap in the adjacent bathroom ran for twenty-eight seconds, the toilet flushed twice, and they were ready. What would the morning bring? Not that they were "brought" anything. These were not passive creatures. The first order of business was to drag their older sister into the day.

Bobby was eleven, almost twelve. She was protective of her sisters and the three would circle the wagons in any society outside of family, but she was also a girl on the cusp, and as such she lived in and out of a realm that was remote to the younger girls, and mysterious, and a bit regal, and sort of awe-inspiring; and at times she had little patience for childish enthusiasms. Celine and Mimi sensed the imminent departure of their sister into the mists of womanhood and were determined to keep her in the land of the bare-foot and the tomboy as long as they could. Their favorite pre-breakfast sport was to sneak into her room while she slept, approach their prey like two leopards, and pounce.

The ensuing battle often ended in tears. Someone might go flying off the bed, someone might get tickled to within an inch of peeing, someone's head might knock someone's elbow, some other might let out a blood-curdling scream that was instantly muffled by hands or pillow—because the very worst outcome would be to arouse the attentions of an adult.

So when Celine and Mimi cracked Bobby's door—she had tried to barricade it with a chair but the two succeeded in sliding it back—and found the bed empty and the window screen propped against the wall, they were shocked, as sisters, but excited, as hunters. They stuck their heads out the window to find the espaliered pear tree forming a perfect leafy ladder, and found it also to be irresistible and they descended it without accident—Mimi could climb trees like a monkey. They ran like escaped convicts down the lawns to the beach where the fog still moved in a living cloud. They thought they would find Bobby collecting sea glass, but she was nowhere in sight. They trotted up the beach and back. They were still in huntress mode and so did not call out, but they didn't have to: They heard, between the moans of two foghorns on the sound, a softer groaning.

Grayson's dock was at the south end of the beach and formed a boundary. At slack tide it was eight to ten feet off the water. Their father had always loved to dive from the deck, and though they had never all been to the island together, he promised in his letters to put each on his back and jump off. He told them it would be like parachuting without a parachute, which for some reason drove them crazy with anticipation. Mimi and Celine followed the sobs to the dock and found Bobby washed onto the beach like a shipwreck, her face covered in blood.

She had dived right off the end, as she imagined her father dove. She had thrown herself off, unaware that Harry only dove at high tide and knew the bottom well enough to avoid the bigger rocks.

Anyway, she didn't really care if she died. Her father had made the big trip back from France and rather than making a beeline to Fishers to celebrate their reunion as she would have expected, he seemed to be looping right around them. Seemed to be sidestepping his own family. Why on earth would he maneuver to avoid them? It surpassed all understanding. Maybe he was angry with her, or hurt that she hadn't written back promptly or often enough. Could that be it? Maybe in Paris, in something so serious as a world war, he had lost his taste for fatherhood. Maybe little girls were too trivial a thing anymore.

The harder she tried to reconcile this behavior with the father she adored and had been missing, the more she felt uncertain that anything would continue to act as it should—her mother, for instance, or the sea, or stars, or the sun. And that made her angry. So. If he was not going to come back as promised and put her on his back and jump off Grayson's dock, she would do it herself.

That morning she had woken earlier than usual. It was barely light and the whip-poor-will was still lashing at the fog with her incessant call. Bobby had been crying. She knew she had because her pillow was wet. She put on her bathing suit instead of her shorts and climbed down so as not to chance meeting the house-keeper, Anna, who also got up very early. She ran down to the beach and across to the high dock and executed an impressive swan dive off the end. She skinned her arm on a boulder four feet beneath the surface and struck the side of her head. Very lucky that the rock was mostly covered in a thick mat of slippery seaweed. Still the crack sent lightning through her brain and she remembered a flash of a thought: *"Ne pas s'évanouir*! Do not pass out! You will drown!"

Still, she was a very practical little girl and calm under all circumstances that had nothing to do with her father, and though she was out of her mind with grief and anger she really had not meant to kill herself. She struck the rock and lightning forked and all went black and then she found herself clawing for the surface where the fog was more luminous than the dark of the seabed, and she gulped water and air and choked and coughed and kept swimming until her feet scraped bottom and got cut on the barnacles and she somehow crawled onto the sand of their beach. She was choking and sobbing. She tried to get to her knees and threw up on the sand and lay back down. She curled up. She cried. Her father didn't love her anymore. She had tried to prove that it didn't really matter, that she could survive on her own, and evidently she couldn't. She was a total failure. She sobbed. She couldn't even cry because she kept choking. Where was she anyway? She hated America.

Celine ran out of the fog and found her sister curled and bloody. With the flash of intuition she would come to rely on all her life, she understood the whole scene. She was precocious, too, in caring for fallen nestlings and stray cats, and she knew to put pressure on a bleeding wound. She did not panic. As soon as she saw her sister's head she peeled off her shirt and pressed it against the cut that welled above Bobby's left temple. *"Même chose!"* she said briskly to Mimi, who wanted only to be just like her big sister and who tugged off her own top, and Celine took the striped shirt and still holding pressure rolled it three times and wrapped it around Bobby's head and tied it as tightly as she could.

"Okay," she said to Mimi in English. "Now run! *Vite!* Fetch Mummy!" Mimi ran back up the beach and vanished in the fog.

Celine got off her knees and sat beside her crying sister and very gently lifted her head into her lap and stroked her bare shoulder. The fog moved in and out of itself slowly, and tiny waves lapped the sand. Peepers throbbed peacefully in the marsh, the foghorn moaned. Her sister cried quietly and trembled under her hand. Celine bent her head down as far as she could so that her hair hung in Bobby's wet face and she murmured into her ear, "He still loves us. He does."

The next one to go to the hospital was Alfonse the gardener. Nobody liked him. The girls couldn't understand why Gaga kept him on. He wore khaki coveralls that were stained with dirt and oil, and he coughed and spat, and he was mean. They said "Hello" and "Good Morning," and he only scowled back. They spied on him sometimes from the dark shade under a stand of pines. They crept through the tall grass at the edge of the lawn like leopards. The light through the needled limbs broomed across their backs and they pretended they wore spots. They watched Alfonse pulling weeds. He yanked them out like he was mad at each one. There was a rumor that once he had had a wife and child, but that they had left, or died. The girls could see why they might have fled. Sometimes while they spied, he lifted his head and looked straight at them, his eyes narrow. Whoops. He also smoked a pipe when he was sitting alone in the shade of his toolshed in the afternoon. It stank. Sort of. He smoked and coughed and spat.

A few days after Bobby's accident, the sisters decided to go fishing. Another enticement their father had mentioned. They had hooks and sinkers and they needed worms. The three of them went into Alfonse's shed looking for trowels to dig them up. They wrinkled their noses. The shed smelled of dirt and moss and maybe vanilla pipe tobacco. They had just found one rusty trowel when the doorway darkened with Alfonse's bulky shadow. "What the *hell,*" he said. "You should ask me first." They did not ask, they squeezed past him and bounded like startled deer and added his curse to their list of indictments. The next day Bobby said, "Let's pull a prank—*une farce*—on the stupid man." They were in the telephone closet off the pantry, under the stairs. There was a corkboard on the wall of the tiny room on which their grand-parents had tacked important phone numbers. A half card of shiny thumbtacks lay on the shelf. Bobby picked it up and ordered, "*Venez! Vite!*" She still commanded allegiance despite the shaved patch on the side of her head and the twenty-three stitches.

Alfonse had a small Harvester International tractor he used to mow the extensive lawns and to haul compost and straw. He parked it in a grove of maples in a simple lean-to at the lower end of the property. The girls walked the path as if they were going to the beach and veered off early and ran to the tractor shed. Bobby handed out the tacks—two each—like a resistance fighter handing out bullets. She asked Mimi if the coast were clear. Clear! Then she placed her tacks point-up on the tractor seat and nudged Celine. Celine made no decision but mimicked her older sister. Mimi did the same. Celine told Hank decades later that in the moment she set the tacks on the tractor seat she knew, or saw— she said it was just like seeing a night landscape in a flash of lightning—that the world was divided. "On one side is the good and just, on the other is the bad and cruel. That simple. I felt evil breathing on my neck and I went ahead. It was a charge, a thrill, like perhaps a shot of heroin is to some. I can imagine. I understood nothing about addiction, but I could feel that a person might seek that rush again. It was a great moral failure."

The next day the cook found Alfonse hanging from a beam beside his mute tractor.

The third one to go to the hospital was Celine. At least she came back. Alfonse, of course, never did. The cook, Aggie, told the sisters one morning that Alfonse had indeed once had a wife and daughter and that they had died of tuberculosis. He had contracted it too but survived, though his lungs were weak, which was why he only smoked one pipe in the evening and was not in the army fighting the war. He had tried to enlist four times and they always discovered his frailty.

Harry Watkins, Celine's father, had just now been at the breaking edge of the war. He had fled just before the Germans marched on Paris, had traded in his Hispano Suiza for a bicycle on the clogged roads, had pedaled up the shoulder of the highway carrying a large leather satchel of Morgan's most important papers, and once out of Paris he had been hailed by a passing black Bentley sedan. "Harry Watkins, is that *you?* Get in! Get in!" It was the Spanish ambassador to France and he had Harry crouch on the floor of the rear compartment and they covered him with a travel rug and smuggled him across the border into Spain.

A fitting, glamorous, and dashing end to the

French chapter for this star hockey player from Williams, this legendary dancer. Harry was a man of action, not of words. When he got across to New York it was mid-July. He checked into the Yale Club, which was open to Williams men, and called his daughters. He was not calling his wife. What Baboo and Harry had to say to each other was written in an exchange of six letters, three each. Mimi answered the phone. She happened to be in the phone closet rifling through the umbrella stand in the corner looking for something she could turn into a parachute. Who knew what method she was devising for her own trip to the emergency room.

"Papa!" she screamed. *"Papa! Viens! Quand est-ce que tu viens?"* Harry was not demonstrative, but he loved his daughters more, possibly, than anything in his world. That comes across in the letters to Baboo, which Celine finally read after her mother's death. He and Baboo had swiftly come to terms. It was not only in their upbringing but also in the makeup of their temperaments that they would prefer death over making a scene. Whatever objections they each had to the final settlement—informally described in a few lines in their last letters—they swallowed. Baboo's last inducement was to remind him of his duty to his children: *I suppose you could come. We would all be together again one last time as a family. The girls, of course, would be beside themselves. They adore you; you are the brightest star in their firmament and I can only encourage you to do your upmost to maintain their affections and strengthen their love. I would not see them stunted. But I'm not sure, frankly, if I have the stamina, nor the necessary élan, to play the part. I fear it would all come crashing down in some horrible way that would scar everyone. And then there is the matter of where you would sleep.*

Now, on the phone, Harry asked Mimi if she had been swimming and she replied that oh, yes, she had, she had learned the crawl and could breathe to both sides and had won her race at the Hay Harbor Club. *"J'ai gagné une médaille!"* she crowed. He said he was very proud of her and that he loved her very much. "Please remember that," he said.

"Are either of your sisters nearby?" he asked.

"Un moment—" He heard her scream for Bobby. He heard a muffled shout in response—he could picture his gangly eldest at the top of the stairs. *"Papa!"* Mimi cried back in answer. A beat, a shout, dropping in tone, then Mimi: "Papa . . ." A hesitation. "She said to tell you that she is indisposed." Which was their code for using the bathroom.

"How about Celine?" he managed to ask.

"She is at the beach learning to sail with Gustav."

"Oh, good. Good. Well you tell them both how much I love them. Now I better hang up. I love you very very much. Remember when you breathe to keep your head down. Just turn it side to side as if it were on a pivot."

"Yes, I do! I do!" she said, hoping to keep him on a little longer. And the phone clicked off, and she heard the even note of the dial tone.

Later, it would occur to her that certain dial tones and the flatlining of certain hearts sound almost the same.

He did not call back. He did not talk to them for months, and then it was formal phone calls and meetings on birthdays, at Christmas. Only Baboo might have understood that the degree of his reticence masked the depth of his loss. He never did anything in his life halfway except for the upholding of his marriage vows, and he couldn't figure out how to manage it. Also, he was a kinetic, physical person, not a man of conversation or verbal gestures. He had loved his daughters by *doing* things with them, and in a regimen of occasional weekend visits, he could never gather the momentum to make things go smoothly, or right. There was one attempt that November to take them all to the Central Park Zoo, which ended with long awkward silences and Bobby trying to feed her arm to the lions. He abdicated to Baboo. He probably felt it was less confusing for the girls, and less painful in the long run if they began their independence from their father earlier rather than later. He was probably also wrong.

The morning of the call, Celine bounded out of the honeysuckle and bayberry bushes on the beach path to find out from an addled Mimi that their father had phoned from New York. Her younger sister was on the back lawn frowning down at a broken umbrella. Her face was swept alternately with excitement and confusion and fleeting sadness. Celine said she looked exactly like a windy hillside being swept by cloud shadows and sunlight. She knew her sister better than she knew her own reflection and instantly she panicked.

"What? What?" she insisted. "*Dis moi!* *Qu'est-ce que s'est passé?*"

"I don't know," Mimi said. "Papa called. He wanted to speak with you. I don't know." Mimi raised her eyes from the wrecked umbrella and met her sister's gaze and burst into tears.

Celine could not believe she missed the call. She charged into the house. Baboo was upstairs in her bedroom winding her magnificent dark hair before a triple mirror. Her hair had come from Gaga. Evidently she had known nothing about the call. The Thin Pink Line was already being drawn: Her daughters were beginning to search out an object of blame for the building absence of their father. But when Celine told her mother that she had missed her father's phone call, Baboo's face told enough of the story. The anger and grief there—worse: the confusion. Perhaps not for any other child of seven, but for Celine it spoke volumes.

She tumbled down the stairs, clapped the screen door, and tore back down to the beach. The wind was up. Gustav, the sailing instructor, had gone back to Hay Harbor. The tiny catboat they had just used was pulled up on the beach and tied with cotton rope to a heavy driftwood log. Celine untied it and pushed the bow around, shoving it over the sand with all her strength and digging in with scrabbling feet like a rugby player in a scrum, and when it was pointed toward the water she went to the rope and put it over her shoulder and hauled it to the wet sand. The westerly wind was stiff and it blew her hair across her face. The green water of the shallows yielded quickly to serious dark blue, deep water, and out there the sound was choppy and the swell met the wind and raised whitecaps. She waited for a bigger wave to float the keelless boat and shoved again; then one more time on the next wave and the little boat was floating.

She stood waist-deep, back to the small breakers, and was knocked by the waves as she yanked loose the ties that cinched the folded sail to the wooden boom, and she gave a great final push the way Gustav had showed her and leapt aboard the liberated dinghy. She picked up the varnished centerboard in both hands and knocked it down snug in its slot. The boat was rocking dangerously just at the edge of the little break and swinging sideways. She needed headway right now, so she made sure the sheet was free and hoisted the halyard and pushed away on the tiller with her hip, and it was just enough pressure to force the bow back into the swell. With the two of them sailing she had not realized how many things there were to do at once to launch her little boat. She had always hoisted the sail with the big Dutchman's help and the weight of it surprised her, as well as the sudden living flapping of the canvas as it rose to the breeze. The boat had become a powerful living animal and it frightened her.

But Celine was Celine. She had been working hard to learn to sail not just because she was drawn to open water and wildness and had always loved sea stories but because her father had promised to sail with her and she wanted badly to show him that she could skipper her own boat. The sail slapped and snapped violently, then fluttered as it rose, bellied an instant as the boom swung away, swung back, came taut and she cleated down the line fast like a pro and thought *Sheet and tiller!* and began stripping the slack-line in fast while keeping the teak handle of the tiller away with her knee, and the sail caught and filled and the boom swung away and slammed hard against the sheet and the boat tipped up to star-board and lurched forward like a wild stallion released from a pen.

In reflex she leaned back out of the shallow cockpit to counter and snugged the sheet down fast in the slot of the keeper and reached blindly for the tiller. She caught it and was surprised again at the living pressure against her palm as she forced the bow into the oncoming sea and leaned back. And was surprised at the loud slapping of the hull bounding against the chop, and the crash and lunge of spray as she hit a whitecap. She was doused and didn't care. Still, she held the dinghy close to the wind. She tugged the sheet from the keeper and gripped it in her left hand. The little boat flew and pounded into the quartering swell. She was more terrified and more thrilled than she had ever been in her life, and she was heading for the open black water of the sound.

Celine was far enough into the channel to make out Las Armas and Grayson's dock and the line of other houses in their clearings on the low ridge, and see Simmons Point and beyond it the open Atlantic. She knew what she had to do to come about, to fall off the wind and slow and head back, but she couldn't make herself go through the motions. She had clung to the mane of a runaway horse in Blois and it felt the same. Except she wanted this. Part of her did. To sail away from everything that had to do with her father leaving them. When the gust hit and threw the upwind gunwale to the sky and burned the sheet through her palm and launched her from the cockpit she cried his name.

So Celine knew what it was to be abandoned by a father. And to what lengths a child—even an adult child—might go to bring him back. After years of turning her great capacity for empathy toward Harry Watkins, she understood, too, the despair that might be visited on some fathers who had made the choice to leave.

thirteen

North of Jackson Hole, the Toyota pickup jounced over a root and stopped. The campsite they chose was right on the shore of Jackson Lake. Dusk was moving over the water with a stillness that turned half the world to glass. The wall of mountains had gone to shadow as had the reflections at their feet. In the stillness the rings of rising trout appeared like raindrops. Slowly, in silence, the dark water tilted away from the remaining daylight. Celine stepped down from the truck and stretched and walked to the water, smelling its coldness and the scent of someone's cooking fire. She saw an older man casting a bobber on the closest point and a younger man shaking a tent out of a stuff sack three campsites down. She thought that peace reigned in the world—might reign. But only where love had no ferocity. Where there was the love between mothers and fathers and children there would be no peace.

Pete came up behind her and put his hands on her shoulders and was wise enough not to say a word. Maybe it wasn't wisdom: The thought of saying anything after arriving at camp after a long drive probably never occurred to him.

After a while Celine said, "It reminds me of Lake Como."

"When you were proposed to by an earl? The year in college you went back to France?"

"He was a duke."

"Hmm."

"Wouldn't it be nice to be simply retired?" she asked. "Like that couple there? And over there? We could come down to the water tomorrow morning and throw out a bobber and hook with a marshmallow on it and sit in a beach chair."

"Hmm. I'm not sure they use marshmallows."

"We could tell that young man who's following us that the game is up, we're not playing anymore, he can go home to his own family where there is probably a house with a little girl inside who misses him terribly."

"That man there?"

"Yes that one. The one next to the pickup who is studiously unrolling his tent under that big pine."

The second night in the camper was more peaceful than the first. They made a pot of Lapsang souchong and drank it slowly at the little table and flipped through the *National Geographic*s in the imperfect light from the little bulb on the wall. Celine turned the pages of a long feature on Chile shot by Lamont, and now she was struck by the sensitivity that had impressed Pete. The susceptibility to wonder was clearly not confined to impressions of his wife. There was one picture of a Chilean *huaso* in furry goatskin chaps and a flat-brimmed hat, riding a gray roan in the rain. He was riding in green woods along a white-water river, and he had a chain saw tied behind the saddle and was holding an infant in one arm. Something about the ease of the scene, the rightness, the green hardwoods and the rushing river and the man and the horse, spoke to her like a poem. Maybe it was simply the attitude of the man: his bearing balanced to the rhythm of the horse's gait; his hat tilted to the trail, to all the work to be done. But it was more than that: There was something wholly protective in his posture. No matter what happened, now or ever, he would cradle this child. Nothing could be more clear. Celine huffed out a breath, turned the page.

On the next was a spread of the presidential palace and the National Gallery, which she skimmed, but at the bottom was a photograph that stopped her again. It was of a painting: It seemed to be a scrim of rain over mountains. Storm in late spring, maybe, greens and a black sky riven by a jag of light. If it were a sky. She wasn't sure, but she felt a rhythm in this too, a music, and a kinship with the elements, and realized the same sensibility that had loved the cowboy now loved the abstract. The painting reminded her of Clyfford Still, the same surprise and mystery. Fernanda de Santos Muños was the name of the artist, and according to the caption she was one of Chile's national treasures. Celine could see why.

"Pete," Celine said.

"Yes, love."

"Look at this painting. It must have been strange shooting in Chile in the seventies. Chile, Argentina, Peru. Those were dark times. I had a cousin who was an economic attaché at our embassy in Buenos Aires and he used to talk about it. He was not a reactionary at all and he said it was awful."

"Mmm," Pete said.

"Not our best moment, was it?"

"No."

"Terrible terrible dictatorships and we abetted them. So many murdered, tortured, gone missing. Ward said several of his Argentinean friends were disappeared. Poof." She took off her reading glasses and polished them on the hem of her shirt and glanced at her husband who was particularly thoughtful and serious. Pete opened his mouth to speak, closed it. Sometimes when he was very upset or angry he did that—shut his mouth hard. As if the fury of what he was about to loose into the world would do more damage. He went back to reading. He, too, had been looking at Lamont's photographs, but he soon got caught up in another article called "Bear Attacks!" It was in one of the magazines from the period that did not have a story shot by Gabriela's father. He read that more than one person had been mauled because they had left food in their RV, which a hungry grizzly had opened like a sardine can. "Note to self," he murmured. "Do not leave empty tuna tins in the camper."

Celine looked over her reading glasses. "What was that, Pete?"

"Nothing," he said. He didn't want to give her any ideas. "Listen to this. I paraphrase: In the summer of '74 a tourist from North Carolina was at Denali with her two small children. They saw a grizzly with two cubs at the edge of a meadow and pulled over and, of course, approached. Face off. The bear—of course—was not amused and made several false charges, building up to the main event. Thinking fast, the woman pulled out her brand-new can of pepper bear spray and sprayed it all over her kids. She thought it worked like Off! They had to go to the emergency room."

"What did the bear do?"

"She fled. Who would eat somebody that dumb?"

They drank their tea. Celine said, "I notice that we have a pretty comprehensive catalogue of the years he was a shooter. Maybe we should make a list and see what months we're missing."

"Good idea," Pete said. He wasn't sure if it was or if it wasn't, but it couldn't hurt to see every one of Lamont's stories, and he was long past questioning her hunches. They pulled out his notebook and jotted down the months and years of the ones they had, and added the dates of the magazines they'd already checked at the library and left behind because they had no Lamont photographs. They found they were missing only five. "I'd like to find those," Celine said.

They finished their tea and climbed into the loft, and were lulled this time not by rain but by the gentle sipping of the lake water against the shore and the shirr of wind in the tall pines. They kept the door wide, latching only the screen, and left all the mesh windows around the upper bed open to the breeze. Celine got up to pee once and for a long time stood in her wrapper in the chilly dark—there would be frost in the morning, she thought—and marveled at the depth and texture of the stars. Like some infinite woven fabric. Which it was. The Milky Way ran through it like the unfurling and whimsical thought of the weaver. It was very still. She took a short walk, a sort of errand, and finally, her toes numb, she went back to bed. No truck woke them in the middle of the night because, of course, the truck was parked forty yards away. Celine kept the Glock 26 under the edge of her pillow.

Pete was up before her and she woke to the smell of strong coffee and the first light through the screen making a luminous bowl of sky where three then two stars gleamed. It was cold, the cold edge of fall and she adored it. She breathed—her lungs felt clear today, despite the altitude. She was almost content. I am lucky, she thought. Very. I could die right now, under this warm flannel with the smell of French roast and a couple of ducks muttering on the lake and my husband puttering below. Die fulfilled.

Maybe. There was a case to solve and something nagged her about her working theory on Paul Lamont. Which consisted of two alternative possibilities: 1) Lamont was eaten by a bear; or 2) he wanted out—of his marriage, of the fathering at which he was a failure, and maybe even from our own Great Game of undercover intelligence in the Americas—wanted out of all of it so badly that he had staged his own death and gone underground.

But lying there, listening to the waking day, another possibility occurred to her: Lamont may not have abandoned Gabriela, after all. He may have been taken. She sat up.

Pete was happy to see her up so early. She held the handle at the edge of the bed and her right foot found the storage cabinet and he gave her a hand down. He hummed and he poured her a cup of black coffee and opened the small electric fridge under the sink and pulled out a pint of milk and poured a generous slug into the cup.

"Thank you, Pete," she said. "Why do you think everybody who camps has to have blue enamel cups?"

"Tradition."

"Hmm." She sat in the chair at the side dinette. The smallness of it, and the little table, reminded her of a school desk, one of the ones the kids got in first and second grade. "I've been thinking," she said. She leaned forward and looked out the open window. The pleasant-looking young man was already up. He was stripping the tent fly from its poles. He wore his baseball cap and a green Carhartt canvas coat. "That man is bothering me. He's starting to feel like a horsefly." She left the cup on the table and stood. "Pete, where did you stash the shoulder holster?"

Celine slipped on the shoulder rig with practiced ease, and snugged the Glock into the holster and shrugged on her plaid wrapper. Bell tartan, the pattern of her family, the Scottish branch. She wore sheepskin slippers. She smoothed down and patted her silver hair into some semblance of shape and took up her enamel mug. No, this wouldn't do. She put the cup back down and reached for her purse, which dangled from a hook. She took out a compact and lipstick and carefully applied the makeup, compressing her lips and glancing at both sides of her face in the tiny mirror. She found a stick and applied eyeliner. She took . . . as long as it took. That was the wonderful thing about applying her face in the morning:

time vanished; it was a kind of meditation. Pete watched her without comment. What could he say? You look great in Glock, dear?

"Back in a minute," she said finally.

She strolled down the dirt track in her robe, carrying her coffee easily, at home in the world, and with the luxuriant pace of someone who isn't quite awake and is strolling over to the house of a familiar neighbor. On the way she stopped to pick up a brilliant blue feather. She had never seen anything like it—it was small and delicate and shimmered from gray to blue to green. Perfect. She'd use it to adorn the top of a turtle-shell mask she was making at home. She tucked it into the pocket of her robe.

The young man focused on folding his orange nylon tent lengthwise on the rough ground, but he was aware of her, she could tell. He had great peripheral vision. Like a basketball player, she thought.

"Good morning," she said.

The man stood. He was tall, maybe six one, slender but broad-shouldered. His short black beard was trimmed but not too neatly.

"Ma'am." He did not smile. She saw for the first time that his eyes were gray, nearly blue but not. Like slate. Eloquent, in that they registered keen intelligence but no warmth. Like a husky. No, like a wolf. Celine studied them for a long moment, unflinching.

"Would you like some coffee? We've just made a pot. It's very good, French roast, much better than the stuff we've all been drinking in the diners."

His eyes did not flicker. "Ma'am, no thank you. I've got the makings started." He glanced at the tailgate of his truck. She noticed the hissing of the camp stove and the Pyrex French press beside it. A bag of Peet's ground beans. I'll be damned. Probably stationed in a cosmopolitan city somewhere and grown used to the finer things. But his accent had a touch of country south of Pennsylvania. And he had said "makings." And the irritating use of "ma'am" suggested ex-military.

"Okay. You probably have oatmeal or eggs or something, too?"

"Yes, ma'am."

"Yes, I see now, that insipid old Quaker on the box. I'm guessing that you make a very fine oatmeal, but prefer ham and eggs. Like the poor man in that Hemingway story, I can't remember the title."

" 'The Battler.' "

Celine raised an eyebrow. "You didn't say ma'am."

"No, ma'am."

He held a small stuff sack filled with what must be tent stakes. He was wearing a wedding ring, a simple gold band, scuffed and dulled to brass. There was that. She tried to imagine those eyes looking into the eyes of his beloved. She could not imagine their mineral gray ever holding any real warmth, but of course they might change color in her arms. Celine was now genuinely intrigued. Not only was he erudite but he had wit, if not humor. Probably both. Clearly these people, whoever they were, had a very deep bench.

"I bet you know that I am carrying more than a cup of coffee," she said.

"Yes, ma'am."

"And that if you keep saying ma'am I might pull it out. I will turn into a complete lunatic." She coughed. It rose in her chest and spasmed her throat. She lifted her arm to cover it, but it gathered force and shook her so violently it spilled her half-full cup. Damn. Her lungs had been so quiet since they'd landed in Denver. The dry air had been good. When the convulsion was over she collected herself and just breathed, pursing her lips. She had great class: She did not apologize to the man or even acknowledge his presence. This was a private matter. She collected herself and gave herself time to return to her normal state of elegance. Then she swallowed a sip of coffee from the bottom of the mug.

Thank God, she thought, he had the tact to keep his mouth shut. He held the bag of stakes.

"Would you like help folding the tent?" she said.

"I think I've got it."

"You know," she said, "you have an almost perfect cooking setup. Except. Just a sec, I had an idea—" She wrinkled her nose, turned on the heel of her slipper, shook the dregs of her cup onto the ground, and was gone. He blinked. She didn't take long. Four minutes later she was back.

"You need one of these," she said. "My son's camper came with one, so we have an extra. Go ahead, take it. I'd say the coffee gets twice as good." She held out her hand. He hesitated, took the thing, rolled it over in his rough palm. It was a battery-powered coffee-bean grinder.

"Fuckin' A," he whispered.

"I didn't get that," she chimed.

His eyes flicked up, a fleeting light—of amusement, or gratitude, or wariness, she wasn't sure. Maybe all three. He nodded once, in thanks, she supposed, and his eyes found their old level, the one that looked a little like granite. Well, she had years of experience dealing with taciturn men.

"If you know where we're going, why not just meet us there?" she said.

He didn't say anything. His expression didn't change. He was looking at her with the same neutral steadiness. She understood that this was a man who could quiet his heartbeat and would not easily tire at the flat distances seen through a rifle scope.

"I mean if you are not trying to intimidate us. Clearly you want us to know you are here, but you don't seem that intimidating." Celine smiled at him. "I mean that in the best way." She sighed. "Well, I suppose. I should probably be polite and ask you if you prefer camp breakfast or a road café. But that would be letting the tail wag the dog, truly." She turned to go and turned back.

"What is it?" she said.

"Ma'am?"

"Arrgh." She smiled again, this time her brightest, true smile. "What am I carrying?"

"Glock 26."

Celine was in a state as they drove up the shore to the Jackson Lake Lodge. They would eat breakfast there, in deference to their travel companion.

"He's too skinny," Celine had said. "He can't survive on oatmeal boiled on the back of his truck. Don't look at me like that."

Pete had not been aware that he was looking at her like anything. "Anyway, he's clearly on expenses," she said. "He can order the Lumberjack

Breakfast. When we all get there, I think I'll just have one sent over."

She did not have one sent over. But she did scribble a note on the back of a pink dry-cleaning ticket and ask their waitress to give it to him. It said, "I couldn't bear, after all, to think of you eating nothing but oatmeal." She nodded at the man as he took his table in the corner—the gunfighter's table, she thought, the one with a clear view of the room and no angles of fire from behind; must be habit—and he read the note and touched the brim of his cap. She and Pete drank their coffee and ate their eggs and pancakes under a massive bull moose who looked out longingly at the young willows at the edge of the shore. Celine just couldn't get over that the man had known her gun, make and model, through her bathrobe.

"I mean it wasn't a *negligee,*" she objected. Either his people had bugged Hank's house in Denver when she had asked for his gun, which seemed very far-fetched, or he had guessed. "I suppose he knew that a Glock is what I have at home and of all the guns it's the one I'm most comfortable with. And of course if it had been a 19 it would have been more bulky. So: a 26. He's *not* clairvoyant."

"Hmm."

"He's a cocky SOB. He knew *The Nick Adams Stories.* Probably a frustrated English major who graduated from college qualified to drive a cab."

They made to leave and stood at the table and Celine waited courteously until their chaperone took his last sip of coffee and plucked up his own bill before proceeding to the cashier at the front. They paid their check and they were half out the door into the lobby and she waited again until she saw the man hand his own ticket to the cashier. Then she said to Pete, "You go ahead, I've got to make one last stop." Which was a euphemism. She headed for the heavy wooden door of the ladies' room and waved at the young man as he followed Pete out the glass front doors, and then she doubled back and went straight to the waitress. She held her digital camera in one hand.

"I'm sorry," she said, "may I have a receipt for breakfast." Celine could see the restaurant copies skewered on a spindle by the register.

"Didn't I give you one?" sighed the waitress. "It's been one of those mornings. My littlest kept me up all night with stomach pains."

"Is she eating enough fruit?" Celine said. She looked carefully at the girl's face. Young forties, a bit too young. It was a habit to study all women who might have been born in 1948. Anyway, her bone structure was all wrong.

"Come to think of it," the woman said, "she eats zero fruit. If it's not a Cocoa Puff or a chicken finger it's a flying object."

"Well."

"Hold on, I'll print you out another."

Celine leaned on the counter and slid a box of charity Life Savers to the edge on the waitress's side and then nudged it over. It hit the floor with a clatter. "Oh!" the waitress cried. "Oh, terribly sorry!" Celine countered. The woman bent to gather up the candy packets and Celine leaned over again, twisted the spindle of receipts in her fingers until the top one was readable and quickly snapped three photos of it with her camera. While the woman was still crouched and showing her broad back, Celine calmly reviewed the pictures, frowned, and on second thought simply snagged the receipt off the skewer and put it in her jacket pocket.

"There," the waitress said cheerfully, setting the box back in its place. "If the day keeps going like this I'll need a straitjacket by lunch."

"I found it," Celine sang, brashly holding up the man's ticket, and placing a thumb over the hole. "My bad." She gave the girl her movie-star smile, overpaid for a box of stale Life Savers, and went out the door.

Pa was impressed. "Why didn't you just take a picture of it with your camera?" he asked as they approached the gate at the south entrance to Yellowstone. A short line of five cars was ahead of them.

Celine sucked the candy in her mouth. "I did,

but the color was terrible. And what if you dropped my camera in the cat dish?" Ouch. He had done that a month ago with his new mini Canon—out of his breast pocket and into Big Bob's water dish. Big Bob weighed no less than thirty-two pounds. He was presently at the Cat Hotel in Red Hook, where he was a celebrity.

"William Tanner," Celine said, reading again the man's breakfast receipt. "An alias if I ever heard one. Not a real name, not possibly. His generation are all named Jacob. We'll have to do a search. Do you think Cooke City even has Internet?"

Pete now understood that her bathrobe visit that morning, and the maternal stuff about the man tailing them not getting a good breakfast, was all about getting to a restaurant and obtaining his name. For the ten thousandth time he marveled at the wits of his wife. But then again, he thought, she probably was truly concerned about the young hunter's caloric intake.

fourteen

Celine had learned these skills looking for her own child. Hank had suspected it all his adult life, but was wary about ever asking his mother again. And then Aunt Bobby came home from the hospital with her brain tumor to die. What she told him before she passed was that Celine had always been the one to hold the family together. It was often the role of the middle child.

"She always kept her wits about her," Bobby said. The eldest sister lay comfortably in a hospital bed in the living room of their stone house outside Lancaster, Pennsylvania, where her husband, David, was the president of a large regional bank. Celine had gone to the store to get Bobby's favorite ice cream, Rum Raisin, which was all she felt like eating. Hank had flown out from Denver to say goodbye to his aunt. They were close. His junior year of high school, when his mother was in a particularly rough place with her drinking, Hank had stayed with Bobby and his cousins for winter break and then half of the summer. His aunt was not sentimental, she had strict rules that she enforced fairly, and he had grown to appreciate the unspoken consistency of her love. Of the three sisters, he thought she was most like Baboo—in her self-discipline, in her reflexive rebellions at convention. She kept her hair short, right at the collar; and she had the strong Watkins nose and jawline, but her features seemed a little harder than her sisters'.

Bobby was in no pain, not more than a headache, and she was lucid if exhausted. Always no-nonsense and practical, she now had a softness about her Hank had never seen. "Celine had to be strong, I guess," she said. "I was usually off in my own world and she felt she needed to take care of Mimi. She practically raised her. During all of our growing up, nothing really could derail her except Papa leaving. And losing that child."

Hank was sure she had not seen the jolt that zinged through him. She was gazing out the window to the wide lawn that ran to the line of old maples and oaks that strung along the brook. What he'd noticed at the end: this reaching back. He'd seen it with Baboo and he'd seen it with Mimi. In the final slow dance with Death there were the long looks over his shoulder. Why wouldn't there be? Hank was not a cunning person but he let a beat go by and said, "The child she had to give up at Putney?"

"She told you? Good, I shouldn't have mentioned it." Hank didn't answer. Her eyes were vague, and still on something beyond the summer stream. "It was afterward. After. She took a year off to have it. It was a Christmas baby. Same birthday as Mimi. Isn't that strange?"

"Nothing seems strange anymore."

She turned her head and her eyes found his and regained their focus. "Amen," she said.

Over the next few days Bobby told him the story: about Celine seeing the doctor, about Mrs. Hinton and Baboo and Admiral Bill, about Celine leaving school. And coming back. She wanted to tell it, needed to. It was as if Bobby were trying to lighten herself for the big trip across the water. She told it in the pieces she could tell when Celine was not in the room, which was often enough. The younger sister was often in Bobby's back office, on the phone with doctors and hospice, or out picking up ice cream and medicine. Hank never got the sense that Bobby felt she was betraying her sister, but rather that she was bringing into relief the difficulty of the decisions Celine had had to make and the almost heroic stoicism with which she made them. At such a young age. But Hank knew as she told the story that Celine had been less stoic than true to her own ideal of protecting the vulnerable and blaming no one and burdening as few people as possible. In this there was true grace. Bobby repeated that her younger sister would never ever betray the identity of the father. Which made him think that this must have been someone vulnerable too. Had it been a teacher, say, exploiting a student, Celine would have given no quarter and forced him to take responsibility. Hank thought that his mother, like her own mother, had an infallible sense of what was right and what ought and ought not to be done. Leaving a predatory teacher free to victimize another young girl was definitely in the Ought Not To category.

So as Hank spelled Celine and sat with Bobby in the elegant sitting room with the prints of hunters and hounds and the stone hearth with the unlit fire laid on brass dogs and the sashed windows open to the screens and the sounds of July crickets—as he sat and watched his aunt sleep, his imagination traveled again back to that Vermont ridge in early spring where he and his mother had both gone to school: patched snow over mud, the first shoots of brazen grass; the weathered clapboard houses needing paint, smell of wet earth and leaf rot—the students on the paths between buildings, one group stopping to talk to a teacher in a plaid wool coat who carries five books—Hank's own mind scanning, scanning for the culprit. Who would it be? Who would Celine never betray? Someone also vulnerable and at risk, not necessarily young nor old, but essentially innocent, as she was. Would it be another student? Maybe. A teacher? Maybe. But if a teacher, that man would carry a frailty or tenderness that would not withstand exposure. He would need, for some reason, more protection than she did. Celine worked every morning on the farm and came back in the afternoons to care for a lamb. Could it be the older farmer who carried the sadness of a widower? The skinny local boy who ran the early milking?

Who, when she returned to school, did she now studiously avoid? Whose eyes met hers and flickered away as she navigated the flagstone walk between the library and the science building?

Did the father of her child even know or suspect? Did he wonder at the sudden breaking off?

In the end maybe all that mattered was that she carried the child and labored and gave birth and gave it up. Was it a boy or a girl? Did Hank have a brother or a sister?

He had asked Bobby about the boating accident, too. She came alive at the memory. She pushed the button on the motorized bed and brought herself up. Her smile made her younger. The blood flowed to her cheeks.

She said, "Do you remember when you were staying with us and you and Ted ran the canoe over the dam and nearly killed yourselves?"

Hank grinned. Ted was Bobby's third son and a good friend growing up. Hank was smiling but it still contracted his guts, the memory of being recycled again and again in the hydraulic below the weir, knowing he was going to die.

"Remember how mad I got?"

Hank nodded.

"Well, you come by it honestly. I'm about to tell you another story about your mother. You know you guys destroyed your grandfather's handmade canvas canoe."

"Sorry." He reached out and held her thin hand.

"You heard about me diving off the dock?" she said.

"Everybody is eager to tell everyone else's story."

A shadow crossed her face. "You heard about the gardener? Alfonse?"

He nodded.

"Oh boy."

He waited.

"It was my idea," she said. He nodded. "I have prayed and prayed about it. Not just what I did to the poor man but that I enlisted my little sisters in what is tantamount to murder." She reached for her sippy cup and took a long suck of apple juice. He noticed that the cup trembled as she set it down. "You know, your mother and I were brought up to believe in Hell."

"Baboo told me that Gaga had her baptized Catholic. Which scandalized the Cheneys. Do you believe in it now?"

"Certain Hells, definitely." She turned to the window. On the lawn were three deer grazing as

216

if they owned the place. The one buck was a spike, just a year old. When hunting season came he would not be a legal take. Reprieve.

"I don't think you murdered the man. It was a prank. At that point anything could have set him off. He had already relinquished any shred of happiness."

"Is that the point? Happiness?"

Hank didn't say anything because he didn't know. She turned her face to him and said, "Sometimes now I think just making it through a day is the point. Practically a triumph, don't you think? If you don't melt down or kill anyone or just give up? If you happen to be kind, or help someone else, or create something beautiful, well, you've really done something to crow about."

He squeezed her hand. Bobby had been a fine-arts photographer and he thought some of her pictures were magnificent. There was a self-portrait reflected in the stainless shine of the back of a toaster oven—herself holding the camera of course—that he thought was one of the best portraits of an artist he had ever seen. Something about how the object tried to stretch and bend her figure—did bend it—and how beautiful and intent she was anyway. There was a metaphor there about what the imagination does to the world, and what the world does back to it, but he wasn't sure what it was. She looked bemused at his laughter. "You will get a blue ribbon," he said. "What an artist you are."

"I will meet the man," she said. "I don't have a doubt in the world. We can shish kebab our toes together." She said it lightly and he knew she wasn't joking.

"Don't you think," Hank said at last, "that children get a certain dispensation? Limbo, wasn't it? Green meadows and sadness."

"No," she said. "Children always take the brunt."

Bobby asked for some tea, green tea, weak, in a real teacup, and joked about what life had come to when all you wanted was green tea. She had been a devotee of single malt scotch before she quit drinking and enjoyed an occasional cigar. Not a cheroot, either, but a robust Churchill or torpedo. Which men found slightly terrifying, also sexy. It was how she met David—smoking on the balcony of a wedding party. He had not been intimidated at all but approached her, leaned against the railing, and lit up his own Partagas. They smoked in silence for a couple of minutes, enjoying the surprising lacuna and relishing their smokes, when Bobby finally said, "Trade you." And they swapped cigars and were married ten months later.

Hank brought her the tea. Celine was out on her longest errand, which was grocery shopping for the next few days. She wouldn't be back for a while.

"You asked me about her sailing escapade?" Bobby said, setting down her cup.

"Yes."

"It was the afternoon she found out—or maybe she intuited it, I'm not sure. But in any event she knew that Mummy's marriage with Papa was truly over."

"Right."

"I won't say she was impulsive. She was, we all were. Diving off the dock into shallow water was impulsive. Ha. With Celine, the mot juste might be *intractable*. She got an idea in her head and she was damn headstrong. But the ideas always had a certain, I don't know—*rigor.* She didn't just fly off. There was always a certain poetic logic to whatever your mother dreamed up."

"I get that."

"This had something to do with Harry promising to take her sailing, but also the idea that one might be able to sail to another land where fathers and mothers stayed together always. She ran down to the beach and launched the catboat. You know she'd been taking lessons with this fabulously handsome Dutchman. We all thought he was."

Hank had poured himself a cup of her green tea, and he raised an eyebrow over the rim of the cup.

"He was terribly serious. He hadn't a clue. Why did your mother and I sometimes simply stare at Gustav like rabbits when we were supposed to be trimming the sail or coming about? He thought we were terrified." She laughed, the hoarse con-strained laugh Hank hadn't heard in a while. "Well, of course we were! Terrified we might miss a single ripple of his countless muscles! Or that profile! Those hands! God. He had no idea. Which drove us even more wild. He got very stern when we spaced out. He thought we needed more backbone. 'Sailing,' he would say, 'is serious business!' That was his motto."

She took a long thirsty sip and managed to spill very little. "He was the most single-task person I've ever met. Wonderful—an absolute absence, completely, of any sense of humor. Made him very safe." She smiled as if she regretted it.

"Despite these distractions, Celine was a quick study. She sailed three times a week, and by the time of the accident she was mostly skippering and he was teaching her the finer points of tack and trim. Amazing for a seven-year-old, but then she was always surprisingly strong. She had just had a lesson and she ran down to the beach and managed to get the little boat into the water and the sail up. There was quite a blow on the sound. It was why Gustav had cut their lesson short. She headed northeast for open water and

220

rounded Simmons Point and was making her way onto the wide Atlantic. Imagine. I wonder if she were planning to sail to Greenland." Bobby shook her head. "*Refractory,* that's the word. Eliot uses it about the camels."

Hank remembered again how erudite all three sisters were. Bobby had attended Vassar, like her mother, and majored in comparative literature. She dropped out when she married David. A lawn mower started up from the other side of the house, muffled, a comforting summer sound.

"Of course she'd been pushing her luck from the outset. It's a wonder she even got the sail up and the boat under control. She capsized. A rogue gust I think. She had the presence of mind to hold fast to the sheet. She hauled in on it and pulled herself back to the boat. She actually tried to right it the way Gustav had taught her, standing on the upwind chine and hauling back on the halyard—amazing. The grit. But she didn't have the weight or the strength. On a quieter day she might have managed it, nothing ever surprises me when it comes to your mother."

Bobby suddenly looked very sad, and Hank wondered if it was because she was feeling how much she'd soon miss her sister.

She smiled. "If there hadn't been the Round the Island Regatta that day, I am certain you wouldn't exist. They came around the point while she was flailing with the mast. As luck would have it, the life jacket she was supposed to be wearing was clipped to the boat and it was bright orange. A Mae West from the war. I think they were the reason Admiral Bill would never go sailing with any of us in the years after: because he couldn't look at that life jacket. It reminded him of all the sailors he'd left behind in the water.

"In any event, though she was close to a mile off their course she unclipped the jacket and stood up on the wallowing hull using the halyard for balance, and she waved in the lead sloop. Heavens!

"After the lead boat turned they must have all wondered what the hell had gotten into him, and then they must have seen her, too. At the time a rescue must have seemed more glamorous than winning the race. I wish so much I'd have seen it, the line of thirty-odd sloops and yawls and ketches falling off the wind in a graceful turn and running down on little sister. It wasn't a class race, it was just for fun. It was Jib Rafferty in the lead. Very dashing, a redhead like all his clan. He literally scooped her up. Took one look at the skinny shivering girl, made her put on his itchy sweater, and said, 'You are a Cheney, not a doubt in my mind. I know right where you belong.' He had grown up with Baboo, after all. I guess we have a certain look. He towed the dinghy and dropped her off at the beach at Las Armas. The Rafferty place was just two docks south. They called the race and everybody anchored off and they had a party that afternoon and night that went down in island history."

Hank loved hearing that story. It fit with everything he knew about his mother, and he loved the transformation that came over Bobby as she told it, how she was transported from the room. She was in the past, so he gently said, "Aunt Bobby, do you know anything else about Mom's baby?"

She studied him. The eye of a photographer must be always framing and focusing, and he thought that the soft gaze with which she had told the story was now tightening down on his face, sharpening the features and calibrating the distances, the depth of field. How much of the background behind him should be revealed?

"She didn't tell you at all, did she?"

He shook his head.

"Not even that you have a sister."

"A sister?"

"Yes. Isabel. What she called her."

"Isabel," Hank stammered. "Does she know where she is? Has she maintained contact?"

"No. No idea. It's why she got into the whole PI thing in .the first place, I think. Finding her daughter was all she thought about. She tried for years."

"No clue? I mean she gave her up and has no idea?"

"She had agreed with the whole plan, under

duress, mind you, and then once they laid the baby in her arms for the first and last time, she went crazy. She would have run away with her. But she was sedated and they had the sheets like restraints the way they do and they just laid her on Celine's chest for two minutes and then they took her. Whisked her away. She howled. Mummy told me before she died—we seem to have a tradition of these deathbed confessions, don't we?—she told me that Celine's howl burned itself into her soul. Mummy never forgave herself."

"But who did they give her to? Did Mom have no idea?"

"There was one lead—"

The door that led to the kitchen swung open and Celine swept in. She carried a two-pint tub of Rum Raisin and three spoons. She was tired, Hank could see it around the eyes, but she was cheerful and she brought with her the scent of mown grass. She took one look at her sister and her son and knew that they had not been making idle chitchat.

"You two are thick as thieves. Is it too early for rum and ice cream? They say the alcohol is cooked out or something but I always get a little giddy. Maybe just because it's so good. Here." She handed the spoons around and pried off the lid.

Bobby died that night. Hank never got to hear more about the one lead.

fifteen

"I'm pulling over, Pete. I want to get to know Mr. William Tanner. Do you think that lodge has Wi-Fi?"

"I don't see why not."

"Because we're in the middle of Yellowstone? And I almost just collided with a bison?"

"Ey-yuh. Still."

"I'm getting peckish anyway, aren't you? The sign says Fishermen's Restaurant."

Set back among tall pines was a long log building with a wide-plank porch and a carved sign on posts featuring a steaming coffee cup, a rainbow trout, and an arched fishing rod. Suspended below it was a white painted sign: BREAKFAST SERVED ALL DAY. Who in their right mind would not pull in?

They had spent the last hour driving around Yellowstone Lake, and when the trees on their right opened up, they looked across wrinkled blue water to big views of the Absarokas. The lake was big, the mountains were big and ragged with snow, the sky was big. Big big big. It would make anyone hungry. Celine parked next to a one-ton pickup with diesel tanks mounted in the bed and a sign on the door that said KELLER DRILLING SERVICES, JACKSON HOLE. The truck had one of those stickers in the back window of a little boy peeing. The word he was peeing on was "Hippies."

"That's not very nice," Celine said. She stopped on the gravel and rifled through her purse and pulled out a plastic mini bottle of Elmer's Glue and a vial of gold sparkles, the kind young girls sprinkle in their hair for fairy dust. She also found a Q-tip. She smiled at Pa. "Leftover from the detective thing I did at the school," she said.

Pete was immune to this sort of behavior from Celine and looked on with professional interest: He was an artist, too, after all. Celine switched out her big oval everyday glasses for even bigger rounder reading glasses and carefully dabbed specks of glue all over and around the stream of pee and affixed gold dust to each dollop. It looked like the little boy was pissing fireworks.

"Kidney stones!" she said proudly. "It'll wash off. Still."

They made their way into the café. The place was almost full and smelled of bacon and coffee. The waitress took them to a table that looked over a dock with a dozen rental rowboats tied to cleats and a view back across the lake. Pete slid their laptop out of its neoprene case and propped it open on the varnished pine table.

"How long do you think before our friend shows up?" he said. "Taking bets?"

"I didn't see him at all in the rearview. He's

probably relaxed a little since he fixed the GPS tracker to our chassis."

Pete smiled. Sudden and surprising. "You *know* that?"

"Uh-uh. Nope. But why wouldn't he? I already put ours in the base of the coffee grinder I gave him. I also put one under his truck. I hope the magnet's strong enough, I'm not sure it's made for four-wheel drive."

Pete's grin got even bigger. "That's why you were fumbling with the grinder. *When?* When did you put a GPS tracker on his truck?"

"When I got up to pee last night. I was very quiet in my moccasins. It's why I brought them, you know. Not because I needed to have my sheepskin slippers wherever I go. He had no idea. I heard him snoring through the tent the whole time."

"He snores?"

"Young-man snores. More of a whoosh. They'll be terrible when he gets older."

Pete reached his hand across the table and squeezed hers. The joints of her fingers were knotted and knobby with arthritis. "Right," Pete said. All in a day's work.

"I put the one on his truck for him to find," she said. "A man with his training will sweep it once a day." She turned her hand in his and gave it a squeeze.

"I've got a signal. Maybe you can ask the

waitress for a password. Shall we start with a general search or do you want to go right to the federal database?"

For an old fart from Maine, Pete was pretty tech savvy. He had linked their laptops and could run their home PC with either one. All their documents were uploaded to the building's server and could be accessed remotely. They logged on to Dale Earnhardt—what they called their home PC because he was super-fast—and went straight to a database of federal employees, nonmilitary. This was one of the most expensive data collections they bought and once in a while it turned out to be extremely useful. William Tanner came right up. DOB 05/04/1969, Lafayette, LA. Vet tech, USAID. The age was right, thirty-three.

Celine tapped at the jiggly yolk of her egg with a piece of crisp bacon and burst it and scooped up as much of it as she could. Yum. Pete had asked her if she meant to eat breakfast again, which was a silly question. Sometimes she ate eggs and bacon for dinner. Since she'd quit smoking she figured she could do whatever she wanted on the gastronomic front. She said, "What the heck is a vet tech, do you think? And for USAID?"

"I know exactly what it is," Pete said. "What it might be. Do you remember that story about swine fever in Haiti? More than a million pigs were euthanized."

"Ahh."

"The U.S. Department of Agriculture has what are essentially sniper teams that can hunt and quickly dispatch wild animals, too. Say if a case of brucellosis were to start spreading in a deer population."

"I see."

"So sometimes these guys are sent to other countries to help them with their eradication programs. Then, I guess, they might be under the auspices of USAID. 'Vet tech' is a pretty title."

"He seemed former military to me. He kept calling me 'ma'am,' which you know I can't stand. So he might be a killer, hmm. Of animals. In foreign countries."

"Or he might be on loan to help poor countries neuter their pets."

"His ears must be burning." She nodded toward the door where Mr. Tanner himself appeared carrying a stainless travel mug. The same waitress smiled broadly at him and led him to a table in the middle of the room. Celine noticed that she put her hand on his forearm briefly when she asked if he wanted coffee. "He's a charmer," she murmured. "Without even trying."

"What?" Pa said.

"Nothing. How do we check if he really is military—former or current?"

"We don't have access to that database, but law enforcement does."

Celine brightened. "So we e-mail Harold! Slide that over, will you please? Wouldn't young Bill"—she tipped her head toward their tail—"be tickled if he knew what we were doing twenty feet away?"

She happily drank her coffee and composed an e-mail to her former AA sponsee. Celine had quit drinking twenty-five years ago, when Hank was a senior in high school. She had been very active in Alcoholics Anonymous, tapering off in the last two or three years as her own family needed more of her time. One core principle was that one of the best ways to stay sober was to be of service to others, and Celine took it seriously.

Newly sober members came in shaky droves to ask if she would be their sponsor. She had mentored a bunch of sponsees over the years and, remarkably, most of them had succeeded in staying off the sauce, and their loyalty to and love for Celine was always touching to see. In their eyes, she had saved their lives. Hard to imagine anyone else garnering that kind of devotion except maybe a great platoon leader.

Harold was particularly fond of Celine. When he met her he was a homicide detective for the 84th Precinct, Brooklyn, and he was on the ropes—suspended for driving a department car into the East River while on a bender. Right off of Pier Two, when it was the dock for the Columbia Line, the big freighters that brought in the net loads of bananas and shipments of cocaine. He had been on a stakeout. The one lucky turn of the whole night was that neither he nor his partner were in the car when he reached in for his shotgun and hit the lever that knocked the transmission into Drive. He was so drunk that he tried to dive in after the car— maybe to put it in Reverse—but his partner tackled him. That was a time in the NYPD when the Thin Blue Line wasn't all that thin, and Harold's captain gave him a choice: get sober for good or get fired and pay for the car, and the two other vehicles he had deliriously reconfigured. The day he came into the church basement on Henry Street, Celine was qualifying—telling her story. She was thoroughly honest, but nobody knew that she was only telling a carefully constructed selection of highlights. She never mentioned having a child as a teenager, but she did talk about getting into investigative work to help reunite broken birth families. Harold perked up when this elegant woman talked about working for a detective agency, about her first cases and the surreptitious drinking that went with them. "Imagine!" she implored. "I was doing, finally, what I'd wanted to do my entire life—detective work! And I was going to drink it into the trash bin. I can't adequately express the shame that caused me." Harold actually straightened in his seat, leaned forward. The woman said she had been sober for seven years. If he was going to learn from anyone in this odd outfit, it would be this striking private eye.

Harold was a captain himself now and he ran a section of the racketeering division. What section, for some reason was never discussed. He was overweight and diabetic and one of the most deeply happy men she had ever met. He must be, to generate the kind of infectious gut laugh that came out of him with such ease.

Celine knew how much he owed her—how much he believed he did, because of course the accounting was all his. In fact, according to him, he could never repay her. And so she was extremely sparing in asking for favors. So. Well. They had Wi-Fi but no cell service and given the sensitivity of his job she couldn't just e-mail him her request. In plain language, that is, and on his government e-mail. She used a Yahoo e-mail address and wrote: "Harold: How is William doing? And his father, Tanner? I met them both long ago, around about May 4, '69. I would love to meet them again. They were military men, I think, and it affected their bearing for the rest of their lives."

That would do it. First name, last, DOB, and focus of data search. The code was nothing formal, nothing even that they'd ever agreed on, and certainly not elaborate or hard to decipher. It was more of a game, and not too tough a one, and it was meant simply to keep the lawyers and Internal Affairs people at bay. No one could ever prove that she'd requested information from Harold, or that he'd ever shared any with her, because he always arranged to have her call him at a certain time between random phones.

sixteen

God may have made the world for the last week of September. Celine had thought that about Vermont when she was a child, and she thought that now. They drove along the Yellowstone River in mobile sunshine that tugged cloud shadows over the ridges and into the canyon. The river flowed low and clear over the gravel bars and the willows were yellow and orange and the box elders and cottonwoods loosed their leaves over the water when the wind blew.

When the wind blew, the aspen groves sent gusts of leaves into the road. They drove slowly. They saw the silver V of a beaver cutting across a pond banked with alder, and saw his stick lodge covered in mud, and saw one the size of a bear cub clamber out onto a rock ledge and glare. "You are king of the river for sure," Celine murmured. "But how on earth do you get the mud onto your house?"

She liked to give a quiet running commentary as she drove, it was a habit Pete thought charming. The leaves stuck to the windshield and they drove with the windows open and the smell of sage and grass pouring in with the cold. They saw a grizzly bear running flat out across a meadow. He was huge and humped and he more

234

flowed than ran, and the long sun rippled over his sleek fur like water and changed his colors. He stopped at the edge of the spruce and began digging. "Jesus," Celine said. She had no idea a bear could move like that. Or that his shoulders would be so massive, or that he could throw up dirt like an excavator.

They drove over a wooded rise and when they came out of the spruce they could see a hundred bison grazing in grass in a bow of the river and white trumpeter swans on the slate-blue water. "Do you think," she said, "that the whole country was like this once? I mean these mountains? Or is this like some game park? It's incredible. Living was easy." She imagined that the Shoshone who had lived here would never have gone hungry.

They lost the river to her canyon and the road rolled through hills of burned lodgepole and down into a broad open valley with a thin creek threading the meadows and stands of black timber like islands. When they smelled sulfur and saw plumes of steam and big parking lots they kept driving. Celine had no desire to join throngs of people; the usual attractions of Yellowstone were not for them. At Canyon Village they pulled in for gas and coffee and beef jerky and bought a book on Yellowstone's wolves. The store clerk saw them studying the maps in a spinning rack and came over to help. She wore an olive ranger shirt and thick glasses and a pin that said, *Ask*

Me About Bison! "Are you guys on a bus tour?" she said. Celine turned to her and smiled and said, "That would be nice."

"They have round-trip day tours right from the village, just two miles down the road. They serve lunch at Old Faithful."

"How lovely."

The girl looked pleased with herself. "I can get you the brochure if you'd like."

"What we'd like to know is who handles law enforcement for the park." This would be a good person to get to know. There would probably be a file on Lamont, even if he went missing just outside the park boundary. A sketch of the case and a discussion of jurisdiction, if nothing else.

The girl frowned. "Is there a problem?"

"No, but we'd like to know where the law enforcement headquarters are."

The girl was puzzled.

"Just in case," Celine added helpfully.

"Oh, right," said the girl. She'd pretty much seen everything; once a Taiwanese man in a tour group asked her in excruciatingly composed English at what age a deer became an elk. "Well," she said, "I'd just recommend you call 911?" It sounded much more like a question than a recommendation. "If you have reception that is. There are emergency phones at all the restroom facilities."

"How convenient. But what we'd really like to

know is where your chief law enforcement ranger resides."

"Oh," she brightened. A lightbulb, high watt, seemed to have gone off. "We have a law enforcement ranger right here. I think I saw Chad in the interpretive area."

Celine knew when she had been whipped. She beat a tactical retreat. "We'll just take the book," she said.

It didn't matter. They weren't ready for that talk anyway. Celine and Pete liked to get the lay of the land, literally, at the outset, before they dug into a case. And of course they could find the headquarters and the park's chief officer in two minutes with another Wi-Fi connection. They bought travel mugs in the gift shop that said *MAMA GRIZZLY* and *PAPA GRIZZLY,* and filled them up in the small restaurant. There was a good cell signal, so Celine called Gabriela. She wasn't worried about a possible phone tap, as everything she needed to know now was old news.

"Without the file in front of you, do you remember the names of the people you worked with up here? Both in the sheriff's department and in the park?"

"Yes, of course. There were three main people. I can text the names to you as soon as we hang up."

"Good, text me everyone you can think of. The sheriff you mentioned, the tracker, the bar owner who knew your father, the name of the bar if you know it. Anything you can recall. Pete wrote down a few when he first talked to you, but I'd like the complete list."

"Okay."

"Gabriela, do you remember where your father traveled to most? Did he tell you? Or did he bring back gifts from the same countries over and over?"

"His favorite place when I was really little was Peru. He did a big spread on Machu Picchu for *Nat Geo* in like '68. You've seen the images probably. Pretty classic. And then he went more and more to Chile. Chile, Argentina, Paraguay. I have gaucho ponchos and maté cups, and pink flamingos from the Atacama. Plastic ones. He loved the coast of Chilean Patagonia more than anything, the fjord country south of Puerto Montt."

"Was he working for the magazine? On those trips, do you remember?"

"Yes. Yes, he was. Do you want me to hunt down the stories?"

"Could you? That might be a big help. I think we may have most of them but I don't want to miss any. I'm not sure what the research facilities are like at the Cooke City Library. Or if they even have a library."

"They don't."

"Oh, and one other thing. Can you tell me about the Ice Mountain?"

There was a startled pause. She hadn't expected the question. When Gabriela spoke again her voice was fraught with probably more than one emotion. She said, "It's way up north in the borderland. There's a lake there, the color of his true love's eyes, and there's a castle there for princesses and their families. Pop said he would take me there. He said the lake sounded like birds and the mountain was the king of mountains."

They drove north and east into the afternoon. Along Buffalo Creek they had to slow and negotiate a traffic jam on a steep hill where someone must have spotted some charismatic megafauna. The line of cars wasn't moving so Pa and Celine got out and stretched and walked to the shoulder and squeezed between a heavy woman in camo with a graphic of Bin Laden in red cross-hairs on the back and two boys in Duke T-shirts holding beers with insulators that said *Vaginivore*. A mama black bear was eating pop-corn flowers, shouldering her way slowly through the small white blossoms and competing with two butterflies who hovered in and out of the sunlight that streamed through the poplars. One landed for a moment on her ear. Two cubs trundled after, climbing over a log and falling onto each other.

Pa said, "It looks like a Disney cartoon."

"It won't look like Disney when she gets pissed and eats a frat boy." Celine's breathing was labored and her eyes were shiny. Pa wondered if the boys' can holders had set her off. Celine couldn't stand conspicuous expressions of dominance. The young men were already princes of the universe, if not masters: They were white, male, athletic, tall, attending one of the best universities; they had great teeth and good skin and they didn't seem to be blind or hitch. They had it made. Why did they have to advertise a contempt for women? Pa knew that it would enrage her and he sometimes thought that she took her rage out on herself. The two boys didn't even know they had skated: At lower altitude, where there was more oxygen, he was pretty sure she would have ended up in possession of the beer cozies, after speaking to them about respect and their own mothers.

There was no shade where they were standing and she shielded her eyes with one hand and placed the other on her chest and struggled to get a full breath. She blew out through pursed lips. She closed her eyes and when she opened them they were very wide as if she were looking for air.

"I think we're pretty high up," Pete said. "Do you want a shot of oxygen?"

"I guess." She was frustrated. That she couldn't just stand out here with a group of dumb tourists in the sun and watch a bear.

"I can get it."

"That's okay." She gave Pete her hand and they walked slowly back across the narrowed road and he pulled the small oxygen condenser out of the backseat. He turned it on and it hummed and Celine's hand shook as she tried to untangle the transparent tubing. Pa took the tubing from her gently and loosened the coils and handed her the cannula, which she worked into her nose. Her hands stopped shaking almost immediately and she placed the split tube over her ears and just stood against the truck and breathed. "Okay," she said finally. "I'll just use it a little longer while we drive."

They turned east at a sign that said LAMAR VALLEY—SILVER GATE, and now they didn't see another car. Celine breathed easier. She unhooked the cannula from her ears and handed it to Pa. "There. Good," she said. They drove upstream along a creek that flowed over stones of many colors, rusts and greens and blues. Just before dusk they came over a rise and down into the Lamar Valley.

The sun was almost down, fighting through dark clouds and lighting the new snow on the highest ridges. In the filtered light she saw the river lined with red-stemmed willows threading through a broad valley of tall grass. The meadows flowed out of a distance where night had already settled, but islands of aspen, flame-colored, stuttered in a sundown wind. The slopes that held the valley were blanketed in dark spruce and fir.

And over all the open country, wherever forest gave way to grass, she made out the herds: moving or grazing, the elk in their hundreds, bunched and heads down; pronghorns in little groups; the dark shadow of dozens of bison moving slowly together and the black humps that were the huge single bulls, scattered over the valley like boulders, unafraid of anything that lived. Celine and Pete pulled over and shucked on goose-down sweaters and stood at the edge of the road in a cold wind and scanned with binocs. Pete spotted a pale coyote trotting down a game trail between rock ledges. Celine found two foxes on the riverbank, ruddy in the last light. They saw mergansers in a pool and a heron in the reedy horsetails across the river. On the wind they heard bird cries, very faint, and realized it was the closest elk, mothers calling to their calves.

"Jeez," Celine murmured. "All these animals. It's like a diorama at the natural history museum. When I was little I just wanted to walk into them."

Pete would write that night in his journal that when they came over the rise and down into the

242

reach of the Lamar they seemed to enter another time. It felt as if the rest of earth might suffer through its eons of fire and ice, and this valley would remain: Dusk would gather as it always had on an autumn evening, and the elk would bugle and cry, a harrier would beat her wings over the grasses. The wolves that thrived here now would watch them all from the blowdown at the edge of the forest.

Celine said, "I was looking at the map. This valley pretty much runs all the way to Cooke City. A tributary does. If Paul Lamont is dead, he might have died in this drainage. It's strange to think it."

"There are worse places to go, I guess," Pete said. "I just don't get the feeling he is here. Or ever was for very long."

Celine reached for Pete's hand. Her own was icy and his felt warm. He'd been keeping them in his pockets. "I don't either," she said. "If he had died here then why would our handsome young friend be so interested?"

"Speaking of whom, where is he? He seems to be slacking."

"When we get back to the truck I can tell you."

They decided to wait until Cooke City to track down Mr. Tanner. They wanted to drive the remaining twenty-five miles before full dark. They unfolded the map and drove up the Lamar.

The road and the river skirted the base of Druid Peak, a dome of forest glades and rimrock where some of the first Canadian wolves were reintroduced in the nineties. A tributary branched off to their left and continued north-northeast and they followed it. Soda Butte Creek was smaller and the valley was narrower and the black woods ran down off the steep ridges almost to the banks of the stream. The mountains loomed over the river bottom and were walled with high broken cliffs. The rock was striped with seeping water and runneled with thin waterfalls. High up were flecks of white that Pete said must be mountain goats. Jesus— nothing up there but cliff. It may have been the thickening dark or the first patter of rain, but this upper valley felt ominous. Pete had his file of notes open and their GPS in his hand, and he said Lamont's car was found just about eight miles north. They would hit the spot at about the same time of night that he had probably come through. Even the weather might be about the same.

Up ahead they saw two white vans parked on the shoulder and a group of people milling. Curious, they pulled over, got out. It was a safari, a group of wildlife watchers just packing up their spotting scopes. Maybe eight of them, in expensive outdoor gear.

A young woman guide in a black fleece jacket

shoved one last tripod into the back of a van and turned and said, "That's right. Rafaella asked about Tala, the legendary she-wolf. Come over here, all of you, and I'll tell you." The eight crowded around her. She wore a knit wool hat and her dirty-blond hair stuck out from under it in a ponytail. She had a round face and a chipped front tooth. "I told you about the Soda Butte pack. One of the first in the valley. Tala came from that bunch. By then there were three established and active packs centered around this area and they were thriving. But Tala had an independent streak from the get-go. She was big and fast, and she was very very smart. Wily, cunning, playful. She began to hunt by herself. The biologists were amazed. The pack would be lying around and she would just get up, stretch, and it was as if she were saying, 'See ya later, I'm going to go get an elk.' Incredible. She is one of the few wolves ever documented that could bring down a full-grown adult elk on her own. Again and again. It's very dangerous work and she did it with ease." The guide raised her voice over the cold wind.

"She broke away. Went off to start her own pack. An alpha female if there ever was one. Of course every alpha male in the country wanted to mate with her. She had her pick. And you know what she did?" The guide was very good. She had them in the palm of her wool mitten. She noticed Celine and Pete standing at the edge of her group and nodded. "She went and picked two gawky, gangly adolescent brothers. Who didn't know crap, excuse my French. She could have had her pick! Did have. And she picked these two youngsters that didn't have much skill and she mated with both of them and taught them how to hunt. One of the great stories. They got very good at hunting, too. And the pack got strong. That was the beginning of the famous Cache Creek pack."

"What happened to them?" asked a man in an Australian safari hat.

The guide frowned. "One fall she led the pack out of the park boundary, in Wyoming, and a hunter with a legal wolf permit shot her. The pack fell apart after that, disintegrated."

The whole group swayed. The guide took a second to recover as well. Finally she said, "That big black female we saw just now, trotting into the shelter of the trees with her own family, that's Tala's granddaughter."

"Wow," one lady said, just the way Celine would have if she hadn't been speechless.

She turned to Pete. "We just missed wolves. Wow." Pete squeezed her hand and they climbed back into the truck and drove north and west. Celine couldn't stop thinking about Tala and her pack. How easily parents can disappear and families fall apart.

• • •

The open valley ran out with the remaining daylight. They entered dark woods and the road turned due east. Somewhere they crossed into Montana. They drove through an unmanned park gate. The road narrowed. The tall firs leaned over it and they lost the sky.

"There," Pa said. Ahead the painted wood railings of a small bridge flashed in the headlights. Celine slowed. As she did, two then three shadows ghosted across the road.

"Coyotes!" she said.

"Wolves. Much bigger than coyotes. No bounce in the gait."

"This feels a bit like Little Red Riding Hood, don't you think?" she said.

She pulled over on the shoulder. This was it, the bridge where the biologists had found Lamont's truck. With his good parka still in it, his wallet, his knife. Somewhere off to their right, across the stream, the searchers had found drag marks, pieces of clothing, blood on a tree. She turned off the ignition and they got out. The wind rushed in the tops of the trees. The stream lapped and gulped. Night had fully descended and with it the chill of a certain frost. For a while they just stood there.

"This feels like a place of death," Celine said finally.

"Wildness or death?" Pete said.

"Death." They stood there listening. "Well," she said, and shivered. "It's good we're here on a similar night. Now I know that if this was all Lamont's idea he had brass balls. Imagine heading out alone on a night like this."

"Imagine being married to Danette," Pete said.

"Good point. Let's go on into town. This is out of the park. What are we in? Unincorporated Park County? We need the sheriff's report."

They decided to stay at the Yellowstone Lodge in Cooke City. It was not in Yellowstone and it was not a lodge, and the closest city was very far away. The motel was a collection of log cottages strung along a rutted dirt driveway. They could have stayed in the camper and poached Wi-Fi from someone, but frankly Cooke City looked like it could use the business. Anyway, the motel had Internet and it might be good to have an HQ and spread out. So they asked for a room with two double beds so they could use one as a map table.

It wasn't hard to find a place to eat. Cooke City had one short main street carved out of thick woods and they had two choices: a pizza parlor with a pool table that smelled so strongly of stale beer that they did a U-turn in the doorway, and Poli's Polish. There was also a bar with a neon flashing Pabst in the window. At least there was cell reception. They sat at one of the six vinyl tables in Poli's and as soon as Celine turned her phone back on it dinged with a new text and a new voice mail. The waitress brought them bowls of iceberg lettuce with lumps of shaved carrots on top. "Comes with dinner," she said with a thick accent. Her name was Nastasia and she was from Latvia. She had a round face with baby fat around the mouth and skeptical violet eyes, all of which made her age impossible to determine. "I thought this was a Polish restaurant," Celine said.

"Actually, most of our customers think Latvia is in Poland," said Nastasia, clattering down two small bowls of white borscht floating with rounds of sausage. "Also comes with dinner."

The text was from Gabriela.

> Cam Travers, Sheriff. Still there, I checked. I guess Park County constituency doesn't change much so he isn't going anywhere. Helped me a lot. Trust him.

> Timothy Farney, U.S. Park Ranger, Yellowstone Lamar District. Led the search and rescue and signed off on death certificate. Saved my ass. Pitied me I think. Knew I could not inherit or move on for seven more years without ruling of death, so signed. Very grateful to this man.

> L. B. "Elbie" Chicksaw, professional tracker. Lives in Red Lodge. Probably

disputed findings of the Park Service report. Seemed troubled about the tracks, to me. Ask him. He's kinda loony.

Lonnie and Sitka Fuzile, owners of the Beartooth Bar. You've seen it already, I'm sure. Name sounds Italian but it's South African. Not going anywhere either, I think they're Afrikaner refugees disguised as old hippies. They knew Dad well as you can imagine.

Ed Pence, lead bear biologist, man Dad was profiling when he disappeared. Lives in Helena.

That's it for now. I looked up some of Dad's old stories. The most famous one from that time was the one he did on the horse country of the Manso River in Chilean Patagonia. All the farms along the river are connected by horse trails only. It's a gorgeous spread. Came out in the January '74 issue of Nat Geo. Okay. Let me know what else you need. I wish I could be there.

The voice mail was from Harold: "Twenty-two fifteen" was all it said. She looked at her watch. That was in six minutes. It was the time, New

York time, when she was meant to call their prearranged number. That's how they worked it. She waved over Nastasia and asked if she could use the restaurant's phone to make a call to New York, it was very urgent and the call would be no more than a minute and she'd be glad to pay. "Of course," Nastasia waved her to the counter. "Comes with dinner." She smiled. The phone was on a narrow desk behind the front counter and the register. Celine waited two minutes and dialed.

"Hi doll," came the gruff voice. Harold always thought he was in a police movie from the sixties. Why not make the most of his job?

He said, "Master chief, Seal Team Three, based Coronado, California. Specialist: sniper. Enlisted '87. Deployments redacted. Hope that helps. Love ya."

"Love you, too."

He hung up.

Celine left a five-dollar bill on the counter and made her way back to the table. She repeated the information to Pete and watched the slight up and down movements of his bushy eyebrows. "No surprises there," he said as he finished jotting in his little steno book. "Wonder where he's gotten to. You were going to tell me."

Celine propped open the laptop and scooted to Pete's side of the table. There was an open network called "Kielbasa" and she logged on. The GPS tracker she had stuck to the underside of Tanner's truck was the same model recently used to track a great white shark from South Africa to Australia. The shark surprised the researchers by making the 6,900 mile journey in 99 days. Celine thought that was fitting. She was sure the shark didn't irritate his trackers by calling them ma'am.

The technology really was wonderful. It worked with Internet, and when they were on the road they had a small map screen that connected via satellite, but it was very expensive to use. She typed in the code for the first tracker and clicked on an icon and a map began to constitute itself. The boundaries of Yellowstone National Park appeared, there was the Yellowstone River and Highway 89, there to the south the Grand Tetons, Jackson Lake, there was Jackson Hole—and there was a pulsing blue dot. In Jackson Hole.

She blinked. Couldn't be. The man had made a U-turn.

Maybe he was sick of diner food. Maybe she had scared him with her plaid robe! Why was her first emotion disappointment?

"I'll be damned," she said. "Pete, I feel abandoned! Isn't that weird? Empty nest all over again."

Pete chuckled. "Not so fast," he said. "Didn't you listen to the man's job?"

"Yes. Starving," she muttered and took a

spoonful of the borscht. "Mmm, wow. Wow. So what?"

"He's a trained hunter. Maybe at last you've met your match. A real James Bond."

"Humph."

"If he is that good, he knew you put the tracker on him. He's surely trained to sweep his vehicle every day, as you said. Remember the Piss on Hippies guy?"

"Of course."

"Wasn't that the last place we saw young William?"

"Uh-huh."

"Didn't the driller's truck say Jackson Hole on the door?"

Celine stared at her husband. Incredible! Pete seemed all fusty and distracted and he didn't miss a single beat, did he? Tanner might have simply moved the GPS on its magnet to the redneck's truck. Damn. Still, it was just a guess.

"Maybe," Pete said, "he is done jogging out in the open, trying to intimidate us. Maybe he is going dark. Trying to."

She blew on another spoonful and swallowed it. Pete said, "Maybe he is hunting us now."

Celine dipped a piece of store-bought roll into the soup. Pete said, "Why don't we check the second one, the one his surrogate mother put in the coffee grinder. Let's see how good he really is."

Celine twisted her lips and ladled up more borscht. "This soup is really delicious," she said. "You should eat something." Pete grinned. His wife, he could see, was delaying the moment of truth. "Okay, okay," she said. She patted her lips with her napkin and typed in the code for the second tracker. The map vanished and reformed and there was the blip in the middle of it, pulsing away like a headache. "He's at the bar next door!" Celine said, triumphant. "Either that or he's making coffee on his tailgate a block away."

"Did you want to invite him over for dinner?" Pete said dryly.

"He kept my present!" she said. "Oh, Pete, you're getting jealous!"

Pete didn't deign to respond. But he did say, "He may simply have known where we were going. Where else would we go? But maybe in the morning we should do our own sweep."

Celine pushed her salad bowl an inch closer to Pete's side of the table. "I don't think so," she said. "I mean, sure, to see if something's there. But if we are lit up, it may have a use later."

"Hmm," Pete said. And she knew by the timbre that she wouldn't have to explain.

"But how do we know," he continued, "when he has begun to really hunt us? When the fun and games is over with?"

"We don't," she said.

seventeen

It was too late to call anybody. Celine wanted to talk to Sheriff Travers first, but that would have to wait until morning. Before they could order, Nastasia brought out two plates of hamburger steak fried flat and smothered in sauerkraut, two small dishes of creamed spinach, and a bowl of mashed potatoes.

"Is this included in the meal, too?" Celine said. They hadn't had time to order.

"Actually, yes." The waitress leveled her world-weary violet eyes at Celine. "Actually, it *is* the meal. There is one meal." Her eyes were neutral, waiting for the challenge.

"Great."

"Okay. Well." Nastasia relaxed just a little and picked up the salad bowls. "By the way, I noticed that you were walking here. Be careful back to the motel. There is Problem Bear."

She must have been sitting in the window waiting for a customer. Cooke City suddenly seemed even sadder.

"What is Problem Bear?"

"He is big griz. He is eating garbage and he charged Sitka on the street, since three nights." There was only one street.

255

• • •

They walked back slowly. They held hands and walked down the middle of the dark county road that served as Main Street. There were no streetlights, only the neon in the bar and the lights from the motel sign and the windows of the two restaurants, a few houses. The rain had stopped but there were no stars, and the thick clouds were keeping the air from freezing. It smelled of woodsmoke. They could see the pale plumes rising from stovepipes into the stillness. Winter was coming fast and people were stoking their stoves, the air was thick with it. Celine wheezed a little as she walked, the thin reedy note on the inhale that almost sounded like a cat. Everything seemed sad. They heard a garbage can clatter somewhere behind them, but they were not scared of the bear because Celine was packing, though she knew that a nine millimeter round would more likely piss off a grizzly than stop it.

It occurred to her as they walked that they were looking for a father who had disappeared more than two decades ago, but that he had truly left his child's life long before that, that the young woman had grown up for all intents and purposes fatherless. As she did. That finding him now might resolve something in the woman's heart but would not change the essential sadness. And that was the business she was in. She had had to accept it long ago: that her job was enabling just such

256

reunions. That though they could not change someone's childhood, still—there was a great raw need in her clients to know their parents and to meet them again. There was something in that resolution that was very important. To the child, and often to the parent. She certainly knew about that. And sometimes they—the parent and the child—started again. Rarely did it work, but sometimes it did. And then a child would have a mother and a mother a daughter.

The saddest part was that parents would keep disappearing, and children would cry themselves to sleep night after night, for months, for years. And that mothers would have their babies taken from them before they had a chance to smell the tuft of soft hair, their ears, before they had a chance to say, "Oh how I love you! Forever and ever." That the baby was taken before she had a chance to kiss her and wrap her properly in her arms.

Pete guided her around a deep pothole partly filled with gravel and she gripped his hand more tightly. In the wan light from the motel sign she could see their truck, the only vehicle in the drive. The only guests. At the end of the street she could see the dark bulk of the Barronette rising against the night sky. Yes, sad. How it felt. She thought that one might not make a dent in the Great Sadness, but one could help make another person whole.

• • •

That night in the overheated motel room Celine dreamed of Las Armas, the villa on the hill. She was returning after a long sojourn, she was not a little girl anymore but she was not a grown woman either. She was running down the shell drive and she was looking for Bobby and Mimi. She had something important to tell them and she wanted badly to run with them down to the little beach, to tell them away from Baboo. She wanted to tread water beneath Grayson's dock and tell them.

She got to the house and pushed open the door and there was a woman in the front hall picking the heavy receiver up from a black phone. The woman turned, startled. She was blond, handsome, her wrist glinted with a gold bracelet, she had the air of having everything she wanted in the world, but Celine didn't recognize her. She wanted to call out for Gaga, but she was afraid of upsetting the woman who clearly lived in the house, and she was afraid Gaga would not answer. Celine looked past the woman to the main parlor and saw scaffolding and sheets and lumber. Broken plaster.

"I . . . I . . ." she stammered. And then she was clawing at her throat, clawing for air. The *I*'s would not come out and they would not go back in. They came up from her lungs and hit the dead spot that swelled there like a bubble and they piled up, backed down her esophagus and up into her sinuses and her head. "I . . . I . . ."

She must have been thrashing because Pete startled awake and his arm flung over and he felt her shaking, her whole thin body taut as tightened cable and shivering, her chest arching upward. Oh God.

He hit the light and he saw her face drawn in a mask of terror, her eyes half closed and rolled back, and her face was blue. He did the only thing he could think of: he rolled over onto his elbow and forced himself to his knees and bent his face to his smothering wife and sealed his lips around hers and blew. He blew hard. Felt the resistance, Jesus, and turned his head to the side and kissed her again and blew harder and he felt something release and when he turned his lips to the side again a rush of hot air blew against his cheek and she cried out. As weak and searing a cry as he had ever heard.

He sat her up. Her eyes were glazed but the blue was almost gone from her cheeks. She breathed. A little. At least she breathed. Shallow and quivering, but inhale, exhale. Her strong arthritic hands gripped the crumpled counterpane as if she were holding herself to a cliff. Pete placed his open hand on her chest for a split second, she gave the barest of nods, and he let himself off the bed and made his way to the oxygen condenser on the other bed, tried not to shake as he unwound the tubing, turned it on, came back. Hooked the cannula gently over her ears, inserted it into her nostrils. She did not move her head, she held it rigid on her neck as if any movement might jeopardize the airway, but her eyes followed him. "Oh," he said. "Inhaler. Red inhaler first," and he saw her shut her eyes a second which meant No.

"Okay, okay."

She breathed. Barely. Her chest moved as rapidly as a bird's. She looked scared. Terrified. That's what got to him the most, he didn't know when she'd ever looked so frightened. And then her breathing hit another hitch and her eyes went wide. Oh God. Pete felt the world freeze and teeter. And then she released, whistled out another breath.

Pete usually never panicked but now he did. He touched her again and rose and scrabbled his hands over the low bureau feeling for his phone, which he found and flipped open. No reception. Damn. Of course not. And the Yellowstone Lodge may be the only motel on the planet with nophone in the room. Pete did not easily succumb but for a moment he cursed. What the hell were they doing here? Cooke City was seventy-five hundred feet and it was cold and the air was thin and all the woodstoves cranking up were thickening the night with particulates and smoke, just about the worst recipe—he shook it off. No good going there. What they needed now was a doctor.

Pete found his pants on the scarred armchair and pulled them on and shucked on the wool-lined Carhartt jacket without bothering to put on a shirt and said, "I'll be right back, three minutes," and she nodded, just the barest tilt of her chin and he was out the door and trotting as best he could over the rough pitted gravel of the parking lot. The motel office. Someone there would help, they would have a phone. A single bulb burned at the door. He knocked. Tried the knob, locked. Damn. Knocked harder. Nothing, no light. Maybe the owners didn't even live here like every other motel-owning family. He went out onto the road, the main street, careful not to stumble on the frost heaves. For the first time he noticed that the night had misted, gone into low cloud, the moisture touched and needled his cheeks, maybe it was frost. Across the street he saw a light burning in a second story. It was the Polish restaurant, who knew who lived above—any harbor in a storm. He moved as fast as his stiff knees would carry him, could not bear to think of her struggling for breath in the room alone. He pounded now. Knocked as hard and fast as he could. He did not stop.

A light flicked on, in the restaurant, over the counter. He saw through the small panes of the door Nastasia pulling tight a white terrycloth robe, knotting the belt. Her black hair was wild and she still wore traces of smudged mascara and she looked alarmed and suddenly many years older. Well. She came to the door at an angle like a gunfighter, tilting her head and peering the whole time, trying to make out the visitor—or intruder. She found a switch on the wall and Pete was suddenly rinsed in white light and her face relaxed. She even managed to quiver one corner of her mouth into a smile. Unlatched the door.

"Wha—"

"It's my wife, Celine. She's having a crisis—her breathing—"

"*Ja ja*," she knew, she remembered, she'd noticed.

"I need a phone. Better, is there a doctor, a doctor right in town?"

She shook her head, emphatic. "He is bird hunter. About maybe five kilometers he has a cabin, no phone, he comes from Bozeman."

"Oh God, I don't drive. Do you?" For the first time he saw her unmasked: Her eyebrows were up, arched, her mouth in an O, her broad cheeks flat, eyes resigned and scared and excited all at once, she looked like a child who has been asked to jump off the high dive and knows she will do it. "Jimmy's truck, he is owner, we will try. He showed me."

Pete did the math and it occurred to him that it was the same calculus Lamont must have done on the morning of the drowning. If they went back to the room to check on her it would eat up five or ten more minutes. But she might be having another seizure now and without help she would die. The thought hit him like a gust of hail. He may have never allowed himself to utter those words, even in his head, and the chasm it opened up was too wide and too deep. He flinched, shrank back. The truck was parked outside, a battered Nissan, and Nastasia yanked open the stuck front door like she was goading a stubborn ox. She had not dressed, she was naked under her robe, and she did not even go back in to find a coat. She must have been freezing, and it filled Pete with gratitude for the no-bullshit people of the earth, the people who knew what had to be done and would find their own damn coat later. She overcranked the starter, grated it again, got the truck going and then lurched it into the post that supported the steps. He could see her shaking her head, heard the gearbox chunk as she found Reverse, and then the pickup heaved back twice and stalled. Then he heard the bark of a Baltic curse and the door flew open. She was pissed, almost smoking with outrage. Pete felt paralyzed. He needed to get back to the room. Her violet eyes now black in the dim light flashed up to his and she saw everything, said, "Go! Go back! I know where! I will get Stumpy to drive! Go!" And with that she tore up the street to look for a driver—in a wreath of fuming frustration and whirling terrycloth like some Halloween ghost.

Celine was not dead when he got back to the room. She was still struggling for breath but her head had relaxed on the pillow and her eyes were closed and the compressor was making rhythmic chuffs to boost each of her breaths. Her fingers still gripped the blanket. Pete sat beside her and placed his cool hand on her forehead and murmured that a doctor was coming. He wasn't sure—not sure of anything: whether Nastasia would find Stumpy whoever he was, whether they'd get to the doctor's, whether he'd be home—but that's what Pete said: The doctor was coming. And when he said it, he thought he heard the tempo of the condenser slow, and thought he felt her forehead relax. Fear, he thought, is the enemy of breath.

Who knew how much time had passed, it didn't seem like much. Nobody even tapped. He heard the drum of several feet on the steps and the creaking wood of the porch and the door was shoved inward. A burly bearded man in a camo parka strode straight to the bed, carrying a teal daypack in one hand. He wore insulated L.L.Bean boots and at his heel was a bronze Weimaraner. Pete blinked. The two looked like they were about to prospect a hillside for grouse. "Dr. Arnold," the man said. *Sit. Stay.*

Andy. Internist, hospital admissions, but we've done our share of ER. Huh." Behind him was a scarecrow with a drawn pitted face and a scraggly mustache and one arm: must be the driver, Stumpy. And following them both was Nastasia, crossing her arms over her robe and beginning to shiver. Behind her was a heavyset woman in a native wool poncho whom Pete thought he had seen shooting pool in the pizza bar. Pete had no idea what the woman was doing here, but crises in tiny towns seemed to gather a crowd. Nastasia huffed and stepped behind the woman and slammed the door.

Sometimes all a breathing attack takes is reassurance. What Pete thought. And a shot of prednisone. And two huffs of the red inhaler, then the white one. And a big burly doctor who looked a little like Ernest Hemingway to place his hand on an arm and keep repeating, "Just a reaction to the altitude, maybe the mist tonight and woodsmoke combined. You'll be fine, fine. There now." And a Latvian in a bathrobe—Oh God! Pete noticed now that she had bare feet! She had not even stopped to put on shoes—a barefoot Latvian to intone, "So beautiful, you really look like an angel," and a one-armed hero who reeks of cigarettes and pot to keep saying happily, "Fuckin' A, look, look at that, breathing fine now, fuckin' A."

• • •

The doctor took Pete out onto the little rotting porch and told him that the next morning he should get her down to lower altitude and right to an ER if she continued to struggle. He refused to take any kind of payment. Celine slept soundly with her oxygen and woke unsteady and ragged, but strangely refreshed. The morning was windy and clear and had swept away the clouds andthe smoke, and she insisted that they stay. They did not need to hurry down to lower altitude. She felt she'd be fine. Pete didn't argue; he yielded to a predisposition to let people exercise their right to self-determination, even with those he loved most, and even when he didn't quite understand their decisions. Especially then.

They ate breakfast early at Poli's and Celine gave Nastasia her favorite silk scarf, the one with little gold triangles that represent pine trees or mountains on a cobalt field, and the girl was so touched she had to hurry into the kitchen. They used the restaurant phone to call the sheriff in Livingston. Then they spent the morning relaxing in their room and looking over their notes and speculating and napping. There had been a lot of travel and emotion in the last few days and they needed the break.

In the afternoon they roused themselves and called the main number for the park administration and asked for Timothy Farney in Law Enforcement. "By the way," Celine said to the receptionist, "what is his official title now?"

"Oh, he's Chief Ranger," the operator said cheerfully. Good, still around. A career man.

"Of what, exactly?" asked Celine.

"Of what?" the operator repeated, puzzled.

"I mean what district or whatever?"

"Oh! Why, of Yellowstone! Of the park!" The woman was so enthusiastic. Well, Chief Farney had made it to the top! After slugging it out in the districts! Clearly the woman had been living in Mammoth Hot Springs too long. Celine had seen the pictures: Elk lay all over the lawns like sunbathers at a beach. It could drive anyone batty.

"Right. Thank you. Please put me through."

"Of *course!*"

Jesus. The next voice was much less excitable. "Operations," it said. Jaded, almost put-upon. "Timothy Far—" Before she could get out the full name the line clicked and she was transferred. Now there seemed to be a secretary. The secretary must have had an office with a view: maybe a herd of antelope on a hill. Celine imagined a jar full of crumbly toffee on her desk, on a doily. She was much more relaxed. "Who's calling?" she asked, ready to be surprised.

"Celine Watkins. I'm a private investigator from New York." She had no reason to be cagey.

"Oh, how interesting. And what matter can I say are you calling about?"

"The disappearance in or near the park of a man named Paul Lamont."

"Just a minute, please." She almost sang it.

When the woman came back on the phone she sounded like a different person.

"I'm sorry," she said with hostility. Wow. "Chief Farney is on vacation."

"I see. And when might he be back?"

"I'm sorry, I can't divulge that information."

"You can't tell me when the Chief of Enforcement will be back in the office?"

"Security reasons."

"I see," Celine said dryly. "Nor where he has gone, I suppose." Silence. "The Caribbean is very nice this time of year, but of course, it's hurricane season." Silence. Then the phone clucked. The mercurial secretary had hung up.

eighteen

Sheriff Cam Travers met them the next morning at the bridge over Soda Butte Creek, just outside the park boundary. He got out of the truck and unkinked his back and reached into the front seat for a stained fawn cowboy hat. He wore a Sheriff's Department parka and Wranglers. He winced as he stretched and leaned back into the truck for a travel coffee cup that said *#1 GRANDPA*.

"Okay, ready for work now," he said and shook each of their hands. When he saw their own travel mugs—*MAMA GRIZZLY* and *PAPA GRIZZLY*—he smiled. "Just a sec." He got a thermos out of the truck and topped them all off. He was courteous and curious, and Celine liked the way he studied their clothes, their speech, sizing them up and withholding judgment. He had just driven the two and half hours from the county seat in Livingston. When he had heard that morning that they were near the northeast entrance and interested in the case of Paul Lamont, he said he needed to come down to Cooke City anyway to deal with Curly, which is what the residents were calling the local grizzly. He'd meet them at the bridge in the morning, and then schedule a bear recon with Parks and

Wildlife after lunch. On the phone, he had asked for Celine's New York State PI license number. Due diligence.

They all drank from their cups. Travers turned up the collar of his jacket. The wind was raw and felt like coming snow. "You live right across the river," he said. "Right in view of the Twin Towers. I looked it up."

Celine winced, not from the cold.

"Sorry," he said. "Helluva thing. The world changed last year. Still changing. I can feel it like I can feel a coming snowstorm. It makes me sad, deep down." He shook himself off, sipped from his coffee mug. "We didn't meet|in the woods of Montana to talk about that." He waited.

"Sheriff, do you remember Gabriela Lamont?" Celine asked.

"Of course I do. A smart and extremely tenacious young lady. Very pretty, too."

"That's her. She said you were very helpful."

"Kind of her." He sipped and looked them over carefully, glanced at the truck camper. The two didn't jibe.

"She came back up here a number of times over a span of two years?"

"She wasn't satisfied with the determination of the Park Service," Travers said. "Neither was I, to tell you the truth."

"How do you mean?"

Travers looked at the bridge, the creek. "Well. In law enforcement we are all a little turfy, that's a fact. The park is federal, of course, and they assumed jurisdiction. They had legitimate grounds. Lamont's truck was parked"—he turned and pointed at the opposite side of the road, a turnout of gravel just east of the bridge—"there. The bridge is the park boundary. The entrance gate is a mile and a half south but the actual border is here. Chicksaw, the tracker, determined that Lamont had been dragged—or run—into the park. So."

"There were drag marks?"

"Possibly. I'll show you in a minute."

Celine studied the bridge. "Which way was his truck facing when you found it?"

"West."

"Huh?"

Sheriff Travers looked at her with a dawning admiration. She was sharp, no doubt.

Celine said, "He was returning to town after shooting pictures with the biologists at the base of Druid Peak. That's what Gabriela told us. The report concluded that he had likely seen an animal that aroused his curiosity, probably said bear, and he had gotten out with his cameras—they found two cameras and a handheld flash, all shattered, in the trees somewhere there, correct?" Travers nodded. "So his truck should have been facing east, toward town, don't you think?

271

I mean, I'm driving along, there, toward Cooke City, I'm hungry after a long day, probably pretty thirsty, too, I see a bear in the road, he's magnificent, I have no shots of a bear at night, I pull over fast, grab cameras, and run." She turned back to the sheriff. "Wouldn't I?"

The sheriff made a check mark in air. "Problem One."

"There were no photos of a bear in the cameras, were there? I mean Mr. Night Bear, our suspect? If there were, you wouldn't be so uneasy about the final determination."

Travers made another tick with his finger.

"You can't give us the report, can you?"

Another tick. "I'd lose my job. Of course, I'm going to lose my job in December anyway. It's called retirement." He smiled. "I'm actually term-limited. Six terms is the limit."

"Wow."

"It's the termination-without-pension thing that scares me. Why I can't give you the report."

Celine nodded. "Is Chicksaw his real name do you think?"

The sheriff laughed, an easy gut laugh that made Celine trust him more. "Absolutely not. I think trackers have tracker names, *noms de guerre*, the way writers have pen names."

Celine smiled at the French.

"I think the man is from New Jersey. One of the first disciples of that guy in the Pine Barrens."

"He gave Gabriela the feeling that the tracks didn't add up."

"Problem Four. It's pretty technical, you should talk to the man. I believe he's in Red Lodge now. We have used him in many investigations over the years. It's not woo-woo. The man is a scientist."

"It rained that night?"

"Rain during the afternoon, then snow."

"There was blood?"

"On a tree. A dense old spruce. Quite a lot of it. Blood smeared on the bark. Under those thick limbs, the only place it would be protected from the elements for a little while. In the woods, when it's been raining, that's where you go to get your dry tinder, the dead twigs under a spruce like that. So how did the blood get on the tree? Did the bear rub him up and down on the trunk?"

"What else?"

"We found a shirt, most of it, ripped and also bloody. Also a boot, with tooth punctures and blood. Drag marks."

Celine winced.

"I can't give you the report, but I can give you this."

He handed her a manila folder. She turned her back to the freshening wind and opened it. Pete came close and blocked the wind and looked over her shoulder. It was a photocopy of an article from a *National Geographic* dated July

1977. The title was "Bear Attacks!" You don't say. Celine and Pete both flinched, which Travers noticed. Two-thirds of the way through the second page was a circled paragraph: *Searchers found only Leichmuller's right boot and a torn piece of his wool shirt. The boot bore punctures from canines and the shirt was saturated in blood.*

The sheriff said behind her, "He photographed for the magazine, didn't he? During that period? He would presumably have had them lying around."

Pete and Celine glanced at each other.

"Why would a successful *National Geographic* photographer at the acme of his career stage his own death?" She was asking as much to gauge Travers's knowledge of the wider context as to hear his opinion. He would not be able to tell her, of course, but she might get a lot from his reaction.

"You tell me," he said. Completely neutral. Unreadable. He watched her carefully. She got the strong sense he was trying to read her expression as closely as she was trying to read his. He was no fool. Much of the investigating they were now doing, he may have already covered twenty-three years ago. Had he looked into Lamont's travels? His international connections? Maybe.

"How long was the search?"

"Ten days. Neither long nor short. The Park Service called it on account of weather."

"And this guy"—Celine palmed her phone and lit the small screen—"Farney. The enforcement ranger, he signed the certificate of death."

"He made the determination of death. The judge in Livingston signed the certificate. There were several factors. A warm front came through and it rained heavily the afternoon just before he went missing. That evening the temperatures dropped into the teens, and then it snowed. He was badly mauled, clearly, if not dead. I'm speaking now in the terms of the report. The determination was that had he survived the initial attack and some-how escaped the bear, he would not have survived the successive nights of snow and freezing temperatures. A reasonable conclusion when you are in the last fiscal quarter and your budget is wearing thin. Search-and-rescue operations are expensive."

Celine detected a certain dryness in the sheriff's tone, even irony. "Gabriela said something about the kindness of the ranger. 'Taking pity on her' were the words she used. Signing the certificate so she could move on."

"Seven years is a long time to wait, I guess." The sheriff turned away from them and spat. Downwind. "The judge in Livingston went along with it. The hearing took twenty minutes."

"I gather, Sheriff Travers, that you don't think it was kind at all."

"Do you?"

Travers gave them his card with his cell number penned on the back and drove into town to meet the wildlife officer. Celine and Pete got back into the cab of their truck and sat for a while with the engine and heater running and watched the first scattered snowflakes hit the windshield softly, splaying into tiny stars before they beaded and ran.

"I got the sense he was relieved," Pete said. "To talk to someone about it. Someone who clearly didn't buy the party line. What did you say to him when you walked up to his truck before he left. When he rolled down his window?"

"I asked him if he got the sense at all that there was more than just investigative process or budgetary considerations that went into calling off the search and signing the death certificate. He had both hands on the wheel and he stared straight ahead for a full half minute before he answered me."

"I saw that," Pete said. Of course he did.

"Finally he said, 'I've known Tim Farney since he was practically a kid. He played halfback for Shields Valley when I was linebacker for Gardiner. I was always taking him to the ground. And he always got up and rubbed the grass off his neck and said, "Nice grab, Cam. For a fat man." Something like that. And he had an eighty-watt smile. He was my friend. When I asked him why he signed the certificate so fast when there were so many anomalies, he got a look I'd never seen before. Hard and tight. "Because I did," is all he said. Period. Case closed. He'd never talked to me like that.' "

Elbie Chicksaw was not at the address in Red Lodge that the sheriff had given them. No one was. No one, it looked like, had been there for quite a while. The little clapboard crackerbox was on a side street on the north end of town, which it shared with a double-wide trailer and an abandoned body shop. The small front yard was overgrown with knee-high dried grass and sweet sage and there was a tumbleweed pressed against the front door like a stray dog hoping to get in. The windows were boarded up with weather-stained plywood and a plywood sign at the gate said in spray-painted letters: FOR SALE BY OWNER. No phone number, no address. Interesting marketing, Celine thought. To be worthy of buying his house one had to hunt down the tracker. Well, we can do that, she thought. She eased the truck fifty yards down the rutted street to the trailer and got out. A wheelchair ramp led to the front door. She rapped. The little girl who opened it held a squirming puppy and her face, and the puppy's, were smeared with chocolate.

She pushed her lips around, cocked her head, and gave Celine a twice-over while trying to keep the puppy's licks out of her eyes. She thumped the dog on the head; he squirmed happily, and she yelled "No, Tucker, no!," tried to blow a strand of hair out of her face but it was too heavy with chocolate. "We're making moose," she announced.

"Moose?"

"Yep, chocolate moose, with giant antlers. Wanna see?"

"Definitely. Are your parents home?"

The girl turned her head and screamed *"Maama!,"* turned back. "We call him Tucker 'cuz no one gets no rest till he tuckers out."

"I see."

Behind her came an electric wheelchair. The woman driving it was in her twenties, broad-shouldered, with a thick blond braid lying over her breast. Dark circles under her eyes but prominent freckled cheeks, cute in a straight-forward, no-nonsense way. She looked to Celine like maybe a ranch girl who had practiced on the cheerleader squad before heading home to do chores. Her daughter hopped out of the way like a pedestrian in a crosswalk. Celine was going to tell these neighbors that she was Elbie's mother, but seeing the woman she knew that

278

wouldn't wash. She found that some people she met just expected the truth and it was almost impossible, and probably a sin, to tell them otherwise.

"You looking for Elbie?" the woman said.

"How did you know?"

"Anyone looks like you shows up on our doorstep they're looking for Elbie. We pay our taxes, and I can see you're not a Mormon."

"How do you know?"

"You know that hundred-mile stare ex-cons have? Mormons have it too, except they're gazing at the afterlife. Try to hide it but you can tell."

"Well." Celine laughed. "I was a Catholic, though, in the beginning. I always thought that was a great disservice—to teach a little girl to believe in Hell."

"Ha!" the woman barked. It caught them by surprise. "There's hell all right. But you don't need to die."

"Amen."

"Elbie's on vacation."

"Seems to be a pandemic."

"Be back in the spring maybe. You can leave your number with me. I'm guessing, though, you're not interested in the house."

Celine shook her head.

"Well what, may I ask, are you interested in?"

"Helping a young woman find her father." Celine was not smiling. She said it with such pathos the light in the entryway seemed to dim. The words settled on the young mother like a flock of exhausted songbirds.

"We know a little about that," she murmured. Celine noticed the scuffed gold band.

"Your husband?"

"Let's just call him the father of my child. The way I'm feeling lately. Jay's been in the oil fields five months and counting. If he doesn't come back for elk season I'll know we're pretty much toast."

Celine whistled without knowing it. Long and soft.

"You two wanna come in?" said the woman.

Celine wanted to find Elbie before the morning was over. But she had several creeds, one of which was that if someone made the effort to invite one in, well, one went. "Thank you," she said. "We'd love to."

By the time they left the trailer they had eaten enough dark chocolate mixed with whipped egg whites to feel queasy. They helped Lydie and Raine pour the mixture into the little moose-shaped cups and set them on a rack in the fridge, and they both got peed on, a little, by Tucker. When they stepped back out onto the ramp and into the brisk and windy morning they had a detailed map of the logging roads that led to Elbie's camp.

They'd driven half a mile when Pete said, "Can you pull over, please?"

"Pete?"

"Something's bugging me."

Celine pulled half off the road and they got out. Pete went to the back of the truck.

He got stiffly to his knees, then lay prone on the dry weeds and slid half under the frame as if he were checking for an oil leak. He slid himself back out, shook the gravel and dirt off his jacket and khakis, and held out a small black box the size of a Zippo with a little wire antenna poking from one end. The way they were looking at each other, a passerby might have thought he was handing her a rose, or a silver pendant.

Celine said, "Bingo! Let's leave it for now," and back under he went.

nineteen

Hank was just twenty-one when he drove down Interstate 91 along the Connecticut River between New Hampshire and Vermont, back to Putney and the school he had loved so much. He was a junior at Dartmouth, most of the way through an English major that thrilled him, and which he fully understood did not prepare him for the job market the way, say, premed would have done. He didn't care. He was reading Faulkner and Stein, Borges and Calvino, Bishop and Stevens. He felt wreathed in the music of language, and as long as he heard it and could write it down, as long as the pulse was in his veins, he didn't care if he lived out of the back of a truck or in some crappy rent-by-the-week for the rest of his life. The rougher, maybe, the better, because he also understood that somehow hunger sharpened the notes, cleared the static. He wasn't sure why, but he could see that the most comfortable writers—the most well-heeled people, even—were often the most deaf. Ah, youth.

But it wasn't for love that he was coming back to his old high school. Or not love only. It was to find his sibling. He knew that there were two male teachers who had taught both him and his mother. He'd start there.

Hank was shy about showing up on campus when there was still a class of kids that knew him, so he avoided the hilltop cluster of clapboard buildings and went straight to the house of Bob and Libby Mills, on Lower Farm Road. It was a blustery day in late October, biting cold, and he walked across a small farmyard matted with wet maple leaves. He climbed the slate front steps of a tight red clapboard house and knocked. Bob was an unlikely suspect, for, like Pete, he was a coastal Mainer who spent too much time cutting firewood and in a canoe to trouble his life with the shallower pleasures of sin. He also seemed to have a wonderful marriage. They seemed, the two, to be real best friends. He remembered once splitting cordwood with the biology teacher and Bob telling how he and Libby had taken their honeymoon on the Allagash. It was a weeks-long canoe trip through the Maine woods, and at the time river runners were required to hire a registered Maine guide. Their man was Calvin C. Beal. One night they camped at the head of a small rapid and climbed the ridge behind. Big views north and east. Bob said, "Hey, Calvin, what is that mountain just there, with the rocky top?" "Owl Peak," said Calvin. "And what about that far range there?" Calvin thought for a second and murmured, "Don't know." A few more considered seconds later, he said, "Nobody knows."

Bob said he and Libby had to have a coughing fit to keep from embarrassing the old guide. That was the kind of man Bob Mills was, the kind who fought every day to preserve other people's dignity, not erode it, and so Hank did not think he would be the father, but he might know something. He knocked on the green door and waited on the stoop and when it opened there was a tall handsome woman, maybe thirty, wearing a flour-powdered apron and chopsticks stuck in her thick hair to keep it up. Hank almost stumbled back. There was something about the intelligence and curiosity in her dark eyes, something about the strong ridge of her nose, and her palpable kindness, that reminded him instantly of his mother. And she would be about the right age. But no, he must have sisters on the brain, because that would be impossible, ridiculously implausible at best, and so he stammered, "I . . . I was looking for Bob and Libby."

Broad smile. "Another acolyte? And former student? There seems to be a stream."

Even the lilt of her voice. No way. She saw his confusion, misread it. "Sorry!" she said. "How presumptuous. God. You probably have some other business I can't imagine." She put out a work-roughened hand that, he noticed, was stuck with bits of kneaded flour. He also noticed that he was in love. Which couldn't be good. "Leah. Bob and Libby are on sabbatical in Sweden.

Would you like to come in? I'm just making bread." Of course she was. He stammered his thanks and turned to flee. Then it occurred to him: He stopped, turned back.

"Are you a . . . a friend?"

"Niece," she said brightly. "I'm visiting from Blue Hill." She smiled. "You don't have to run away. I'm sorry for being such a prig."

Oh yes, he did—have to run away. Even the way she talked . . . he ran. Actually skidded on the wet leaves as he spun the car back up the road.

So, was the start to his search auspicious or inauspicious? He wasn't sure. He was rattled. It reminded him of those lines in "Journey of the Magi." The wise kings come a long way to witness the divine birth and the one speaking says, *There was a Birth, certainly . . . I had seen birth and death, / But had thought they were different . . .*

Next stop: The young art teacher he never quite liked. Young when Celine was at school, only twenty-five to her fifteen. Late fifties now. But one of those men who never gets over being twenty-something. Taut, tan face, wearing a silk scarf like the French—how ridiculous in Vermont—and a beret! Not like Celine who always looked as if she'd been born with it, but like a poseur of the first degree—and who fancied himself a New England nouveau impressionist, whatever that was. Hank found the man in his

285

studio at the bottom of Putney Mountain. When he opened the door he looked at Hank with dawning recognition, and with a predator's eyes, eyes that measured him immediately on a scale called What Can You Do for Me? How Can You Feed Me? Hank wanted badly to make this brief. He did not have a true investigator's mettle. He said he was back just for the afternoon, he was at Dartmouth doing a family memoir on Putney, and if Mr. Surrey remembers, his mother had attended Putney, too—when Surrey was just beginning his career there, did he remember her? Could he tell Hank anything? If a shadow moved in the man's eyes, Hank could not distinguish it from the other secrets there.

Surrey sat Hank at a table covered in dried and spattered paint and made him tea. Predators, Hank thought, are usually lonely. The loneliness of the hunter. "Of course I remember her," he said. "She was one of the most talented students I have ever had. Is she . . ." The man slid the bowl of sugar cubes to him and Hank registered the copper and leather bracelets, the two silver rings. The collared shirt whose top buttons were open one button too many. Well, vanity is not a crime.

"Yes, she's alive and well."

"Is she painting?"

Hank bristled. He did not, he realized, want to talk about his mother with this man. He felt protective. Well. "She's a sculptor. Very talented." Hank thought he saw the man stiffen. Maybe with the knowledge that there was yet another competitor out there.

"How wonderful. Now what would you like to know?"

"I gather she was a very passionate art student. She has attributed that many times to your brilliant mentorship." The man blinked, almost visibly puffed. Hank had inherited his mother's social antennae and he knew how to hit home.

"Well . . ." Surrey mumbled.

"She has never had a more brilliant teacher ever, is what she said. In anything. Was she a serious student? Did she stay after class? Or take the evening activity?"

"Oh, she did both, often." The man's guard was completely down, obliterated by one small volley of flattery. "Often she would even stay after the evening activity and I would have to remind her of In-Dorms. I mean, if she didn't get back to her dorm by ten, there would be trouble with the dorm head."

"I remember," Hank said.

"Of course. But sometimes she would come back. She was that committed to her work. Amazing, really. She would check in with the dorm and then sneak back out. If she were very involved with a certain painting. More than once I caught her in the studio after In-Dorms, working

God knows how late into the night. I never said anything, of course. Only another artist can know what a taskmaster the muse can be. Yes, she was quite special." The man's eyes did something that approached misting over, and Hank felt nauseous. Maybe the tea on an empty stomach.

"Did you ever help her, I mean one artist to another, late at night? I mean as the only other person on campus who would truly understand the workings of creative brilliance?"

"Yes, we understood that. We had that bond. I would help her sometimes, of course. Once or twice at night I would work beside her on my own canvas, to, you know, inspire her."

I bet, thought Hank. Inspire or impregnate. Jesus. He hoped against hope.

"Did she . . . I mean, do you think—you were such a force, brilliant, probably a genius artist in your own right—do you think she might have fallen in love with you?"

The man touched his hair unconsciously, yes, it was still in place, still looked debonair, a bit messy, a bit bohemian. He seemed flustered, torn maybe between discretion and braggadocio. What a fool. "Well, who can say. Yes, maybe. She probably was. Probably was . . ." The man seemed lost in memory and Hank had to fight not to bolt the many-windowed room.

"Did she . . . did she ever try to kiss you?"

Surrey came out of his reverie, and his feline eyes refocused on Hank. As they did, he seemed to understand the snare he'd almost walked into, and who, actually, the boy in front of him was. He snapped back into his former tautness.

"How ridiculous," he said curtly. "She was my student. Was there anything else?"

Hank knew the door to further inquiry had been slammed shut and he was happy to leave. "No, thanks," Hank said. "You've been super helpful. I'll call if there's anything else that occurs to me."

"Please do," Surrey said dryly and showed him out.

The third stop was the most unexpected and perhaps most helpful. He drove his ten-year-old Toyota truck down the back road to Dummerston and reveled in the windy sunshine and the leaves blowing out of the woods in gusts that stuck to the hood. He stopped one farm shy of the Aiken Farm, at a small farmhouse that had once been white and was now weathered to gray wood, whose pastures were once mowed and were now grown with milkweed and blackberry. The curtains were pulled in all the windows, but there was a long, low-slung old Lincoln in the yard and so he knocked. A very old man with a two-day white bristle opened the door. Clean flannel shirt tucked into high-belted khaki jeans. Rheumy blue eyes.

"Mr. Grey? Ed Grey?"

"Eh-yuh."

"My name is Hank. I went to the Putney School, as did my mother. I am doing a project. I heard you were the farmer between '42 and '71—"

"Seventy-two."

"I see—"

"Bum leg why I didn't go to the war. Tried nine times."

"I see—do you remember my mother, Celine Watkins?"

The man tilted his head. Hank could almost see the name working through a nest of copper tubes, like in an old still. "I do," said the man. Hank was taken aback. How many students had worked on the farm over the decades? Hank had to remind himself again that very few people ever forgot Celine Watkins, even, he was discovering, when she was just a child. "Coltish was how you'd call her. Legs went to her neck and there weren't much between. Had a lamb if I recall correctly."

"Yes! Yes, she did!" Astonishing, the elephant memories of the very old.

"She had a thing for that milk-house boy."

"Milk-house boy?"

"The one that run the dairy those years.

Not much older'n she was. Slip of a kid. Good worker. Real quiet."

"What was his name?"

"Silas Cooper-Ellis. Shyest kid I ever met."

Hank gawped for words. "What happened to him?" he got out, finally. "Do you know?"

"Killed in Korea. Second week. Saddest thing. Went to the funeral in Sandwich."

"New Hampshire?"

"Yep. He lies there. That pretty cemetery looks to Chocorua. You know it?"

"No, no I don't. Thank you so much."

"Any time." The retired farmer blinked reflexively at the sky over the woods across the road. "Snow," he murmured. "Can taste it." And he rubbed his eyes with his palm, as if trying to wipe away all the work still left to do before the real snows came.

twenty

The truck groaned on its springs and bucked their heads into the roof. Celine pushed the Toyota to the end of an unmaintained logging road. Chicksaw lived in a shithole. The "house" may have started as a single-wide but it had been chopped up more than once. And added to with logs and steel framing and plywood. A car windshield had been framed in for a picture window. The front door itself must have been salvaged from a school—it had a push-bar latch. They pulled into the dirt turnaround with their windows down and could hear loud yelping and howls. The door jerked open and Chicksaw stepped onto the pallet porch with a shotgun. A small beagle shot out of the gap and jumped down to the dirt and began to bay. The man spoke to it sharply and it hopped back up to his side and sat, tail thumping the porch.

Chicksaw was tiny, maybe five foot three, with a long gray beard like an elf. Skinny. He was the most elfin man Celine had ever seen. They hadn't meant to surprise him: They tapped the horn half a dozen times before they even got to the yard. He held the gun in one hand and shielded his eyes with the other. When Celine stepped out of the truck in her short Austrian felt jacket and beret, with her gold bracelets and almost every finger bejeweled with rings, his hand dropped and his face betrayed raw skepticism—as if this might be a practical joke. Or some Publishers Clearing House scam. Celine stepped carefully around dried mud cakes in her Italian calfskin boots and waved a hand at him like an old friend she'd spotted on the beach-club veranda. Pete got out a little stiffly and zipped up his barn coat and settled his tweed newsboy cap into its nest of tufts. Gave a straight-across Maine smile.

Elbie Chicksaw had seen a lot of strange things step into clearings in Montana—once he had seen a bull moose with a goshawk perched on his rack, riding it like a mobile hunting platform— but this might take the cake. He set the shotgun against the doorframe and dug a pair of thick wire-rimmed grandpa glasses out of a breast pocket and looped them over one ear then the other and squinted. For a tracker his eyesight was terrible. He crossed his arms like a jinni and waited.

When Celine and Pete got within fifteen feet of the man they stopped. "Helloo," Celine called in her best Hail the Natives register. Elbie couldn't take it anymore. He started to laugh. It erupted out of him and his little frame shook like one of the leaves in the aspen at the edge of the yard. "For fuck's sake," he managed to blurt in a voice like a truck dumping gravel. "Who the *fuck* are you?"

Celine blinked. This man had clearly not been to finishing school, or maybe any school. He probably inverted his fork when he ate, if he used a fork at all. "The question seems a bit vulgar," she said. "Maybe you'd like to reconsider your greeting." Elbie took off the glasses he had just put on and cleaned them with the tail of his dirty flannel shirt. He blinked back.

"Sorry. I meant to say, 'Where the *fuck* did you all beam in from?' You're not going to give me shit now for ending a sentence with a preposition?"

Ahh, Celine thought, a diamond in the rough. There seemed to be a lot of those in Wyoming and Montana. She cocked her head and studied the tracker with her squinty-eye-bird look. "Where's the library at, asshole?" she murmured.

Which set Elbie off into another fit. "Right! Right!" he breathed. "The Harvard upperclassman with argyle socks! Damn! Fuckin' *hell!*"

Celine tugged her wallet out of her front jean pocket and opened it to her license card. "Celine Watkins, private eye. This"—she motioned to Pete—"I mean he, is Pete, my Watson and my husband. Actually, I may be his Watson, but no one would know because he doesn't say much."

Elbie widened his eyes at the new information and let another gust of laughter run through him.

"Oh, *God,*" he breathed. He replaced his glasses and opened three old-school aluminum lawn chairs that were leaning against the indeterminate siding. "Sit," he said. "You've clearly come a long fucking way. I'd invite you in but it's Tuesday and the cleaning ladies are wreaking havoc."

They sat. Elbie broke some dry sticks from a stack on one end of his makeshift porch and piled them with some crumpled *Red Lodge Advertiser*s into an oversize semitruck hubcap and lit the pyre. As the flames licked and rose he held his hands over them and rubbed them together. Fun, thought Celine. We can pretend we're homeless right here on the porch. A little like pitching a tent in the backyard.

He tapped a Camel unfiltered out of a hard pack and offered it around, then took it himself and lit it on a burning twig. He coughed once, hawked and spat, and said, "What can I do you?"

She had to admit it was pleasant sitting around the fire in the shelter of the man's porch with a few dry snowflakes blowing onto the planks. Chicksaw seemed to be pieced together like his shack, which was growing on her. The place looked haphazard, but on closer inspection everything seemed to have a function. The fifty-five-gallon drum at the east corner, for instance, which caught water from a guttered rainspout. The scrap-lumber framework on the other side of the porch, which she thought at first might be a lattice for vines but then realized was where he tacked out and stretched his hides. There was a beaver hide under the eave, drying right now. She recognized the fur from one of Baboo's stoles.

The same for the man: If he'd been a quilt it would look at first glance very primitive, even crazy in its pattern. But study it a little closer and one might see some fine stitching and some very curious patches. Celine began almost immediately to revise her first assessment of his education. He had clearly been to some school somewhere. The closer she listened to his fitful outbursts, the more she thought: College. Yes, definitely. Then: English lit. Then: Northeast somewhere. Then: Ivy League, probably. Ending a brief discourse on the inevitability of corrupt law enforcement, he said, "*Plus ça change, plus c'est la même chose.*" At one point he said that winter in Red Lodge was "colder than Winter frigging Carnival." Finally, being Celine, she interrupted him and asked point-blank, in French, if he had studied comparative literature under Professor John Rassias at Dartmouth. Chicksaw's cigarette fell from his mouth into the fire. Stopped him cold. It was either the precision of the question or the perfect, even beautiful French.

"*Ouais, ouais,*" he said in the vernacular, on the inhale, like a true Frenchman. He smiled and pouted his lips and assumed a completely different persona. Pete said it was like watching a brown octopus pass over a bed of green coral and almost disappear. *"C'était réellement un maître, ce professeur. Un vrai don du ciel pour éclairer la littérature française classique, Molière, Racine, Voltaire. Vraiment."* Deep sigh. *"Requiescat in pace,"* he added, shifting smoothly into Latin. Celine was surprised he didn't cross himself. Damn. What a weird world. Wonderful, really.

"What bothered you about the disappearance of Paul Lamont?" she asked abruptly, also in French.

"The tracks," he said without hesitation in English. "The fucking tracks were all wrong."

"Just a sec," he said.

Chicksaw got up from his lawn chair and went into the house, came out a minute later with a bag of marshmallows and three long barbecue forks and handed them around. "No Graham crackers or chocolate. Still." He browned himself a perfect treat and began to give them a lecture on grizzly tracks. He said that grizzlies walk with an "over-step" in which the rear track will appear just ahead of the front track of the same side. "The tracks will be offset, anglewise, something like twelve degrees and the rear track will be just a little deeper on account of the bear carrying more weight in the hind end. Now when he's dragging something, usually a carcass, the rear tracks will set even deeper and the front tracks tend to lose their regular offset and may smear. If you get on all fours and try dragging that branch across the yard with your teeth you'll see why."

"We might skip that part," Celine said with a sweet smile.

"Right. But the Lamont Bear—that's what everyone calls him—his tracks ran in and out of the drag mark with the normal offset. Also, the depth of the impressions did not change."

"Hmm."

"Hmm. That's what I said. Also, the impressions of the toes. Over uneven ground and especially dealing with cargo, so to speak, the toes will flex and move and the space between them will vary. Not to the untrained eye, but if you look closely."

"And these toes stayed put."

"Perfectly. Kept their spacing to the millimeter."

"But you didn't have that many tracks to check," Celine said, peeling the blackened skin off her burned marshmallow.

Chicksaw looked up sharply. "What do you mean?"

"Well, it snowed the night he would have encountered the bear, didn't it?"

He stared at her. "That's right. I had the set beneath the big spruce by the road, the tree with the blood on it, and that was it. Five prints. A drag mark. The rest all covered up by snow in the night."

"So if you were going to plan your own

disappearance you'd pick just such a night, wouldn't you?"

He studied her for a long beat. He had pieces of toasted marshmallow stuck to his beard. "Kinda what I was thinking," he said.

"What does L.B. stand for?" Celine said.

"Lawrence Burton."

"Lawrence Burton Chicksaw?"

"Chillingsworth." He picked the bits of goo out of his whiskers. "In Montana you gotta pick your battles." He took a flaming marshmallow out of the fire, blew it out, and gave it to the dog.

Elbie explained that a plausible track could be carved. "I knew an eccentric painter once in Colorado who carved a set of huge clawed tracks and glued fur between the toes and bolted them to a pair of running shoes. Jim Wagner was a character. He stomped all over the mudbank of his favorite fishing hole and it worked. Scared the crap out of everybody and he had the place to himself. People thought he was crazy for fishing there in the evening. The rancher brought in the game wardens who just scratched their heads, they'd never seen anything like it." He laughed his gravelly laugh.

"Couldn't you see human impressions off to the side? Of the Lamont Bear?"

"There were plenty under the snow. It's the first creek and first pull-off outside the park. It's pretty,

I guess. Seems people pull over to picnic and pee."

"Did you share your concerns?"

Elbie squinted at her. "I'm not at all shy."

"And?"

"Travers hired me. The sheriff. This is before he got overruled by the park. I gave him my report."

"Did you ever talk to Farney?"

"Farney is ex-marine. Kinda the charge-the-beach mentality. I'm not saying he can't be subtle because he can. But his first instinct is to go straight ahead. Go for the simplest and most plausible explanation of anything. *Lex parsimoniae.* The more assumptions there are, the more out of his depth he gets. He's a good man, and I guess over the long run, all things being equal, he gets more right than wrong. Going with the simplest explanations, maybe he comes out ahead of the rest of us."

"Occam's razor."

"Right. Bear tracks, drag mark, bloody boot, case closed. Plus, he really looked pained every time the girl showed up."

"Gabriela?"

"Right. That was her name. We had a meeting, the four of us."

"You *did?* Who?"

"Travers, Farney, Gabriela, and I. At the site. She kept insisting and finally Farney thought it was the least we could do. Show her how they found everything. Give her a little closure."

"Good God, the sheriff didn't mention that."

"I don't think it was anyone's finest hour."

A gust blew along the pallet porch and sent sparks against Celine's and Pete's legs. A few dry snowflakes blew into their faces. The tracker got up and fetched more broken sticks from the stack and built up the fire.

"How do you mean?" Celine said.

"Well. Farney set it up. I wasn't invited but Travers called me in. Like he knew what all Farney was going to tell her and he wanted me to be there. Like maybe the conscience of the outfit, I guess. She was so young and I gathered now she was an orphan. It was heartbreaking. But she was sharp as a tack.

"The sheriff wasn't allowed to give her his report and he never expressed his doubts about what all the park concluded. He had to keep a united front for so long—especially with the media. I mean. Imagine if he had broken ranks and started bringing up questions. What a media clusterfuck that would have been. And what would it have accomplished? Pain and doubt for the girl. Suffering, that's what. Everyone knew they would never find this guy. Not dead, not alive. Whatever the hell happened that night it was for keeps. Sometimes you can just feel it, in your bones like a change in weather."

He shuddered. Celine could see that, like her, he took his assignments to heart.

"So we all met," he said. "She came in her own car, a little compact out of Bozeman probably. We parked at the bridge and walked the short distance into the trees. Cold, mid-November, a dry fall so far—except that one week—and not much snow, a lot of patchy dirt showing through. She was wearing a hooded parka that was too big for her, it had patches that said 'Smithsonian-Arctic Institute Antarctica Expedition 1975.' I guess it was her dad's. And she wore mittens, I remember, and held a little picture in a frame. I asked her what it was and she showed me: her mother and father, close up, arms around each other, leaning close and smiling big as anything. There was a railing in the picture, looked like they were on a boat, their hair was blowing around. Lord, they were a handsome couple."

"So the four of you were under that tree."

"That's right. And she was so skinny in the big parka. I mean I should talk. Farney and Travers are both big men, football players, and she looked like a child next to them. She pushed back her hood so she could hear better and the impression was not dispelled. I mean she looked so young and she was wearing mittens and holding on to that photograph. It broke my heart. I mean. I am not a sentimental man."

"Don't be so sure of that," Celine said.

"Well. How she was, it may have had something to do with what happened. Farney cleared his throat and proceeded with about as much alacrity as if someone were holding a gun to his head. He went through all the details, the boot here, the blood here, the tracks, the cameras, the drag mark, not looking at her, not able to, then he'd glance over fast and bite his lip and clear his throat some more.

" 'The conclusion—bla bla—is that he did not survive the initial attack. We have data on these sorts of attacks, bla bla bla. More than a very brief initial engagement, they are almost always fatal. Especially when equipment or clothing are separated from the, well, ah.' He shut the fuck up. He was beet red. It wasn't the cold. 'I'm sorry,' he said. You could tell he wanted to put a hand on her but he didn't. Her eyes were big and shiny. You knew she was using all her strength. Farney clears his throat and looks over at Travers and says, 'Sheriff?' I told you how it was. Imagine the scene. Do you think Travers or I was going to pipe up and say, 'Well, gee, young lady, who just lost your last remaining parent, there are about ten fishy things with this whole fucked-up disappear-ance—' Wasn't going to happen. We caved. I admit it. Not my finest hour. She deserved to know the truth. I thought it then and I have thought it often since. A little time passes and it's, well . . . sleeping dogs." He turned and spat off the porch.

You let the sleeping dogs lie. Celine glanced at

the beagle curled at the man's feet, and the piece of marshmallow stuck to its black nose.

They drove in silence back down the forest track. When they hit the county road Pete said, "What was that about argyle socks?"

"Oh," Celine said, "you honestly don't know that one? Your alma mater and all."

Pete shook his head.

"Well, the kid from Arkansas arrives at Harvard and is trying to get his bearings and sees an upperclassman striding across the Yard—wearing argyle socks and smoking a pipe. 'Excuse me,' says the kid very respectfully, 'can you tell me where the library's at?' The upperclassman peers down and haughtily says, 'Young man, at Harvard we do not end our sentences with a preposition.' 'Oh,' says the boy, mortified. 'Let me rephrase that: Where's the library at, *asshole?*'"

Pete's soft chuckle was the best part of the day so far. "I do remember it now," Pete said. "I guess I just wanted to hear you tell it. Speaking of libraries, I think that should be our next stop."

"You're reading my mind again." She licked clean two sticky fingertips. "We need to read a little history and find the *National Geographic*s we are missing. Lamont was in South America a lot, and I have a hunch he was there at just the worst time."

twenty-one

In Red Lodge they decided that they needed more than marshmallows to fuel a research session. Pete knew that if there had been cotton candy it would have rounded things out for Celine. Instead, they were enticed by fourteen Harleys parked along a hitch rail outside a log building called Billy's Crab Shack. The crabs would be very far from their native habitat, but the bikes looked right at home. They were mostly black, three were fully chopped, and four had death skeletons painted on the tanks: two Grim Reapers were in flagrante delicto with buxom naked babes, one skeleton was shooting up, and the last held binocs and looked like he was bird-watching. They pulled in next to the bikes.

Celine was excited. Pete could tell because she unwrapped two sticks of Juicy Fruit. "Look, Pete," she said between chews. "The Boy Scouts are in town." As an artist steeped in the iconography of death who often used skulls and bones, she cast an aficionado's critical eye over the airbrushed art shimmering on the Harleys. "Not anatomically correct," she said.

"The skeletons or the girls?"

"I would say both. Do you think they really have crabs?"

"I hope not," he said simply.

They got out. The clouds were scudding fast and the day was warming and for a moment they were in full sun. Celine stopped on the sidewalk and let the sun soak in for a minute and then they pushed through the batwing doors. It was not like in the movies where every head turned. The bikers were too engaged with the business at hand. Six were shoulder to shoulder at the long bar, which was probably built to accommodate fifteen normally sized humans, three were playing darts under a lobster pot hanging from the ceiling, two were at a pool table in back with two thin biker babes, and three were hoisting one of their leather-vested girls onto a small table where she began to dance to "Free Bird" on the jukebox. Every one had Sons of Silence colors on the back of his leather jacket. A thin-faced local with a gray ponytail was drawing draft beer behind the bar, and a pretty young girl served fish-and-chips in baskets to the dart players. She wore a blue checked short dress with frills at the sleeves, white sneakers, an apron, and she moved with the flitting, hesitant grace of a springbok in a lion pen.

Every head didn't swivel, but every eye did glance at the posh elderly tourists who came through the front door; the eyes, registering neither threat nor opportunity, went back to the party. Celine made a head count in an instant and tallied it against the motorcycles out front. All males accounted for, no one in the bathroom. It was habit. She also saw that she and Pete made about as much of an impression as two flies. Well. But. She would have to ask one of the men what the skeleton was doing with the binoculars.

The place was an odd mix of family lunch spot and bar. The round tables were covered in red checkered vinyl tablecloths and bottles of hot sauce and ketchup, there were fishing nets and lobster buoys and boat hooks on the walls, and Foster's Ale and Budweiser neon blinking in the window. Celine wrinkled her nose. It didn't smell of stale beer like a frat basement, at least, but she thought several of the nice bikers could really use a bath.

The bartender waved them to one of the tables. Celine chose the one closest to the dart players. Thankfully the music was not so loud as to kill the possibility of conversation. Two bearded Sons holding beer mugs watched the third brother throw. One was saying to the other, "Yeah, I went to J.R.'s funeral in Denver. The chaplain stood up in front of two thousand One Percenters, I shit you not, said, 'Every day I thank *Gawd* that today I haven't killed anyone, or maimed anyone, or robbed anyone—and then I get out of *bed!*' "

Laughter. Celine gestured to the round patches of their colors—an eagle spread-winged over a Latin phrase in cursive.

"*Donec Mors Non Separat*, Pete. Pretty much the same as the wedding vow, *Donec mors nos separaverit*. Till death do us part. Something like *Semper fi* is less . . . marital, don't you think?"

"Maybe you shouldn't mention it."

"Humph."

They watched the waitress arrange three baskets on the table by the dart board. She waved at Celine. The bearded bikers smiled and thanked her. She fled. Not fast enough. The tallest, clean-shaven, with a long ponytail and bare arms and spiderweb tattoos at the elbows, reached out with the hand holding the dart and pinched the hem of her dress. He was lightning fast and it stopped her cold. She took another step against the pressure as if not willing to register the grab and Celine saw the cotton stretch flat against her thigh and stomach.

"Not so fast, girl. I said: Did you have *salsa?*"

The girl spun around. She was flushed under her freckles. "I didn't hear you, sorry. There's hot sauce on the table, sir."

Spiderwebs cracked a grin. Two gold teeth flashed. He looked her up and down, sheathed in her twisted dress. He held the hem up between his fingers as if he were pinching a butterfly. Her leg was now exposed to the upper thigh. Celine could see the flower pattern on her underwear. *"Sir,"* he growled. "That makes me feel almost old. Hot sauce ain't salsa." He didn't let go and the girl panicked. Celine could see it in her eyes. She muttered, "Sorry. I think we have some in the kitchen." Celine could read her lips, and the girl's hands went nervously to her hips where she tried to smooth down her tangled dress.

Pete saw his wife's breathing become labored. She pursed her lips. He had carried in the oxygen condenser over his shoulder just in case, and now he turned it on and handed her the tubing. She was annoyed, but her eyes were big the way they were when they were looking for oxygen, and reluctantly she took the cannula and hooked it over her ears. She took two breaths, unhooked the tube, and stood up. Pete did not entreat her to sit back down. Nope, not in his job description. He simply turned the condenser off.

Spiderwebs had balled the hem of the girl's dress into his fist, and she made to twist away. His free hand darted to her open button-collar in a fluid, practiced gesture. He hooked two fingers, covered the little gold crucifix that hung on a thin chain in the notch between her breasts, and he pulled just enough so that she had to take a stumbling half step to him. She looked wild, like a horse in a burning barn.

"Where we going? I ain't in no hurry. Let's talk about condiments. Sauce and the like. You got sauce, I bet. Hot, too."

Celine took one last deep breath and slipped between two wooden chairs. She reached up and tapped Spiderwebs on his shoulder. He jumped. *"Fuck!"* He let go of the girl and wheeled around, fists up, and didn't see anything until he looked down.

"Fuck was *that?"* he said. Across the fingers of one fist, one letter to a digit, was a big blue "FUCK"; across the other "OFF."

"That's very clever," Celine said. "Fingers that make words. Remind me to tell you my tattooed-penis joke."

The waitress took a second to register that she was free, and she gaped at Celine and shot across the floor to the swinging doors that led to the kitchen. Pete saw heads turn now. The Sons at the bar swiveled on their stools. The dancing girl on the table frowned. She had unbuttoned her vest and she was naked underneath.

Without breaking the man's stare, Celine reached for a plastic bottle on the table beside her and held it up. "Salsa," she said. "I guess no one noticed." Spiderwebs unclenched a fist and took the bottle. He blinked. He had zero idea of what to make of this little old lady. Celine could see he was trying to summon his warrior's rage but it had fled him in his confusion. Well, she could bring it back.

"That wasn't very polite," she said. "Do you always grab young women by the dress? Or hair, maybe? Maybe the only way you can ever get them to pay attention?"

The man's mouth closed and his face hardened. His black eyes went opaque. Just like shutters clapping shut, she thought. He was a very tough customer. One of his buddies unplugged the jukebox.

"Granny," he said. "I strongly suggest you sit the fuck back down. That's me being merciful. Big-time." Celine took three steps back. The 26 lay beneath her jacket under her ribs. If she had to draw down on the man, she didn't want to be within his reach. She gauged the distance. She looked around the strange Montana crab shack. Half of the bikers were grinning.

"That's right," said Spiderwebs. "Back off. Be a good granny." And he grinned, flashing the awful gold teeth.

"I think you should apologize," she said. "To the girl. You can do it to me. I will represent my gender." Celine straightened. She looked straight at the man, her eyes very serious, completely devoid of fear. She was very regal.

The space in the bar went taut. Pete heard a faucet behind the bar turn off, heard water dribble in a metal sink. He smelled now the full brew of sweat, unwashed clothes, beer, a lit cigar.

Spiderwebs licked his dry lips. Slowly, as if in a trance, he slipped something out of his leathers pocket—a clip knife, five-inch blade—and he thumbed it open. No hurry, almost savoring the practiced movements. Celine understood that the man was very dangerous.

"Granny," he murmured, "do you want to die? I can help you with that."

The faces of the men watching went to stone. No more big smiles. It was the anticipation of serious blood, or the fact that in three minutes they might all be running from a murder beef in Montana. That would take some fast tactical maneuvering. They were watching and listening with an intensity that was as ferocious as their death's-heads.

Celine did not break his gaze. She licked her own dry lips. Everyone in the bar saw the gesture, tried to read it. "Young man," she said finally, very clear, "I am already dead."

The words hit the assembled watchers like a gust. It was the Samurai creed. The Legionnaires'. Their own. It hit them with a force of recognition: It was uttered with conviction, with simplicity, and with a total lack of fear. In every warrior's heart is an absolute respect for simple courage, and every Son saw it in the woman, and it cut through even Spiderwebs's trance. The knife no longer looked at home in his hand. Celine thought he could go either way.

"Just a minute," she said. Her high cheeks had gone hollow and her eyes were shiny. She held to the back of a chair and breathed. Nobody moved. She nodded to Pete. He switched on the little condenser and handed her the cannula, which she pressed to her nose. She breathed for a full minute, handed it back.

She looked around the room. "I strongly suggest you boys quit smoking while you still have the best of life ahead of you."

It was like letting air from an overinflated tire. Bikers all around the room let out a breath, shook their shaggy heads, murmured "Fuck was *that?*" One or two laughed, awkwardly, but nobody was having fun anymore. The bearded elder touched Spiderwebs on the shoulder and he folded his knife and jerked his head like he was clearing it from a dream. Pete heard somebody say they better saddle up if they were going to make it to Big Timber for happy hour. A giant man with a chevron patch, the sergeant at arms, paid the tab. One by one the Sons of Silence filed out. The jukebox was mute. In the suspended stillness left by their absence Celine and Pa heard the cough and roar of fourteen Harleys thundering to life.

twenty-two

The Red Lodge public library was a new building with a deep porch looking over the river and a bronze grizzly bear looking over the parking lot. Where a young hippie couple was openly smoking pot. The cars parked there seemed to be an even mix of beat-up Subarus and pickups with gun racks—hippies and rednecks, the oil-and-water demographic of many small Western towns.

Pete set up their laptop in a carrel and Celine asked the librarian at the front desk where she might find thirty-year-old *National Geographic*s. The woman wore a turtleneck and turquoise earrings and rimless hexagonal reading glasses. Her long gray hair was in a ponytail. Her blue eyes came up and settled on Celine with a certain recognition, the way one blue heron might look at another in a marsh. She was probably raised in Connecticut. "You know," she said, "I'm old enough to remember when young boys would ask the same question. And they weren't at all interested in tectonic plates or cave paintings."

"Well, I'm actually terribly interested in both of those subjects, how did you know?" Celine said. The woman came from behind the counter— she was wearing Danish clogs—and Celine knew she had an instant ally. "What year?" the librarian said over her shoulder. "Actually," said Celine, "it's five issues. March 1973, January 1974, February 1975, September and October 1977."

There was the spread. He was not in the other magazines, but he had a huge feature in January 1974. Oh, he was good. He was very very good. This was another, later, story on Chile, but this time entirely shot in the Manso River valley in Patagonia. The one Gabriela had mentioned. The place must have made an impression on Lamont the first time around. More shots of *huasos* on horseback in their signature flat hats, the farms along the river linked by horse trails and shrouded in low clouds, women sharing a cup of maté at an outdoor fire, one of a cowboy pushing horses up into the treeless saddle of a mountain pass with nothing but a storm-black sky as backdrop. Stunning. And there he was, Paul Lamont, his picture on the contributors' page, hatless in the sun, handsome and solidly built in a black T-shirt. The short graph said he had spent the entire previous Chilean winter photographing in the Manso valley. That is not the only place he had been, Celine thought. I'd bet my hat. There was no mention at all of the political upheaval in the country that had taken place at the end of September.

She brought the magazine back to Pete who began a search on Chile in the winter and spring

315

(Southern Hemisphere) of 1973. He quickly selected and saved a score of articles. On the morning of September 11th, General Augusto Pinochet ordered an infantry and armor assault on La Moneda, the presidential palace in Santiago. Pinochet would dislodge, once and for all, the socialist government of the democratically elected President Salvador Allende. In the afternoon, when the palace's defenders finally surrendered, the sixty-five-year-old Allende was found dead in the Independence Salon—the official version of events being that he committed suicide with an AK-47 given to him by Fidel Castro. The coup installed a military junta of which Pinochet soon became the sole leader, and he launched one of the darkest periods in the history of any modern nation: a regime of torture, disappearances, and political murders that inflicted tens of thousands of casualties.

The U.S. government had been implicated in laying the groundwork of Allende's overthrow, and a report directed by the National Intelligence Council in 2000 concluded that while the CIA did not "assist Pinochet to assume the presidency," it had "ongoing intelligence-collection relationships with some plotters, and—because the CIA did not discourage the takeover and had sought to instigate a coup in 1970—probably appeared to condone it."

"Appeared to condone it," Celine repeated

dryly. She swiftly scanned the rest of the articles. "Lamont saw something he shouldn't have seen. Or recorded it. Call Gabriela," she said, finally. "I'll call her. We need to know if her father had access to La Moneda. If he ever mentioned it. Jesus." She coughed, loud and long, holding her arm up to her face. Some kids and parents on beanbags in the Kids' Corner looked over.

"Sorry," she breathed. "Will you call her now?"

"What about the ta—"

Celine nodded, her hand still covering her mouth. She caught her breath, barely, and got out, "Maybe ask her to call you back using the phone of a nearby coffee shop. Have her call the library number. Maybe offer them twenty dollars. They couldn't set up a tap—wait, yes they could. Hmm—" She gasped for breath, coughed again. "Look," she said. "The Chile link is the key to this whole thing. He was there. Those rumors about his sideline work. It makes sense. Explains our friend, young Mr. Tanner. *Wow.* Wow, Pete. You couldn't make this stuff up."

Pete smiled. *Wow* is what she said when she was really impressed. She was really impressed. So was he. Pete lay his hand gently on her back and let the convulsions pass. He was used to this. When she could breathe easily again he rubbed her back and said, "Maybe we don't need to call her and put her under more scrutiny, or danger. What more can she tell us now?"

317

Celine breathed. She stood unsteadily and looked over the carrel around the rest of the library. The kids and mothers had gone back to their reading aloud. There was a mountain-man type checking out a book at the desk, an elderly woman carrying some quilting magazines to the counter, and the stoned hippie couple from outside was now on one of the desktop computers at the front of the large open room. That was it.

"I don't get it," she said. "There are no secrets. Not anymore, not by now. Who really cares? Everybody kind of knows what the CIA did down there."

"Maybe not."

She raised an eyebrow. She was swift. Pete could almost hear the finely tuned gears—Swiss watchmaker gears—ticking. She said, "All these stories point to funding for disruption of the socialists, encouragement of the plotters, intelligence. What if there was more? Something even more . . . shameful?"

"More direct," Pete said. "You think Lamont was involved?"

"Seems to be heading that way. Or he was there. He was a *photographer.* He had a *photograph.* I'd bet my hat. Oh, Pete." She sucked in a few more breaths. She was too excited.

"But it's all supposition," she said. "All bits of hearsay, coincidental timing. There must have been thousands of Americans in Chile in the winter of '73, many with reactionary political inclinations."

"Sure," Pete murmured. "But young William Tanner is real. And he seems to have gone dark."

They checked for Tanner on the tracking screen and there was no pulse, nothing. Well. He may have parked in a narrow canyon, or in a structure, underground. It was easy to temporarily lose a signal. They took a walk. Something in the library, maybe a cleaning solvent, was aggravating Celine's breathing, and at this point in their discussions it would be good to clear the air. Take a fresh look. They needed a plan of action and they didn't have one.

They had always found that walking together was an excellent stimulator. Often at home they walked up along the East River, around the River Café, by the old brick spice warehouses, and into the cobbled streets of Dumbo. They'd walk past the little stone beach and up into the Navy Yard and back. Sometimes they'd stop for a thick hot cocoa at the chocolate shop on Water Street. And more times than not these ambles brought them a fresh perspective on a case.

So they walked up Red Lodge's main street, slowly, past Gents Barber Shop, and the Butte Diner, and Faye's Taxidermy, and Ben's Sporting Goods, and they turned right down Elk Street and walked to the banks of Rock Creek. The

319

cottonwoods and alders were every shade of fire-orange and pumpkin and yellow squash. The sky was clearing, showing blue, and sunlight swept the trees of the far bank like wind, and the wind smelled sweet of falling leaves. Celine thought that sometimes it was sheer wonder to be alive. What more could there be than this?

Well. There were great mysteries. Wouldn't it be good to solve at least one?

What they talked about when they talked was the efficacy of any next step. They would have to tread delicately now. Several things were becoming clear: 1) Gabriela's phone had been monitored. 2) Something in her first phone calls with the two of them triggered a break-in. 3) Her file of her own research on her father's disappearance had been taken. 4) A man named William Tanner who was a trained SEAL sniper was following them, and likely not because he was a groupie or wanted to write an approved biography. 5) The official on-site investigation into the disappearance of Paul Lamont was screwy and had been skewed for some reason toward a conclusion of Death by Bear when evidence pointed, possibly, toward other explanations. 6) The man in charge of that investigation, Ranger Tim Farney, had acted uncharacteristically brusque in hastening that conclusion, showing signs of possible outside pressure. 7) Paul Lamont had been in Chile on assignment for *National Geographic* in the winter of 1973. 8) At the end of that winter a U.S.-backed coup, with help from the CIA, toppled a democratically elected government and installed a dictator.

"Let's think of two more, Pete, there must be two more. Wouldn't it be elegant to have an even ten?" Pete's murmur. They walked slowly.

"What is that bird we keep seeing?" Celine said. "Flying back and forth along the bank, lilting like that? He's lovely."

"That's a kingfisher."

"He's very beautiful."

So: 9) Something about Tanner. The man is really disturbing. Oh, of course: He was practically in their faces as he followed them, and then as soon as they turned the tables and began to hunt up information on *him,* he went dark. Just vanished.

"It makes me uneasy."

"Me, too."

10) The sum of all these bits of fact and supposition suggests that someone with substantial resources and power wanted Paul Lamont to stay dead.

They got ice-cream cones at the Big Dipper on Cooper. Pete got a chocolate cone and Celine taught the young staff how to make a Dusty Miller, which she strongly advised they make for themselves, "But be careful, it is highly highly addictive. Enough said!" It was the sundae she and her sisters clamored for every weekend at the beach club on Fishers, named for the low, dusty green plant that spread over the sand dunes. Baboo adored it, too, and allowed herself one a week, and she always got one for Gaga, who pretended indifference. Coffee ice cream, marshmallow sauce, Hershey's chocolate syrup, a generous dusting of malt powder on top. Enough said.

They sat at a picnic table in the shade of a big cottonwood in front of the ice-cream shop and ate. The day had turned almost warm. What Celine loved about fall: You could only depend on it being wildly unpredictable. She was enjoying herself now, greatly.

Perhaps most mothers and grandmothers her age do not like change much, or sudden swerves, or bearded assassins on their tail. Celine loved it all. She pretended that Tanner made her nervous, but Pete knew that she was thrilled. She thrived on it. He was the most immediate challenge and he sharpened her focus. He did not just fall off the map, give up, go home. She could smell him, as she could often smell coming rain and danger and goodness.

"Pretty good," Celine said as she scooped up another spoonful of heaven, dusted in malt. "I bet if we come back in a year it'll be on the menu. And all those kids will be fat."

Pete was serious. He said, "It seems to me that our concern right now should be making sure we're around in a year. I think we are beginning to touch on events and sensitivities that are bigger than Gabriela and her lost father."

Celine frowned. Casual passersby—like the teenage couple walking along the river path—might have thought that Celine was angry. A very glamorous older woman perhaps peeved at the shoddy service in a Podunk dairy stand. Her lips were tight and her eyes were big and her cheeks taut. She breathed heavily. She was not angry. She was steeling herself for a fight, as she had had to do her entire life. She was certainly not going to let this one go. When she took the case, she had nothing to lose. Mimi's extra morphine had beckoned from the gun safe.

Now she had the safety of the girl to think about, and Pete's safety, too. Her husband's course was not yet run, not in the least; she knew he could live out the next two decades happily writing memoirs about life on an island in Maine, and about being a Finder of Missing Persons. She *was* mad, part of her, that anyone would have forced the situation to the point where a father felt he had to abandon his daughter. Danette certainly had something to do with that, and Lamont's self-destructive behavior as a dad, but so probably did larger pressures and circum- stances—Celine felt sure of it. Lamont, she suspected, had gotten himself in too deep and wanted out of it all, and the only way to do that was to die.

But he was not dead. She smelled it on the wind. She did. Just like a scent hound.

"We need to find him," she said. "Now. I want to call Gabriela."

"What about Tanner?"

"Tanner will be Tanner. That's one thing we can be sure—"

The streetlight over their table exploded. The air thinned and cracked—could only be a second bullet. That whanged hard off the steel post. And glass rained. It bounced off the picnic table like bad hail. Shards hit their hats and stuck on their chocolate sauce in glittering sprinkles. Celine was mid-spoonful. Her head jerked up and the spoon dropped to the rough wood—and in her hand as if conjured was the black Glock. It was not the response one would expect from an older woman, or anyone, really. The kids in the open window of the ice-cream shop crouched and gawked at the customer holding the handgun.

"Whoo," murmured Pa. "It's as if he heard us."

"Maybe he did. We'll have to sweep." Her face was hard. "I do not like glass in my Dusty Miller. I like it less than geen."

"Ey-yuh."

"Anyway, I feel safer. If he had wanted to kill us he would have."

"Um, not so sure. That might be the next move."

"Fuck Tanner. I hope he hears me. We better scoot before the police come and make us fill out forms. Life is definitely too short."

Pete let his thudding heart slow down, chewed on the inside of his mouth, and quietly assessed his undaunted wife. So far, she hadn't gotten either of them killed. She squeezed his arm. "I don't think they have any interest in doing real harm to two little old people, do you? It's scare tactics."

"Hmm."

"I just had an idea," she said as she holstered the handgun. "Getting shot at clarifies the mind."

"For me it has more to do with the bladder."

"Remember that artist, Pete, the one in the National Gallery in Santiago, whose painting Lamont photographed in that big feature on Chile? Remember? The one they called a national treasure? She was there. He may have known her. She would have moved in elite circles. I wonder if she is still alive, Pete. If she is, we need to call her. It's a stretch, I know, but we need to place him there."

They shook the glass out of their clothes and drove straight back to Cooke City. They could try to call the artist from the Poli's phone. And there were a couple of Afrikaner refugees they needed to talk to.

twenty-three

There were gaps in Celine's life that Pete had puzzled over and never figured out how to fill. She had skill sets that were not at all ordinary, reactions to crises that were not at all normal, and it was clear that at some point she had undertaken extensive training. He had asked a time or two and had been brushed off. He wondered if it were really any of his business and decided it might be. Then again, maybe not. As a genealogist and a family historian, his yen for research and investigative rigor competed with his congenital modesty and respect for people's privacy. An inner life, he had concluded long ago, was inner because someone had decided they wanted to keep it inside. Respecting someone meant respecting that boundary. Biography, when it was done well, carried with it a sense of that tact. History, on the other hand, was the story of everything that had been exposed. And a wife . . . well. A wife's mystery must at all costs be preserved. Probably.

He was thinking this as Celine navigated the truck to Cooke City. It was the first time they had ever been shot at, and he was wondering where she had gotten the training to draw her gun that fast, and even more impressively, to stay so calm in the face of surprise gunfire. No, even more than that: To come alive. To quicken and harden. He had seen how fast she reacted, rising instead of shrinking, scanning and searching, reckoning angles and cover. He also noticed that her breathing, if anything, got more relaxed, fuller. He could only conclude that *this* kind of crisis made her *happy.* Kind of a marvel. Well.

Hank had told him once about the second time he had seen her shoot. Celine was in Sun Valley helping Mimi die, and Hank had come up from Denver to say goodbye to his aunt. They were driving through Hailey, it was a breezy spring afternoon, and Celine had noticed a cement-block gun shop by the river and asked Hank to pull over. The man behind the counter was wearing a cowboy hat and coveralls, like a rancher who'd been working on his tractor, except that he wasn't working on a motor, he was cleaning a Walther. He had the pieces scattered on a cloth. His expression became more and more intrigued as he watched the petite, genteel city slicker browse the guns and home in on a very large sidearm under the counter.

"May I see that one?" Celine had said, pointing down, her gold bracelet tapping the glass.

"This? This 1911? It's a Colt ma'am, .45 caliber. A gift?"

Celine looked up, smiled at him quizzically. "For me, of course."

He grinned. "It's a little big. I recommend—you might start off with a .22."

Hank had acted out the voices, it was hilarious, and Pete had managed to emit an audible laugh. "Well, I'd just like to see this one," Celine said. "I've never held it." Which was possibly true.

The man shrugged, reached in with a hand like a paw, and with the barrel facing toward the floor released the magazine and set it on the counter and tugged back the slide enough to check the chamber, then handed it to her on two flat palms the way gun dealers do, like a sacrament. He stepped back and watched her with a certain indulgence; he was now ready to be entertained, and he had the courtesy to not cross his arms. Celine picked up the black semiauto, raised an eyebrow at the man, plucked the magazine from the counter, slid it into the base of the grip, and banged it home with the heel of her palm. Then she wrapped the frame with both hands, left over right, slight pressure of the left against the slightly bent right arm, and sighted at the door. Hank saw the man's mouth work to the side like he was probing a sore tooth with his tongue. He could read his thoughts as if they were in a cartoon bubble over his hat: *Hunh, pretty good stance. Must watch a lot of cop shows on TV.*

Celine is really little according to the tape measure. The gun looked huge as she held it. She brought it down. "Heavy," she said.

"Helps with the recoil," he said. She nodded. He said, "Plus I can see the grip's much too big. We could modify it for you."

"Could you?"

He really did look perplexed. And curious. Who the heck was this woman? She could barely lift the damn thing. He touched the frayed sleeve of his coverall and glanced at his watch. "Heck," he said, "already five. I was closing in half an hour anyway. Let's go shoot this thing. Want to?"

That's how they ended up in Dick Roop Jr.'s Bronco, bouncing up a Forest Service road to an arroyo above Hailey. It was a narrow gully shaded by ponderosas. An old log lay against a dirt bank. A fire pit and scattered empties, a favorite party spot. Dick picked up four cans and three bottles and lined them up on the log in no particular order. He walked back about twenty-five feet and held the gun down and said, "Mrs. Watkins? This is how you rack it. Now you hold it down and away like so. Don't want to shoot your pretty toes off." Celine nodded, very attentive and polite. He grinned and pulled the slide. "Here's the safety, you work it with your thumb like so. It's always on until you're ready to fire. You think you can remember that?"

"I'll certainly try, Mr. Roop."

"Now it's going to kick like a mule so make sure your right arm is locked like I saw you do before." He handed her the gun and stepped back. "Try to hit that first can on the left."

Celine took half a step back with her right| foot and half turned and lifted the pistol and wrapped it in her hands and smiled at Mr. Roop. Then she lowered the gun. She pursed her lips and breathed. Hank's gut tightened. He knew she should be using oxygen at this altitude. Well, she was very stubborn.

"Don't be scared," Dick said.

She glanced at him, and only Hank would have seen in the look the slightest shade of annoyance. "I'll try," she said.

Then she lifted her hands swiftly and fired, concatenate echoes, a blizzard of shots, two then three, then one, then one, the slightest of beats between as if she were firing to music, and cans flew into air and bottles broke and sprayed glass and the log was emptied of targets and the echoes rolled down the gully. The last shot sent a can against the cliff into the air. She turned to smile at Dick Roop the Younger, and his expression was priceless. One could not exaggerate or caricature the disbelief. The shock. The perfect awe. He took off his cowboy hat and ran his hand through his thinning hair, and Hank thought his hand shook a little. He spat.

Celine let her lungs get what fill they could of the cool mountain air and stepped over to the man and handed him the gun, and said, "I like it.

Stopping power is what we're after." Big smile. "Yes, please modify the grips, if you would. I'd like to pick it up next week if that's possible. The background check shouldn't take more than a day I wouldn't think."

It took him a moment to find his voice. They bounced back down the dirt track in his Bronco and on the way he stopped calling her Mrs. Watkins and was now calling her Celine.

The story did not surprise Pete, of course, who knew that she went regularly to the range on DeKalb Avenue and every few years up to the Lethal Force Institute in New Hampshire for refresher courses. But responding under live fire is another kettle of fish. Hmph. He noticed as she drove that she checked the side mirrors often.

Cooke City was hopping, there were pickups and rusting SUVs parked up and down Main. They decided to visit the bar first and make their calls later. They parked at the motel and walked slowly across. Blues Night at the Beartooth was their most popular event. The Choke Setters were all the rage in the valley, all the way to Livingston. Celine realized that they were barhopping today, and what a different vibe this one had than the last joint. The place wasn't bursting at the seams, but there were at least twenty-three patrons ranged along the bar and scattered among the tables. Can a blues band be

331

called a trio? Celine didn't know, but there were three of them: a very fat, baby-faced man on bass in loose jeans and a Sara Lee Frozen Dinner T-shirt; a scrawny teenage kid with hair down over his shoulders and a sparse blond beard on lead guitar; and a woman who might have been his mom on drums—young middle age in a business-casual polyester black skirt and hose and an ivory-colored faux-silk blouse. With plastic pearl buttons. Hair to the neck and curled. All the details Celine had trained herself to see. It was maybe the oddest combo she had ever witnessed.

And they rocked. Wow. It took Pa and Celine a moment to surface through the wave of sound and rich smells. *Rich* was one way of putting it. They stood in the door blinking and got their bearings, and the waitress, if that's what she was, waved them to an empty table. She wore a very short skirt and huge hoop earrings and work boots and a crop top and she must have been at least sixty. Well, thought Celine, she is very skinny.

Celine and Pete sat at the table in the corner underneath an open window where the cigarette smoke wasn't too thick. The kid was in the middle of a lead, who knew how long. The fat man bit his lower lip and stared at the ground and seemed to let the bass in his hands live on its own. Live and squirm and thump and thrum, like some giant genius frog that had just jumped into his arms. The mom on drums—just off work, it seemed, from maybe the insurance adjuster's office—kept an arterial backbeat, and the kid . . . well. The kid had come untethered. His own music was breaking the grip of his sneakers on the stage. The notes poured from the guitar and battered at his feet and shins and ankles in a pitiless current and shoved him backward. He would fall over but for the tide of unresolved and flattened fifths keeping him afloat. Extraordinary. Pete wondered if three people had ever, on this sad planet, spilled forth the blues with such conviction. In Montana, go figure.

They almost forgot what they had come for. They both scanned the crowded room for a handsome young man in a trimmed black beard. Celine counted four, but none were Mr. Tanner. When the waitress, who was muscled and corded like jerky, finally came to take their order, they were back on task. They asked for club soda with lime and Celine called out, "Are you Sitka?" The woman had been mid-wheel, balancing a tray of empties, and she caught her own momentum and wheeled back and didn't tip a single longneck. Pretty good. Her hazel eyes flashed with alarm and swept them both, then came back for a closer study—exactly like the spotlight at a prison camp. Apparently she was not placated by what she'd seen because she tensed for a jump and said, "Who's asking?"

Celine motioned the woman to bend down and she put her mouth right against the ear and its big hoop and said, "We're not here for you. Not anything about you. Can you take a ten-minute break?" It would be just like Celine to ask in the middle of Blues Night, but she did not at all wish to wait until the next morning. She was feeling the heat of the chase and if she'd learned anything in investigative work it was that you struck while you had momentum. Because the universe, she came to believe, was composed of currents, just as a river or an ocean. When you wanted to go somewhere, and the cosmos wanted to pull you forward, you jumped. Especially if someone was chasing you.

And of course for Sitka, the sight of this elegant older woman in her fabulous felt jacket and gold scallop earrings inspired too much curiosity to say no. "Just a sec," Sitka said. The band was in the middle of "Stormy Monday": *Lord, and Wednesday's worse, and Thursday's all so bad . . ."* The harried co-owner of the Beartooth slammed the tray on the bar, whipped off her stained apron. She tapped a younger woman in blond dreadlocks, who was drinking beer at a table with four rough men, and handed it to her. Easy as that. The girl shook her head and stood, dropping her unfinished cigarette into a mostly finished beer bottle and tied the apron on. Then Sitka nodded at the two and strode to the front door, grabbing a parka off a hook as she went through.

The night had cleared. There were stars and it was cold and the cold felt bracing and good after the closeness and smoke of the bar. Nobody else was out on the porch for the moment. Sitka sat her butt against the far railing and crossed her arms in the coat and steeled herself. Her cheeks were drawn and her eyes were large and heavily mascaraed. "Okay," she said. "What can I do you?" Again her eyes traveled up and down the genteel older woman.

"We have some questions about Paul Lamont."

At the words the face transformed. For an instant. It was as if the shadow of a large beast had moved fast through the forest behind her eyes.

"Who?"

Celine said, "You know who. We're trying to find him. For his daughter, Gabriela. Who, I'm sure, you will also remember. She told us her father drank here often, with you and your husband, before he went missing. She misses her father terribly. She has never believed he was killed by a bear."

"And who are you?" Mercifully she omitted the *fuck*. Celine listened for a trace of Afrikaner and heard the slightest flattening of the vowels. Barely there.

"We find missing people. On our own. Mostly we reunite birth families. We only take the cases that we feel have merit and we often work pro bono, for free. So mostly we work for people who can't afford an investigator."

"I know what pro bono means."

Celine nodded. "Gabriela went to my alma mater and saw an article about our investigative work in the alumni magazine. She called and asked if we could help her. She is an orphan, as you know, and she has been tortured these last years by the thought that her father might grow old and die without seeing her again. That he might not know his grandson. You can imagine, it's very hard."

The suspicion in Sitka's face softened. No one, probably, on earth, would disbelieve Celine in that moment. Anyone with half a working antenna would know she was speaking the truth. Pete looked on with mild approval, as if he were watching a German shepherd lick a kitten.

"We know that Lamont came into your bar often over the weeks he was here. And it's a long time ago. But we just wondered, well, what he might have talked about when he was drinking at the bar. I know he was gregarious and sometimes voluble."

Sitka dug a soft pack out of her parka pocket and turned her head and lit up, blowing smoke up into the corner of the porch.

"He talked a lot about the bears. The ones he was shooting. How they were much smarter than anyone gave them credit for, how they seemed almost like people at times. The way they cared for their young, the way they dealt with threats . . ." She turned and blew smoke. "He talked about what an asshole Ed Pence was, the bear biologist he was profiling. How he hogged the limelight whenever he could. How he was ambitious. He wanted his own TV show. I think he thought he was the next David Attenborough. Ha!" She coughed. Celine winced. She could hear a kinship in the hack, sisterhood of the scarred lungs.

Celine glanced quickly at Pete. "Anything else?" she said. "Did he talk about going anywhere after? Or for vacation? Or pine for a place?"

Sitka dropped the butt and found the half-crumpled pack again and lit another. Celine had the distinct impression that she and Lamont had been closer somehow than patron and barkeep. Well, he was as charismatic as they come and he was a ladies' man. Sitka half turned against the railing and looked off down the street toward the deep woods and Yellowstone and Barronette Peak outlined against the starry sky. "When he got pissed"—there it was, the South African emerging—"he sometimes said he'd like to go to the Ice Mountain. The one in the fairy tale. I hadn't a clue. He said there was a lake there, the color of his true love's eyes. And a cabin where a man could find himself again." She turned back to Celine and her eyes were wet. "My eyes are sorta brown, aren't they? So I knew this lake, wherever the fuck it was, wasn't going to be brown, was it?" She dropped the half-smoked cigarette and forced a smile. "Anything else?"

"Did he say that the lake sounded like a bird and the mountain was a king?" Celine asked.

Sitka flinched as if burned and looked up quickly. "Yes," she said. "Like that. Just what he said." Celine doubted he had told her that over the sanded wood of the plank bar. Across a pillow more like. Or from the warm plain of her own stomach.

"He said he would take me there. A day's drive. He never did, did he? That it?" she said. "I better get back."

"Yes, thank you." Celine touched the woman's forearm. "Thank you." She was going to beg her to stop smoking, but thought better of it.

"Any time. The club soda's on the house." She sucked in one last long breath of night air and flung the door open and dove back in.

twenty-four

They walked back to the motel. They'd try to locate the artist Fernanda Muños first, and then call Gabriela who, in San Francisco, was an hour behind. No one shot at them and Celine had a feeling no one would. That had been a warning, stark as the clanging of a buoy in the sound.

The buoy. That had tolled each night through the screen of her open window at Las Armas. Singing out the temper of the sea. The thought of that relentless and lovely bell buoy gave her an immediate ache. Of nostalgia and also grief. How many nights had she gone to sleep to its angelus? Feeling that a hole had been torn inside her? She felt again what it was to miss a father. What if someone could have waved a magic wand for *her?* So that they were together again, always?

Celine did not see her father much in the years she attended Brearley. The three sisters went to his apartment on East Seventy-Fourth Street on Christmas afternoons. He sent a driver in a black sedan to their building off Lexington and the sisters piled in the back with their bags of presents. They were not coerced into it, they wanted badly to see their father on Christmas day and they shopped for months to find him the perfect gift. He received a drawersful of ties and tiepins and silver golf-ball markers and cashmere scarves and even wool sweaters over the years. His daughters wanted him to be warm and play great golf, and they wanted him to love them, which he did. He just wasn't very good at showing it.

He was a principled man, which people sensed from the moment he shook their hands, which is one of the reasons he had been so successful in banking. He was also a natural athlete, a superb golfer, a legendary Montauk fisherman. A man's man in every respect. But not much of a little girls' man. He was awkward around his daughters, and they could see the relief coming over him when he said goodbye to them at the town car that took them home. But they also sensed, because they were those kind of girls, that his awkwardness stemmed from deep love, and deep embarrassment that he had abandoned them in their tender childhoods. He could never accept the less than half—far less than half—presence, and he punished himself for not being a complete father, and in doing so, without meaning to, he punished them.

He saw them at Christmas. And he took each one out on their birthdays—took off from work in the afternoon and took them out to the park, the Met, the circus, ice-skating, and then always to a Broadway show in the evening, followed by a very late dinner at Sardi's. At which the girls invariably fell asleep at the table. There were other weekend days scattered here and there, and an occasional trip out to Montauk to go fishing, which Celine adored. Even with such a limited apprenticeship, she and Bobby got pretty good at surf casting.

Celine missed her father. She missed him with an ache that she could feel in her growing bones. She knew, she *knew,* how much he loved her, knew that in a parallel universe he was at home every night and would sweep her up in his arms every time he came through the door, and would teach her again to fly cast in the park, and to sail on Fishers—she'd a million times rather have Harry teach her than the gorgeous Gustav— and she saw him in this parallel life even help her with her math homework and teach her to be a banker. She railed against the circumstances that prevented this from occurring and sometimes cried into her pillow, but she stopped at some point blaming Baboo. She knew in her bones as she knew the other things that Baboo had not been the cause of her bereft childhood.

One day, when she was fourteen, right before she went off to boarding school, Harry took her to lunch at Mortimer's on Lex. It was the first week of September, still hot and summery but with the longer light gleaming nostalgically off the locusts and maples the way it never does in July; she was due to take Amtrak up to Vermont in

341

a few days, for her first term at Putney. They sat on opposite sides of the little table by the front window and talked sparingly and watched the passersby. She was digging into a Dusty Miller with sprinkles and he was watching her with real pleasure, and she was just happy to be soaking up his approval and attention. He was extremely handsome, and she noticed the effect he had on the elegant maître d' and the younger waitresses. He had the bearing of an athlete, and the wonderful Watkins jaw, which Celine inherited, and also the strong hawk's nose that many blue bloods shared. She had inherited that, too. She was not unaware, happily devouring her sundae, that the two looked exactly like father and daughter. And this made her exceedingly proud. They were playing a slow game of How About That One? One of them would point a spoon at an oncoming pedestrian and they would guess 1) what the person did, 2) whether he or she were married or unmarried, and 3) one eccentricity or attribute or achieve-ment. They had developed the game over the years and Celine thought it was a testament to Harry's integrity and his aversion to ever taking the path of least resistance that he didn't seem to play the same game with her sisters.

She slurped an extravagant mix of melted ice cream and chocolate and marshmallow, and pointed her spoon at a woman coming down the sidewalk. The woman was tall—taller in her showy strapped sandals with very high heels—and she walked with the rhythmic hip swing of a metronome, and her nylon or silk summer dress clung lovingly to her flat belly. She was pretty, too, with wonderful auburn hair that spilled in curls to her shoulders, and a wide sensuous mouth. "That one!" she said. Celine had her own opinion, she thought she must be an actress, maybe even a movie star. "How about *that* one?"

Harry turned in his chair and as he did the woman glanced over into the big picture window and their eyes met and her father's face tightened as she'd never seen it tighten before—with alertness, ears coming forward and eyes sharpening exactly like a wolf when it smells prey—and she thought she actually felt a pulse of heat on the air, and the woman's mouth opened in an O, and her eyes widened, and she turned into the front door. A second later she was overwhelming the elegant maître d' with charm, and a second after that the severely dressed hostess was leading the beauty to their table. Celine thought with delight that it looked like a handsome blackbird leading a brilliant tanager. She turned to her father who was not so amused. She had never seen him at a loss. The wolf on the hunt had gone into a defensive crouch. He was master enough of himself that no one but his daughter would have seen it, for his bearing was the same, his uprightness in the chair, his chiseled, reserved expression, the light of recognition in his blue-gray eyes. But there was something. And then the woman thanked the maître d' and chattered out a big "Hello" and leaned down to kiss his cheek and covered his face with her bountiful locks and the whole table with her rich perfume, and she effused that it was so nice to see him, and "Oh, this must be your daughter. Which one is it? Barbara? I should say *Bobby?* How utterly lovely! What a beauty she is going to be when she grows into those legs, *wow!* Why don't you call me, you big lunk? It's been, what? At least a week. The show is running into the second month, it's ghastly, I'm practically worn out. I could use some entertainment of my own!"

Father and daughter stared at her, their beautifully shaped jaws slack and their mouths open. It wasn't so much the fact that Harry had lovers, which Celine must have guessed, or sensed with her infallible nose, but that here in the flesh was a woman who was absorbing, even demanding, his attention, and clearly occupying a space in his life that could have been devoted to her. Celine got to see him every few months and here was some starlet fussing over not seeing him for a week.

The tears sprang unannounced and irrepressible into her eyes and down her cheeks and she excused herself and got up quickly, knocking into the woman who teetered on her heels, and Celine muttered "Powder room" and fled. She could sense her father standing behind her. She stayed in for much longer than anyone ever did who was powdering her nose, and when she washed her face and finally emerged Harry had paid the bill and was standing by the front door with his hat in his hands. His inscrutable mask had returned, the one he used to cover his embarrassment, even his love. They didn't speak once as he walked her home, and she later thought it was a testament to their odd closeness that they didn't need to.

Celine and Pete walked slowly back to the Yellowstone Lodge. The pace belied their excitement. For the first time in their hunt they both felt that they were properly on the scent. That within a very short time they might have their man. If he lived, that is. If they did.

How many ice mountains are there? The one he had spoken and sang of often to Gabriela when she was small was "up by Canada, in the borderlands." Poetic but probably accurate. How many ice mountains by the Canadian border. Well. Glacier National Park was a good place to start. Wherever it was would have to be glaciated, because Lamont told Gabriela in the fairy tale that the Ice Mountain was ice even in the hottest summer. So where were there glaciers? In the park. That made it easy. But. If there really was a cabin where he longed to raise his family, then it could not be on public land, especially not in a national park. On Forest Service land maybe, if it was grandfathered in.

Suddenly they were not tired, not anymore. They were both wide awake. Pete fetched the laptop from the truck. He set it up on the desk–slash–TV stand and pulled out the one chair for Celine. Who had started up her portable oxygen condenser and was letting the flow cool her sinuses while she sat on the bed and cleaned her Glock. She had a superstitious belief that the extra oxygen would empower her brain. O_2 IQ. Pete watched for a minute, surmising his own surmises, and said, "I don't think that would do much good. For this kind of bear."

She looked up and smiled. The condenser growled like a little generator. "Moral support." She did not field strip the handgun but just ran a solvent brush through the bore. Which she'd already done since she'd last shot it. But. It calmed her.

"You think we might need those hunting vests soon?"

"Definitely," she said.

"Shall we try to find Fernanda de Santos Muños?"

"Just a sec." She finished cleaning the barrel, then she touched the action with two drops of military-grade gun oil and racked the slide. One of her favorite sounds in the universe. Reminded her of one thing she was really good at. Everyone needs one of those, she thought. Then she took the plastic cannula off from behind her ears and pressed the Off button on the machine.

It took Pete all of four minutes to log on and find the leading Chilean artist Fernanda Muños's gallery in New York, to learn that she was indeed still alive, that she had had to flee the Pinochet regime, and that she now split her time between New York and Valparaiso. It was the shoulder season and so no telling where she might be. Five more minutes searching their data banks and they had her unlisted home numbers—at an apartment in SoHo and a cottage on the coast in Chile. Pete handed his phone to his wife. "I don't see why we can't make this call from here. For some reason I have one errant bar. Honors? New York first? It'll be almost eleven there. Too late?"

"Maybe better if she is just dozing off." She took the phone and dialed.

twenty-five

Hank drove back from Putney under reefs of black cloud heavy with snow. The walls of trees on either side were nearly leafless and bleak. He prayed the storm would hold off until he got to Hanover, but by Bellows Falls the first wind-driven squalls were flecking his windshield. He felt as clueless as he had before, even more so. Because each of his interviews had yielded more possibilities, rather than less. Not the way an investigation was supposed to work. For all he knew, the woman who smote him—by simply standing in an open door in a flour-dusted apron—could be his sister. Celine had adored Bob Mills, she had mentioned him more than once, one couldn't rule him out. Maybe for the sake of propriety they had raised her as their niece. And the creepy artist: The ambiguous pedantic relationship with his mother was almost a cliché. A perfect setup. Yuck. But the young herdsman, the kid in the barn and milk house—Hank tingled to his image almost as if he were remembering Silas Cooper-Ellis himself, he could almost smell, across the decades, the warmth between the two of them, the gawky empathic girl and the shy and awkward boy— smell a connection the way his mother might have. But. Of course young Cooper-Ellis was dead.

It was not comforting, none of it was. Where there had been no fathers, now there were too many. Fathers upon fathers, marching on his filial landscape, and not a single one forthcoming. He got to Hanover in a full blizzard, and that night he called information in Blue Hill, Maine, and asked for Mills. He didn't know Libby's maiden name, and if the bread-baking woman at the Lower Farm was truly a niece, then there was a 50 percent chance that she was from Bob's side. So Mills it was. The operator asked, "Frank or Harrieta?" On a hunch he said, "Frank" and then made the call. The voice that boomed "Hullo" might have belonged to his old teacher Bob, and he asked quickly if the man was Bob Mills's brother, and he shot back, "Times I wish I weren't, not often." The same gruff chuckle, the same thick down-east accent, and Hank blurted, "Do you have a daughter? Leah?" "Only for thirty-one years. Who's asking?" Hank had no idea what to say. In a great panic, and with almost equal relief, he hung up the phone. He could imagine the old Mainer staring at the receiver in his hand and shaking his head.

Two weeks later he drove over to Sandwich. The cemetery was on a high ridge, woods giving onto big fields, with a view across the valley to Mount Chocorua. It was pretty, as the farmer had said, and lonely, and cold under four inches of fresh powdery snow. Hank walked the headstones, some so eroded and lichen-covered that they would never again reveal their markings, others from the mid-eighteenth century still barely readable. After a few minutes he found the family Cooper-Ellis, three simple granite stones, the smallest belonging to Silas Henry. DECEMBER 5TH, 1931—JANUARY 29TH, 1951. MEN'S DOINGS ARE SMALL, GOD'S GLORY GREAT.

Nineteen years old. He died midway through Celine's senior year. Had they stayed close? The old farmer had said that the shy boy had been in Korea two weeks. Why did it hit Hank so hard? The epitaph was as eloquent in what it left out: no "In loving memory," no "Beloved son." He took off his gloves and brushed the night's snow off the top of the stone with his bare hands and then he surprised himself. It was as if grief had just touched him on the shoulder and he cried.

An hour later he stepped into the tiny post office on the tiny square and asked the postmaster if he knew any Cooper-Ellis still extant and the man shook his head. He wasn't much older than Hank. Hank asked him who was the oldest old-timer still in town. Dottie Caulkins, must be ninety-plus. He got directions, and a mile from town, in a dark pine wood beside a black-water creek that was not yet frozen, he knocked on the door of a run-down farmhouse with an ancient and rusted log skidder parked to the side. The house had once been white and the skidder yellow,

350

and they were both weathered now to almost the same nameless dun. She came to the door on the fifth knock. She held a bent-handled cane and did not invite him in.

"Cooper-Ellis?" she said in a strong, frayed voice. "I knew 'em all." Nothing about the way she said it betrayed good nor bad.

"Are there any relatives still—"

"Alive?" She actually laughed. "Alive is all anybody cares about. Might be overrated." The laugh again. It occurred to Hank that she might be crazy—with years, with watching so many things pass.

She took a tissue from a pocket on her dressing gown and dabbed the corners of her eyes. "No, they ain't. Not any I know about. The boy died— in the war—then the parents died. Stove fire they said."

"The house?"

"Gone. Gone gone gone. Where Dr. Dixon lives now with that pretty wife."

"Did the boy, the boy Silas—"

"Died in the war."

"Yes. Did he have a . . . a child?"

"A *child?* He died in the war. How could he have a *child?* Don't you remember a thing? If he saw a girl a half mile away he'd run the other way. The boy never said a word. Not a damn word."

Hank thanked her and she slammed the door.

For the next two years, while he was still in

New Hampshire, he drove over and visited Sandwich and the cemetery maybe half a dozen times. He never found out anything he could ever use in connecting Silas to his mother, but he liked walking the dirt road along the stone wall above the big field, and for some reason he liked visiting Silas's grave. He'd sit and speak about whatever was on his mind, and if it was summer he'd often stay to watch the swallows hunt in the long light of the late afternoon.

Fernanda Muños was not at home in New York. Or she did not answer her phone. Nor did she pick up at the number they had in Valparaiso. Dead end, for now. Celine sat on the bed. She did not look frustrated. She pursed her lips and dialed the New York number again. This time an answer.

A sleepy voice said, "*Bueno*?"

"Hello, Señora Muños? My name is Celine Watkins. I am an artist, just about your age, and I am also a private eye . . ."

Safe to say that in the richly colored life of Fernanda de Santos, she had never heard an introduction like this before. She was not put off. Even through a phone line, one could tell immediately that Celine Watkins had heft: She was not going to waste your time. The two chatted for almost fifteen minutes. The conversation might have concluded sooner, except that Fernanda sometimes lapsed into Spanish. She said, "Yes, I remember Paul Lamont. Who wouldn't? The famous photographer from *National Geographic.* He was brilliant. But even so, even then, if he had not been so good . . . *Pues—todavia el nos hubiera encantado.* Even Allende."

"You mean that he came to the palace? The presidential palace."

"Yes, he came to some of the parties. It was not unusual. Many illustrious visitors came. All the embassies invited whomever was in town."

"My God," Celine whispered. She coughed once, cleared her throat. "Excuse me. You say you fled the country *before* the coup?"

"An anteater could have seen what was coming. You know I did a large and rather famous Chilean *Guernica.* This was an echoing of the disgust with Franco, with all fascists. My affiliations were well known. No, I was not at all popular with the generals."

"Wow," Celine murmured to herself. And to Señora Muños: "This is hugely helpful. Thank you so much."

Pete had learned that the hotter the chase became, the more his wife's mind clarified, like warming butter. Now she seemed dazed. "He was there," she said. Her voice was husky. "Lamont. He was a great charmer, greater even than we had imagined. He charmed himself right into the

353

presidential palace." It occurred to Pete that the case had become personal. They all were, to an extent. But this one had become more so; it had had a certain charge right from the beginning, and the Quiet American now understood that Lamont may have been as charming, and as prodigal, as Harry Watkins.

She coughed. She patted her mouth with a Kleenex and straightened. "There is a photograph, Pete. What all this is about. I know. Now we have to call Gabriela. We'll use the phone in the motel office."

The owner of the Yellowstone Lodge was home. He had a gray beard to his sternum and rivaled Pete in volubility. Not much could impress him or ever would. Celine got the impression that when the Grim Reaper showed up with his scythe the proprietor would show him to one of the rooms with a moose print and tell him to cool his bony heels. He waved them to a phone.

Celine had a strong hunch and she was eager to test it. From what she was learning of Lamont, of how his mind worked, she was certain that he would place the two most important photographs of his life in the same frame. The one, of the darkest thing he had ever witnessed; the other, of the greatest love he had ever known, and lost. There was a weird and awful logic there that Celine, who coupled death and

354

beauty in her own art, could appreciate. She would have bet a significant sum. When Gabriela answered, she was brisk. "Remember how your dad would give you pictures of Amana? How he'd slip the one picture behind another?" she said. "I want you to check the one on the ferry, your favorite. Open the frame. And call me back in five minutes at Poli's Restaurant." She hung up. They walked across the street. Celine walked fast and her breathing was clear. The phone rang as soon as they got to the counter.

"I—I have it." Gabriela's voice shook. "Christ."

"Listen, Gabriela, we don't have long. It's a body."

"Yes."

"There's a man beside it?"

"Two . . . two men." The girl was holding it together, barely. Good.

"One looks familiar," Celine said.

"Yes. Oh, God. Younger, young, but. Vice pres—"

"Makes sense. The other?"

"I don't know. Latin. A soldier. Wait . . . there's something here—"

"What? What is it?"

"On the back, something written. It's Pop's hand. Hold on." Slowly she made it out: "It says, Francisco Peña de la Cruz, La Moneda."

"La Moneda is the presidential palace. That would have been the day of the coup."

"Who is he?"

"I don't know, we'll find out. Jesus. Right. Okay. Take your son now. Right now. Is he—"

"He's here, he's here." Gabriela's voice sounded strong and clear again. A bit afraid, but excited, too. That's my girl, Celine thought. This is one to ride the river with.

"Okay, don't pack a bag. This is just for a couple of days, I promise you. I want you to get in your car now and drive. Not to a friend or relative. Take the, the Thing. Park at a bus stop, take a city bus, then another, and change again. Leave the Thing at a random business to hold for a few days. Tell them it's your husband's fortieth birthday and you are going to pull a prank and surprise him, give them some money. Get to a suburb and—"

"I get the idea. Got it."

"Okay, go. Call me in three days."

Had either Celine or Pete thought to hit the stopwatch function on their watches they would have learned that searching for information on Francisco Peña de la Cruz and nearly finding the fantasy hideaway of fairy tales took them exactly seven minutes. *The New York Times* reported that in the chaos of the coup, Peña de la Cruz, the minister of finance, had gone missing. The first prominent casualty in the ugly history of the Disappeared. Well, he had just been found again, murdered with the help of someone very familiar to all Americans. As for Lamont's hideaway—how many ice mountains are there?

They asked the question and the National Park Service's EagleView satellite site told them. A handful. Not mountains but glaciers, glaciers hanging against mountains, and there were only a dozen that would be noticeable from outside the park, and only a handful from the east side. The east side it would have to be, because on the west were the remote lakes and woods of the Flathead National Forest, most of which was not accessible by road. They studied the east side of Glacier, above Babb, Montana, and there was a smattering of black lakes. They would have to be green, the color of Amana's eyes. Many of the glacial lakes high up in the basins were shades of blue and green, but they were in the park. Poor Sitka. So outside the park it was, east side, and there were not too many lakes and ponds to count and there, *there,* was one called Goose and one called Duck, and they were *green.* Well, greenish. *Sounds like a bird.* And when they zoomed in, what was the most prominent peak? Chief Mountain. A great monadnock of a flattop, mesa-like, rugged and standing alone. Everything about it spoke of Paul Lamont. And it was almost on the Canadian border.

Celine sniffed. It smelled too easy, but maybe not. It couldn't all fit together that snugly. But:

Sitka did say that he had told her his cabin was a day's drive. North would make sense. The area was right. Also there were a few snags: The first was that the mountain itself was not of ice. In the winter, in the late fall and early spring it would be snowy and icy, but it had no permanent glaciers. Still. Celine's antennae hummed, her nose wrinkled, her gut fluttered. There would be big glaciers visible from the lakes, and there was Chief Mountain near the border. She saw the lone wolf of a peak, the borderland rock pile, and knew. So they zoomed down close to Goose Lake and there were tiny clearings and a dozen structures on the east and south sides and four dirt tracks twisting down from the county road. Duck Lake had another handful of cabins and three more roads. That was problem number two: If one of these were the lake—and it would be just like Lamont to send a hunter on a wild "goose" chase—even if this was the spot, or spots, they could spend a day running between houses, and Lamont would have friends who would warn him. All the successful fugitives in recent history had local help, every one. They needed to know the exact cabin and they needed to go there, directly, in one shot.

"Pete?" Celine said. "How can we know? This might not even be the right county."

Pete hummed. He enjoyed the tactical problem.

"We need a dog," he said.

"A dog, Pete?"

"How do you hunt grouse?"

"I have no earthly idea how one hunts grouse. Did you hunt grouse, Pete? In Maine? In your Norman Rockwell youth?"

"Ey-yuh," Pete said.

"Should have known. Well?"

"A pointer is best, some use a flusher. You get the dog started in the right direction. You have an idea of the best meadow, the ridge, you've been watching all fall. So you get the dog started, you jump-start him, so to speak, you push him into a clearing and—he takes you right to Mr. Grouse. Points right at him or flushes him out."

"Tanner! Woof! I have been thinking along the same lines, you know."

He knew. Pete's lower cheek tightened. It was barely visible. He tipped up his chin.

Neither of them was sleepy. They were amped. They had paid for the night but they had their house on their back so they loaded up, found a few inches of burned coffee in the Perpetual Pot in the motel office and poured it into their Mama and Papa Grizzly travel cups, and drove. They had been wrong from the start: Tanner knew where Lamont was, had known all along, that was clear. The hunter's bosses could not help but know since the beginning. After all, these were no fools, it would be a lethal mistake to think so. And as long as Lamont was a good boy and stayed dead, well—no harm, no foul. They wouldn't take him off the board and risk triggering the release of the photo or photos. Because Lamont would have been canny enough to set that up. It was all falling into place. But if they jumped, if Pete and Celine drove directly to Lamont's woods, that would be a different story. The shadow squad would have no choice but to beat them there and get Lamont out of the picture, one way or another. So. Jump-start the dog, follow him to the bird. Simple. Maybe.

They drove. Celine at the wheel and Pete with the GPS tracker screen plugged into the cigarette lighter and resting in his lap. And with Tanner's own tracker attached to the frame of their truck. Celine, Pete noticed, was wide awake, more awake than she'd been in the last two years. Her breathing was clear and easy and she drove fast, with the focused confidence of a rally driver. A marvel to behold. They pushed the truck up through Bozeman to Helena where they pulled over at the parking lot of the municipal airport. And here came the blue pulse of their pursuer. Here came the dog running after. They were sure he would overtake them, bound past. But just in case, they would sleep in shifts, Celine with the Glock at her right hand, Pete with the twelve-gauge racked on the bench seat. The timing would have to be perfect or someone, probably Lamont, might die.

Tanner passed them on Interstate 15 at 5:14 a.m. Celine was on watch and she shook awake a snoring Pete. They could see their breath as Pete lowered the pop top and there was new snow dusting the mountains and high passes above town. The lawns and roofs of Helena were covered in a hard frost. They wanted to be close but not too close. If they got on Tanner too early, he might just stop and confront them. A fight would not lead them to Lamont. But if they were too far behind, Tanner might have time to get to Lamont and remove him, one way or another. It was dicey.

After they dropped the top of the camper, and before they climbed into the front seat, Pete said, "We know we've got his tracker on the frame. No reason to lose it, is there?"

"Better not. We need to keep pushing him."

"Ey-yuh," Pete said.

They ate eggs and bacon at the No Sweat Café downtown, joining the dawn patrol of construction workers and loggers, and Celine ate with relish and they barely spoke. Pete chewed his lip and said, "Did it ever occur to you that if we get that close, Tanner could take *us*?"

"Pete, that's so maudlin."

"Seriously. His M.O. seems to be Ambush."

"I've been thinking about it. I don't feel particularly at risk. I said it before: The agency, or whoever it is, wouldn't risk the murder of two

361

elderly investigators. Heavens. Too many loose ends, certainly. He will try to put us off one more time, and then he will go after Lamont."

Pete nodded, but he didn't look convinced.

He propped the tracker screen in his lap and they drove north, through Wolf Creek and Choteau. They crossed the Sun River and the Teton and drove along the east flank of the Bob Marshall Wilderness. The season had turned: The swaths of aspen on the shoulders of the mountains were yellow and in the windless hours of the morning single leaves spun straight to the ground. They drove with their windows half open, relishing the smells of autumn. They entered the Blackfeet Reservation and turned west at Browning and followed the South Fork of Cut Bank Creek upstream. The sharp rock peaks of Glacier National Park loomed to the west, their flanks swathed in new snow. Something about these first touches of winter: The high ledges were limned in ice, the gullies etched, the hanging glaciers dazzled. Reefs of cloud stood off to the west behind the peaks, but the sky above them was lens clear. Celine drove with a lead foot and they got to Babb by late morning, twenty minutes behind Tanner.

Babb, Montana, is a café, a gas station, and half a dozen low houses along Route 89. They passed the airport, which was a grass strip covered in grazing cattle, and they passed a liquor store and a few hunters' pickups with four-wheelers in the beds. They did not stop. Pete was calling the turns and cross-referencing with the topo maps in their gazetteer. Just past the town, Tanner turned east on a dirt road and they passed a mud-green lake on their right, they could see it through the trees—Duck Lake—and they continued on. They drove for a mile. The road forked, and they passed another, smaller lake— Goose. Tanner drove along the east side of it and—forked right again. Drove right past it.

"I'll be damned," murmured Pete.

Now there was only one way to go, one two-mile-long drive to one cabin on the south edge of a much smaller lake. They did not speak. The road got rough, and then it turned into a four-wheel track, just worn tire ruts on grass and weeds. It ran through pine woods, big spruce. A rougher trail, choked with brush and barely wide enough for a truck, forked to the north and Tanner had turned off there and followed a drainage a quarter-mile and stopped. Good. What you'd expect. A half mile farther and three large boulders blocked the track. Whoever lived up here didn't need a No Trespassing sign, there was no way through.

"I make it out to be about a mile and half more," Pete said, looking at the map. Celine chewed her lip.

"I guess it's time to use the hunting vests. We

don't want to get shot by Mr. Lamont. If that's him." She nodded at the boulders. "Something about the whole setup tells me it is."

"I don't think hunting season starts for a few weeks. Big game, that is. Are we going to take the shotgun?"

"You are," Celine said. "I just don't feel comfortable with anything but a high-powered rifle."

"Are we going to load them?"

Celine stared at her husband with the incredulity she sometimes felt sharing her life with a man who grew up in Maine. It wasn't that he was simple—well, yes, he was. Brilliant *and* simple.

"What good is a gun if you don't *load* it, Pete? Heavens."

They got dressed fast—bright orange hunting vests and hats. Pete wore the neon baseball cap; Celine insisted on wearing the goofy Elmer Fudd thing with the earflaps. "Goofier I look, the better," she said, admiring herself in her powder compact. She put on a small belt pack with a pint water bottle, handed one to Pete who shook his head. They slid the guns out of their Cordura cases and Celine levered the action and thumbed the bullets down into the rotating magazine of the Savage 99. She pressed the top bullet back into the mag and slid one more into the chamber. Nobody used lever-action hunting rifles anymore, but she liked it—the feel, and the nod to the past. The safety was on the tang and she thumbed it back. Locked and loaded. Pete, who had grown up with shotguns, fed five shells of double-ought buckshot into the side-loading magazine of the Winchester Marine, pumped the action once, thumbed one more shell into the gate, and pushed the safety button on the trigger guard over to On. Ready. The day had warmed enough that they didn't need gloves. They shut the camper door but didn't lock it. They glanced at each other once, in the way only an old couple can who is about to embark on something risky but important.

"You feel okay?" Pete said.

Celine gave him a thumbs-up. "I feel really good today. Will you remind me later to pick up that little skull just next to the tire there? Must be a rabbit or something, I'd like to use it in a piece."

Pete nodded and they started walking slowly up the track.

They trod in sun and shadow. In and out of it. Slowly. The patches of sunlight were nearly hot, the shade cold. They crunched over old pine needles and they could no longer see their breaths. It felt good to walk. Celine thought the scoped rifle was heavy but she insisted on carrying it. The track was not much more than a path through mostly pines, a game trail, but it was smooth enough.

They had walked about fifteen minutes when they heard a clattering in the woods off to their right. They both turned and a bull elk broke across the trail not twenty feet off. Huge rack. Startled. All three of them. Pete jerked and stepped back, Celine spun to the side and the air split. Crack and boom together and the trunk of the big fir tree beside her splintered. She dropped. Reached out her free hand and pulled Pete down into brown grass and sweet sage. Jesus. They hit the ground. That was no warning, that was a kill shot. Meant to be. She was breathing hard. *Stay,* she commanded.

She went to one knee and brought up the gun and her left forearm slipped instinctively into the leather sling and twisted it taut; her left hand gripped the checkered forearm, and her right thumb punched the safety as her eye came to the scope. The figure was moving fast, running in closer for a finishing shot, a single shooter. She found him with her open left eye and swung. He would have underestimated the elderly lady in the Elmer Fudd hat. He shouldn't have. With complete calm Celine tracked and led the green blur like a loping deer, and fired. He dropped. Without thought she levered the action again, letting the spent brass fly into the dirt, and stood.

"Stay!" she commanded Pete. She moved. When she had to, she could move pretty fast. It taxed her lungs but she could do it. Something about adrenaline cleared the airways. She untwisted her arm from the sling and went. Fast into the dark of the trees where there was no trail and it didn't take long. He was maybe only a hundred feet away. He was sprawled on a duff of pine needles, splayed, his hand scrabbling back for his rifle and a bloom of blood on his right shoulder.

"Don't!" she commanded simply. One word. He didn't. "Where's your backup piece?" He shook his head.

Tanner did not look the same. His ice gray eyes held fear.

"No backup?" Shook his head, watched her, cornered and bleeding.

"You underestimate me." No response, his head very still, watching her. "Big mistake."

She stepped forward so that she was above him but not close enough that he could make a grab. She had the rifle pointed straight at his gut. Her finger was on the trigger. "Safety's off," she said. "If you're lying and you have a backup and go for it, you're a dead man." He nodded. She could see through the pines to the east a swampy clearing, a perfect place for moose. Probably where the elk had been when he startled it. "Where's the sat phone?" He blinked.

"You don't need the oxygen," he croaked, his eyes staying on her face.

"I need it sometimes."

"Where'd you—"

"Learn to shoot like that? Clearly your research was incomplete."

"Jesus." His voice sounded like a draft wind coming through dry twigs.

"The phone?" she repeated. He motioned his chin down to his hip. His eyes were wary and scared.

"Okay," she said. "First thing, you take this stupid hat and make a compress. Then take my beautiful silk scarf and here—" Still covering him, with one hand she deftly tugged free her red scarf and doubled and looped it and tossed it to him. "Put your arm through, yes, and pull it tight. A half hitch. There." He did.

"So sad," she said. "That's Armani."

He stared at her, wary, his eyes like a hundred miles of Arctic ice, but something moved in them. A question.

"No, I am not going to finish you. I meant to. I missed, thank God. You have a kid at home, don't you?"

He nodded, barely. "One I bet. I bet it's a little girl." Suspicious nod. "Well, you better go back to her. We wouldn't want another little girl to grow up without a father."

He stared at her.

"Bill?" He blinked hard. "You're going to call in your support now. There's a clearing through there, you saw it, I bet it's where you parked your truck. Big enough for a chopper. Call it in. You'll be in the ER quicker that way than if we called the olunteer ambulance. By the look of Babb that could take a while."

He hesitated, nodded once.

"You can get to the clearing, right?"

He nodded.

"And this is what you're going to tell your people." He stared. "Listen: Tell them it ends here. Lamont stays dead. The secret about Chile"—he blinked—"just tell them: The secret about the coup stays secret. But—get this very clearly, please—if any harm at all comes to Lamont, or his daughter, Gabriela, or her son, or to me, or to Pete, or my Hank, the photos go to the press. *New York Times*, *Washington Post*, etc. It's all set up, all it takes is the trigger. Otherwise it goes nowhere, everybody moves on. Got that?"

He nodded.

"You all have bigger things to worry about right now, is my guess. We better hope everyone lives long and natural lives. Now sit up. I'm not afraid of you anymore. They will surely kill you if you trigger the release of those pictures." She leaned her rifle against a pine and knelt by the bleeding man and helped him sit up. She got behind him and undid the knot in the scarf and undoubled it and wound it expertly several times over the folded orange cap and his shoulder, and under his armpit, and snugged it very tight. He winced and flinched hard but did not cry out. "There. Better," she said. She tugged the half-quart water bottle out of its sleeve on her belt. "Here." He took it. She noticed his hands were scarred and very strong. Who knew what they had wrought in the world. He tipped up the bottle and squirted half into his mouth. Nodded once.

"You need help getting to the clearing?" He shook his head. Slowly he got to his knees. She stepped to the tree and picked up her rifle. He reached over for his, which lay where he'd dropped it on the pine needles. "*Uh-uh,* Tanner," Celine said, bringing her rifle up. His head came up fast, whether from the sound of his last name or the curt warning. "You'd better leave that. That stays. I've always wanted one of those. It's an M24, isn't it? .308." On his knees he stared at her. He looked like a man who wasn't sure if he were in a bad dream from which he'd soon wake.

"From now on be careful who you call ma'am," she said. "Get going."

She slung his rifle, which was surprisingly light. Kevlar stock. Lovely. And she watched William Tanner walk slowly through the trees, watched him unshuck his satellite phone and bring it to his ear.

twenty-six

Celine made it back to the trail. Pete was there, standing in the shade and looking shaken. She never thought of him as an old man. He was just a few years older than she was, after all, and he was game and had a lively mind and his body still bore the temper and memory of a high-school athlete and farmhand. But she thought as she came out of the trees that he looked old. Something a bit frightened and tentative hovered around him as he stood there in his bright orange hat. Well. Anyone at any age would've been frightened by getting shot at—by a SEAL sniper. The only thing that had saved their bacon was getting startled by an elk. See? she thought. Jumping with fright can have its upside.

Pa looked deeply thoughtful as he watched her come and he held his shotgun at port arms. "I can't believe what just happened," he said as she unslung the M24. It really was a gorgeous rifle.

"You can't?" she said, catching her breath.

"You used your favorite Armani scarf as a bandage."

Her head came around. He didn't seem old anymore. He smiled.

"You saw that? You were watching?"

"Do you kind of fake the emphysema for

371

effect?" he said. "Or sympathy?" Pete's expressions fell into no categories of common usage. "I'm also getting the feeling again that you've had special training in a part of your life I know absolutely nothing about. Not yet." Yes, he wore a half smile, and yes, he seemed deeply amused, an amusement touched strongly with irony, and yes, his eyes were loving and tolerant, also bemused, even concerned. Maybe even a little confused. Well, one just had to let Pete be Pete.

"You had my back," she said. "You were right there. And you were so stealthy the trained professionals didn't notice. Wow." She stood on her toes and straightened his cap. "Let's go visit Paul Lamont. It's a long shot, I know, but I keep being reassured." She tucked some loose hair behind her ear. "Hank's wondrous hat, damn. I just gave it away. Just a sec, my beret's on the front seat." She squeezed his arm and picked up the old and trusty lever-action hunting rifle.

They followed the track for twenty-five minutes and came to the edge of a clearing. The clearing was tall faded wheatgrass and rabbitbrush and sage. A light wind rippled through the grass and in the warming early afternoon they could smell the sagebrush. Also woodsmoke. No sounds but the breeze and the pulse of crickets. A copse of blue spruce and lodgepole pines protected a small cabin and behind the cabin was a small green lake. Green as his true love's eyes. And beyond the lake, west, was the stone and ice ridge of Many Glacier rising out of the trees. There, northwest, was the mesa-topped monadnock of Chief Mountain. It dominated the horizon. They knew from the map that there, too, was the Canadian border. A good spot for a fugitive if ever there was one—if he was in good shape he could find a game trail and trot across the border in a few hours, all in the cover of deep woods. Someone must be home—a thread of pale smoke rose from a stovepipe in the roof.

Celine murmured, "Goose Lake. Sounds like a bird. But one step past it. A crafty SOB." Pete nodded. "Happy hunting," she said. And they stepped out of the deep shade of the trees.

They split up and walked over the open ground just the way two old hunters would: Walked slowly, careful not to twist an ankle, stopping every few steps to sniff the air and scan for elk or deer. And walking on. With their guns and orange vests and apparent age they could be nothing else. They had covered almost half of the two hundred yard meadow when they saw the cabin door open and a man stepped onto the porch and he was studying them with large military binoculars. They stopped and watched him, too. Then Celine raised her arm like a squadron leader and the two continued forward slowly. And the man stepped back into the darkened doorway and came out again holding a rifle. Each step in the sequence was done without haste and in silence. Also without haste the man raised the scoped rifle and leveled it at them. Well. Seemed like a day for getting shot at. Must be how every deer and elk in the county will feel in a month.

They stopped, glanced at each other, Celine frowned and nodded and they stepped forward. Celine waved at the man: an elderly hunter from away encountering an ornery native, trying to be polite. No shot, so they stepped forward again. They continued walking. The man, evidently, would let them live, and walk, until they got within hailing range.

And—just then Celine heard the thwop of a distant chopper. More like a stuttered pressure wave coming through the nearly still air. A beating of pressure in the ears and then the true drumming of the blades and they saw the man's rifle come up to the sky over their heads as he scoped the new threat and they both turned and saw the black Robinson 66 coming fast and low over the ridge and trees. Maybe two miles from them, less, it came around hard in a clockwise bank and hovered. Right over the swampy meadow. Loud now, even at that distance. The bird rocked on air just over the treetops, and then it settled down out of sight and the throbbing dropped an octave; a few seconds later they heard another roar, the ramping up, and the chopper was over the trees and rising. William Tanner did not take long to load. The helicopter had barely cleared the tallest spruce when it tipped and banked and the tail rose and it accelerated straight toward the ridge and maybe Helena. Celine hoped so. Helena and not some black site, the man needed medical attention. She hoped he wouldn't get demoted because he'd gotten bested by a silver fox.

They turned back to the cabin. The barrel of the rifle and the scope above it were aimed straight at Celine. Well, she carried the .308.

They walked on. What else could they do? When they were less than thirty yards the man took his left hand from the forearm and raised it: *Far enough.* He looked through the scope, his face half obscured, but she could see a taut sunburned cheek, a gray stubble on chin, a dark eyebrow, shaggy hair—light brown going to gray. A blue Oxford shirt, untucked, patched, stained. Loose khakis, also stained with sap and oil, hems and pockets frayed. No hat.

"That's it," the man called. "There." His voice was resonant but cracked, sonorous, the voice of a man who could probably sing—maybe a mountain tenor—but who hadn't spoken in a long while.

"Lay the guns on the ground," he called.

"Beg your pardon," Celine objected.

At the sound of her voice the man flinched. He looked up over his scope and blinked and she saw that his eyes were a deep brown. Not hazel, not black. Large, still shiny, impressionable. The eyes of a man who took in the world as image—image sufficient unto itself and mysterious, and in a constant state of composition.

"Hunting season isn't for a few weeks, last time I checked." The voice again. Cracked and even now charming, that frayed resonance charismatic men often carry. "What the hell was *that?*" He motioned the barrel toward the horizon, where the chopper had vanished.

Celine set down her rifle and dusted her hands together. "We're from New York," she said, as if that explained it. "And we've come to see where the Princess of Ice Mountain might want to live with her father, the King."

Paul Lamont reeled back. He lowered the gun and let it fall against the logs of the wall and his hands went to either side of his head. He stood rooted to the porch.

"Celine Watkins," she called. "My husband Pete. We come straight from your daughter, Gabriela."

twenty-seven

Lamont made coffee. He had not had a visitor in twenty-three years so his social graces were rusty: He pulled out a pine chair for Celine at the rough table. The only chair, she noticed. The cabin was log, one room, neat, the plank floor swept, and two jackets—a canvas Carhartt zip-up and a Gore-Tex raincoat—hung on hooks by the door. Shirts and pants and wool sweaters, all old and patched or faded, were folded in wooden egg crates against one wall. A single bed against another wall, under a four-pane window on a side hinge. On the sill of the window, two books. She could read the spines: *Poems of the Masters* translated by Red Pine, *The Great Fires* by Jack Gilbert.

She counted two Aladdin kerosene lamps, and candles stuck to saucers on the windowsills. A very old sheet-metal sheepherder's woodstove in the northwest corner. Two cast-iron frying pans hung on nails in the wall above the stove, and two stainless cook pots. An orange-bodied STIHL chain saw rested on the floor by the front door. Lamont knocked the handle of the woodstove and let the door swing open. He tossed in a couple of chunks of firewood and latched it and ladled water from a five-gallon plastic pickle bucket into the smallest pot and spooned in a pile of coffee grounds from a red tin of Folgers and set it on the stove. Cowboy coffee. He didn't look at them. "Just a sec," he said without meeting their eyes and went out the door. He carried in a pine stump, tall enough to sit on; thudded it down on the floor. Went back out for another. "There. Please." He motioned to Pete.

He concentrated on the coffee and did not say another word. Celine watched him. His whole life must have been boiling up in his mind, his heart, just as the coffee would in a couple of minutes—boil and rise, and the crust of grounds would crack open and the water would bubble through.

When it did boil, he knocked the pot twice with a spoon and sprinkled in eggshell from a bowl. Must be a chicken coop out back. In no hurry, he let the grains settle. A steel sink stood against the back wall. Upside down against the rim of the sink was a chipped coffee cup with a pink Disney World castle. Something about it made Celine wince. He turned it over. On a plank shelf were three jelly jars. He brought two down. Poured the coffee and handed Celine the palace mug. "You," she said. "I'll take the jar." He nodded. Brought down a glass sugar bowl from the same shelf. One spoon.

He sat on the stump. Celine studied him. The tautness in his cheeks was ascetic. He ate lean, lived lean, clearly kept his thoughts lean. An acolyte to past mistakes. His lips were cracked with sun and they quivered just a little as he stirred a heaping spoonful of sugar into his coffee. His one indulgence, she guessed. He was still very handsome. His eyelashes were long, his eyes clear if a little bloodshot, his graying sandy hair down over his collar, which hung loosely and revealed a welted scar running from his left ear to his collarbone. She reminded herself that she did not like this man. He was weak, and he had abandoned his only daughter horribly—and twice. She thought again of the tiny girl standing on a stepstool meant to help children brush their teeth—standing on it and cooking her own dinner in her own apartment, alone.

Celine sipped the piping hot dark coffee and said, "How did you die?"

He told them. But first he looked at them steadily, first Pete, then Celine, and said, "The chopper took off. So you must have settled something."

"We did," Celine said. "I promised them that you would stay dead. I told them that the photographs you took of Peña de la Cruz would stay buried."

Lamont started, flinched so hard that he spilled his coffee. He put the mug down, stared at her.

"How else do you think we're all still sitting here?" she said. "And not being buried by the lake?"

He nodded slowly.

"You took pictures in the palace that afternoon, of the body."

He stared, nodded.

"And next to the body, an American, a government official. Important enough then, but now very high up. Very."

He didn't move. Not a twitch. The absolute lack of motion spoke volumes.

"We've had good—" She stopped. "Well. We've had *long* lives. Full. I don't mind, really. But I was thinking of Gabriela." He nodded. "And her son." Another flinch. Poor man. He started to speak and she held up a hand. "We'll get to that. Good," she said and took another sip. "Good coffee." She took a deep breath. "Salvador Allende did not commit suicide, did he?" She sipped. "Nor did poor Peña de la Cruz. They would not worry about a crackpot adventure photographer who had been drinking too much vodka and maté—sorry—railing about the CIA killing a minister of finance. Who would believe him? Not I. Who cared that much, after all, anymore? Water under the bridge. Sadly. But. Photographs would be a different story. A picture, like the others I assume you've got, of an American, in a suit, a very important American standing with a gun over the dead body of a member of the cabinet, that would be a different story. That would rock the world and rewrite history at just the wrong time. *This* time, this critical time, when the States are swimming in international sympathy and clearly trying to pull together a coalition. Very bad timing. So I told them that if an ounce of harm came to any of the three of us, or Gabriela, or your grandson, or my family, that it would trigger the release of the photographs to the press. I mentioned *The New York Times*, *The Washington Post*."

Lamont stared at her.

"Old poker player." Celine smiled. "We've found one of the pictures, and wherever the rest of those photographs are, you'd better set that up. We can help you."

So they drank coffee. Through the afternoon and into the dusk. No one was in a hurry. He lit the lamps and scrambled up eggs in olive oil—he did have a chicken coop—and they ate them with strips of elk jerky, the best dried meat Celine had ever had. He made another pot of coffee and they drank more after supper. Celine told him everything she knew of Gabriela's life, and of her son, who was now eight. Lamont listened like a man who was half dead from thirst, half dead and now drinking cold spring water. It was like pouring water into the pot of a dried and yellowing geranium, they could see the firmness coming back to limbs, the color. He said very little. What could he say, Celine thought. After everything. He had made his choices. Hard ones.

He told them how he'd died, how he'd studied and carved bear tracks out of wood and picked a night of coming storm, and cut his own wrists for blood. He knew it didn't have to be perfect, because he knew the agency would want him dead and would go to great lengths to put him there, at least in the official records. He did not speak of the bigger decisions except to say, "Gabriela needed a life. Needed out from under the Woman. Needed to inherit. I needed out of the work. With them. They knew I had the photographs and they knew my personality—that I was impulsive and rash and maybe, ah . . ."

"Self-destructive?" prompted Celine helpfully.

He nodded. "Right. That if they even tried to threaten me with say, Gabriela, I would blow it all open. So if they couldn't find me after I disappeared, maybe they didn't try all that hard. Probably relieved to have it all go quiet. But then—"

"Then we traipsed through the ashes. Made everybody sneeze."

He almost smiled. His face, Celine thought now, had been chiseled by sadness. Now it nearly smiled. She wondered if the muscles even knew how anymore.

Celine set down her fork and said, "You had a beautiful family and you screwed it up and caused immense pain." His eyelashes fluttered and he looked down at his plate. "Especially to your daughter. You made bad choices and you were weak. You suffered terribly when Amana died." His hand touched his own cheek, reflex, as if to make sure he was still living. "I get that. But many many people suffer terribly and go on to live lives of grace. You know, I am terribly fond of Gabriela. She's an extraordinary young woman. She's made a good life despite losing her mother, despite the wrecking ball she had for a father. I think she is going to want to come to see you. Soon. I think you ought to get another chair and another coffee cup."

The man turned on his stump away from them, to face the little window. He leaned forward. His elbows went to his knees and his hands went to his face. Celine let him be. Finally, she said, "Will you walk us to our truck now? We're exhausted and it's getting truly dark. We could use a guide."

She could see him nod. "Of course," he said huskily. "Of course."

epilogue

Celine and Pete were reluctant to leave their new hermit-crab home and they decided to camp for a week in Polson, at the southern end of Flathead Lake, and then move down along the Swan River. It was the best time of year. Frost at night and warm, sunny days, when the yellows and oranges of the aspen and cottonwoods did something to the blue of the sky behind them that an artist might never mimic. They took long walks along the lake and the river, and they read, and drank tea in the evening at the side dinette, while the sounds of water came through the screen.

On October 7, Hank flew up to Helena and they drove to meet him. He was between assignments and relished a few days in the mountains in early October. He would help them drive home. He offered to put them on a flight and take the truck back himself, but they seemed reluctant to leave the camper they called Bennie, which amused him. Hank thought he could use a trip away from home in any event. They picked him up at the little airport late on a Thursday morning, and Celine found it amazing that even with a broken marriage and the uncertain future of a freelancer he was cheerful. He was a big strong kid, an ardent fisherman and canoeist, and Celine noticed that under his loose flannel shirt he'd put on some weight, probably beer weight. Well.

Gabriela flew in a few hours later. They met her in the outer concourse that boasted a mammoth grizzly posing full height and growling. Now that they'd found Lamont, the bear was a little less potent, thank God. Gabriela's hair was back in a ponytail as on the first night, she wore a fitted down jacket, and her cheeks were flushed. Her smile when she saw them was instantaneous and bright. Celine was struck again by the fresh contained energy of the girl. And by how easily, after an introduction in which they both seemed shy, she and Hank fell into conversation—excited but relaxed—almost like two old friends. Well, they were both artists in precarious vocations, and they both loved what they did and reveled in the outdoors. He asked about her son and she said, "Oh God, Nick wants to be a writer! He is a born storyteller. Do you think you can dissuade him? Tell him about all those awful jobs you had? Your mom told me about them, you know."

Celine thought Hank's laugh was easier than she'd heard in a long time. "I don't know," he said. "I secretly think pizza delivery and short-story writing are the way to go. Go figure." He slipped Gabriela's carry-on from her hand just the way Bruce Willis had taken Celine's that time. Hmm. Celine thought life was ever more surprising, and never less strange. Who knew anything?

They decided to take an easy walk along the Missouri, which had a split-rock canyon down-stream and meadows of tall auburn grass and cut banks that caught the last sunlight. They walked slowly on the wide dirt path. The evening was not cold. Pete and Celine held hands, let the younger ones lead. At dusk they all climbed into the truck and returned to town and ate steaks at Nagoya. The conversation never flagged. Gabriela and Hank asked repeatedly about the case, the succession of events, but Celine and Pete were reticent. Hank could see that they were experiencing the faintest postpartum letdown, the depression, maybe, that mixes with the euphoria after finding their man, or woman. So mostly the kids talked, about where they lived, their jobs and failed marriages, and mostly Pete and Celine listened closely and held hands.

Gabriela would rent a car the next day and drive up to Glacier, to the cabin under the mountains. Several times over dinner, at natural breaks in the conversation—with the serving of a course, the clearing of plates—Celine noticed Gabriela staring, abstracted, at the tablecloth, or into the middle distance of the dining room, and she knew that the girl was thinking about her father, preparing herself somehow for their meeting. She couldn't imagine. Or she could, and it constricted her chest. Once she couldn't help herself—she reached across and touched Gabriela's hand, and Gabriela startled and met her eyes and they shared a look only the two could share, and that's when Celine knew the case was truly closed.

They reserved three adjacent rooms at the Trout Creek Hotel, ground floor with parking spaces in front, but Pete popped the top: He and Celine would sleep in Bennie. Hank couldn't get over it. They wouldn't think of sleeping in the stuffy room. Hank watched his little mother step down out of the camper to survey a night full of stars before sleep. She had taught him almost everything he knew about moving through the world with some semblance of grace, and he tried to live it and bumbled often and tried again. She had taught him courage in the landscapes of the imagination, and to find the joy in things when he was afraid. But she brought him pain, too. She wouldn't share with him the one story he cared about more than any other.

He had a sister somewhere. Whose heart pumped with his mother's blood, and some of his own. He imagined that his sister would have an affinity for the vulnerable and the lost that surprised the people around her. She probably had a quizzical humor, and a delight in things that were mysterious and didn't quite fit. He wanted to know her. He wanted to make her a package at Christmas, to call her out of the blue and say, "Hey, it's your bro, what's up?" But his mother had stonewalled. Years and years. He had felt the intensity of her pain and had tried to respect her wishes, and backed off. But here they were, under a river of stars in Montana, and Celine had just given Gabriela her father. Gabriela was about to embark on a new life and Hank could sense the excitement, and the strength she would find there.

Celine caught sight of him and turned. "Hank! Come look at Orion with me. We don't see the stars much in the city. I'll miss this terribly. Honestly, I could live in Bennie for the rest of my life."

"Whoa! I said you could borrow him."

"I wonder if the shell would get too tight?"

"Probably."

"Probably."

Hank hugged his mother good night. He squeezed her and whispered in her ear, "Mom, I know I have a sister. I don't blame you, or anyone."

She stiffened, breathed. She stepped back from the hug and held him at arm's length. She said, "Bobby told you."

He nodded.

"How they took her away before I could even smell her hair, put my lips in her ear, tell her what I wanted to tell her. The promises I had to make. I had things to say to her." She pursed her lips, breathed.

Hank found his voice. "Her name was Isabel, right?"

"She told you that?"

He nodded.

"That's right. Isabel. What I called her. She would be—is—ten years older than you. I wanted to promise her that I would find her. One day, I would. I did promise. As the nurse swept her out the door. It's something I live with."

Hank hesitated. He closed his eyes and he could smell the cold water in the creek. "Will you keep looking?"

"I am looking every day. I never stop."

acknowledgments

Many dear friends and family contributed generously to the making of this book. To my first reader, Kim Yan, I am so grateful. Your insight, humor, and literary sensitivity are a great boon. Lisa Jones and Helen Thorpe were constant companions and indispensable, as always. Thank you. And thanks to Donna Gershten for your energy and careful readings. And to Mark Lough. Ted Steinway, Nathan Fischer, Jay Heinrichs, Rebecca Rowe, and John Heller helped all along as they are wont to do. As did Pete Beveridge, Leslie Heller-Manuel, Callie French, and David Grinspoon. Carlton Cuse gave me another creative jolt, which he's been doing since we were fifteen. Jay Mead and Edie Farwell shared their excitement and knowledge. So did Sally and Robert Hardy, Margaret Keith/Sagal, and JP Manuel-Heller. Ana Goncalves saved me at a critical moment. Thanks again to Jason Hicks and Jason Elliott for their expertise. And to Bethany Gassman, Laura Sainz, Lamar Sims, William Pero, and Thor Arnold, who know the territory. And to the docs, Melissa Brannon and Mitchell Gershten. Thanks to my buddies and first cousins Ted McElhinny and Nick Goodman. I'm glad we were there together.

I am grateful to Myriam Anderson and Céline Leroy for their discernment and passion. Your love of the work means the world to me.

To David Halpern, my agent, I raise another glass. This book, like all the others, would not have happened without your keen input, enthusiasm, edits, tact, encouragement, and humor. *Skol.*

And to my editor, Jenny Jackson, well. There are, for once, few words. Time and again I have depended on your intelligence and your grace and I am grateful beyond telling.

Thank you all. What a pleasure and a privilege.

a note about the author

Peter Heller is the best-selling author of *The Painter* and *The Dog Stars*. He holds an MFA from the Iowa Writers' Workshop in both fiction and poetry. An award-winning adventure writer and a longtime contributor to NPR, Heller is a contributing editor at *Outside* magazine, *Men's Journal*, and *National Geographic Adventure*, and a contributor to *Bloomberg Businessweek*. He is also the author of several nonfiction books, including *Kook*, *The Whale Warriors*, and *Hell or High Water: Surviving Tibet's Tsangpo River*. He lives in Denver, Colorado.

Center Point Large Print
600 Brooks Road / PO Box 1
Thorndike, ME 04986-0001 USA

(207) 568-3717

US & Canada:
1 800 929-9108
www.centerpointlargeprint.com